CW01095841

Nottingham Forest FC

Who's Who 1946 to 1974

Garth Dykes

A *SoccerData* Publication

Published in Great Britain by Tony Brown,
4 Adrian Close, Toton, Nottingham NG9 6FL.
Telephone 0115 973 6086. E-mail soccer@innotts.co.uk
www.soccerdata.com

First published 2019

Cover design by Bob Budd.
Photographs from Colorsport, with others from the author's collection.

AUTHOR'S DEDICATION

For Debbie, Alex and James Moat

Printed and bound by 4Edge, Hockley, Essex
www.4edge.co.uk

ISBN: 978-1-911376-13-2

FOREWORD BY TONY BROWN

Garth Dykes has asked me to write this foreword, which, as a Nottingham lad, I am pleased to do. I have also contributed the sections on 1939-1946 and the club's managers, so please do not blame the author if mistakes have been made in those pages. My only claim to footballing fame is that I once played in the same school team as David Pleat, who features later in these pages.

With just a few exceptions, all football clubs have their ups and downs. The cycle tends to repeat itself, in that the gloom of relegation is often followed by the joys of promotions and cups won. In Forest's case, the period under review in this volume saw the club relegated to the Third Division for the first time, promotion to the First Division, an F.A. Cup win, and a second place finish in the First Division. If the successes in this list are overshadowed by what was to follow, then so be it. However, for many of us, the Wembley FA Cup win in 1959 remains the highlight, particularly as Billy Walker's team played the attractive football for which Forest became associated. Admittedly, a look at the match video shows how much the game has changed since 1959. The pace of the game is often pedestrian by today's standards. The passing is somewhat random at times. Also, far be it from me to question the players' fitness, but I think we can all agree that it falls somewhat short of today's standards.

The immediate post-war years were difficult for all sorts of reasons. Although Forest had placed a big emphasis on young players between 1939 and 1946, not all of them were ready for the step into League football. Along with many other clubs of the time, there was not a great deal of money available to invest in new players. Forest made big financial losses in the early war years, only getting back into the black when larger crowds returned to watch the games. The last two pre-war seasons in Division Two ended with the club in 20th place, with relegation avoided on the last day. 11th place in the first post-war season of 1946-47 showed promise, but 19th the following season, and 21st and relegation in the next were disappointing. The game was different in those days, so this did not result in Billy Walker losing his job. Indeed the Chairman patted him on the back and said "get us back up", which he duly did in the second season in the Third Division.

As is often the case, the impetus gained in the lower division led to good performances in the higher one. There were outside chances of promotion in 1952 and 1954, and second place in 1957 with promotion to the First Division, the first time at that level since 1925. The promotion team was not filled with young players as might have been expected from Walker in his earlier days as manager, but instead included well-established players of pedigree, probably rated as "past it" by their former clubs. The same can be said of the Cup-winning team of 1959, where the signings of Chic Thompson, Joe McDonald and Billy Gray helped produced the fine footballing team. However, subsequent League performances were generally mid-table, except for the first month or two in the first season back in the top-flight, when Forest found themselves top. However, 5th place in 1965 indicated things might change, as indeed they did with the club's best-ever finish as runners-up to champions Manchester United in 1967. However, this standard was not maintained. Mid-table became lower mid-table, with relegation in 1972. Thus it was a run-of-the-mill Second Division club that brought Brian Clough to the City Ground in 1974, where we can leave this account to continue in a later volume.

It is worth remembering that throughout the years covered by this book, Forest were the only club in the Football League that was not a Limited Company, and therefore was not "owned" by anyone. The committee comprised local business men, generally running successful concerns, which was just as well since they occasionally had to dip into their own pockets to keep the club in business. Did operating this way affect the club's trading performance, or their results on the field? I would say it did not; the club was run on professional lines, and money for new players could be found when needed. "Forest Limited" finally arrived as a private limited company in April 1982.

Tony Brown
April 2019

NOTES ON THE TEXT

For each player I have attempted to provide the following information: full names, recognised playing position, height and weight, date and place of birth, and date and place of death. It should be mentioned here that the dates of birth and death of some players have been culled from registers that only record such events in three-month periods. Hence the use (for instance) of 'January quarter 1923', denotes a span of January/February/March of that year. Also included are each player's Nottingham Forest debut, full career and biographical details, and a breakdown of appearances made and goals scored. Every player who played in a Football League match, an FA Cup and Football League Cup-tie are included. Appearances listed as 'Others' cover matches played in the Inter-City Fairs Cup, the European Cup and the UEFA Cup.

ABBREVIATIONS

These have been kept to a minimum and are those in general use in works of this type:

App/s	Appearance/s
NABC	National Association of Boys' Clubs
NASL	North American Soccer League
cs	close season
gl/s	goal/s
q.v. (quod vide)	denoting a cross reference
FA	Football Association
FL	Football League
WW2	The Second World War (1939-45)

Forest's 1959 FA Cup winners. Back row, left to right: GN Watson (secretary), Bill Whare. Joe MacDonald, Bobby McKinlay, Roy Dwight, Chic Thomson, Jeff Whitefoot, Tommy Graham (trainer). Front: John Quiqley, Billy Gray, Jack Burkett (captain), Billy Walker (manager), Tommy Wilson, Stuart Imlach.

ADDISON, Colin

Inside-forward 5'10" 10st 12lbs
Born: Taunton, 18th May 1940
CAREER: York City Schoolboys. Cliftonville. York City, amateur 1956, professional May 1957. **FOREST January 1961, fee £12,000**. Arsenal September 1966, fee £45,000. Sheffield United November 1967, fee £40,000. Hereford United player-manager October 1971, fee £3,000. Durban City, South Africa, manager January 1975. Notts County assistant manager December 1975 to October 1976. Newport County manager January 1977 to May 1978. West Bromwich Albion assistant manager July 1978 to May 1979. Derby County manager May 1979 to January 1982. Newport County manager February 1982 to May 1985. Coaching appointments in Qatar with AL Ahli May 1985 and Kuwait. Celtic Vigo (Spain) manager April 1986 to August 1987. West Bromwich Albion assistant manager September 1987 to October 1988. Atletico Madrid (Spain) assistant manager October 1988 to June 1989.Cadiz ZF (Spain) manager March to July 1990. Hereford United manager July 1990 to May 1991. Westfields F.C. manager January 1992. Al Arabi (Kuwait) manager September 1992. Cadiz ZF (Spain) manager 1993-94. Merthyr Tydfil manager October 1994. Deportivo Badoajoz (Spain) manager 1995. Merthyr Tydfil manager July 1996 to 1988. Scarborough manager 1999. Yeovil Town manager 2000. Swansea City manager 2001 to March 2002. Forest Green Rovers manager September 2002 to December 2003. Barry Town manager February to August 2004.
Debut v Cardiff City (h) 21.1.61, won 2-1
In the days when there were five different forward positions, Colin Addison filled them all with equal success, making his mark as a utility forward of the highest class. His lengthy career in the game began with York City for whom he netted 28 goals in 87 League matches. Although born in the West Country, he moved with his family to York at the age of eleven. He made his senior debut at the age of 17, and in his second season assisted the Minstermen to promotion from Division Four. He was one of Forest manager Andy Beattie's earliest signings, and the newcomer took the step up to Division One in confident fashion, netting both goals in a 2-1 win at West Bromwich Albion in his second appearance. Aside from his second season, when he was affected by sinus trouble, Addison was a key member of the Forest attack, leading the scoring charts in 1962-63, 1964-65 and 1965-66. When season 1966-67 opened with successive defeats he lost his place to John Barnwell, and was swiftly transferred to Arsenal for £45,000, as Forest went on to enjoy a memorable campaign, finishing as runners-up to Manchester United for the First Division title, additionally reaching the semi-final of the FA Cup. In a relatively brief stay at Highbury, Addison did not come up to expectations (nine goals in 27/1 League matches) and moved on to Sheffield United in December 1967 for £40,000, linking again with Andy Beattie, the Blades' assistant manager. During his time at Bramall Lane he experienced relegation in his first season, and promotion in 1970-71, appearing in 93/1 League matches, scoring 22 goals. In October 1971 he joined non-League Hereford United as their player-manager, guiding them to their remarkable FA Cup run in 1971-72 and election to the Football League in the following season, in which they were promoted at the first time of asking, as runners-up to Southport. It was to be just the start of a long, varied, and generally successful career in football management and coaching, both at home and abroad. In subsequent media work, he was a pundit with BBC Radio Wales, and also worked with Sky Sports and ESPN. In August 2012 he took a non- executive post on the Hereford board. An area north of the Edgar Street ground, Addison Court, is named in his honour.
Appearances: FL: 160 apps 62 gls FAC: 11 apps 6 gls FLC: 3 apps 1 gl Others: 2 apps 0 gls Total: 176 apps 69 gls

ALEXANDER, Dennis Leslie

Inside-forward 5' 10" 11st 0lbs
Born: Nottingham, 19th February 1935
Died: Apsley, 11th November 2011
CAREER: Hyson Green Boys' Club**. FOREST amateur, professional 9th June 1955**.
Brighton & Hove Albion March 1958, fee £500. Gateshead October 1958 to April 1959. Ilkeston Town *circa* August 1959. Sutton Town. Long Eaton United player-manager. Belper Town.
Debut v Liverpool (h) 20.8.55, lost 1-3
A local boy who began his football career with one of the City's leading N.A.B.C. teams, Hyson Green. As a youth of 17 he won England N.A.B.C. honours, and joined Forest as an amateur, prior to being called up for National Service with the Army, which was spent largely in Hong Kong. Joining Forest's professional ranks on demobilisation, Alexander made his senior debut in the first game of season, a 1-3 home defeat by Liverpool, and held his place for the first twelve matches. The subsequent signings of experienced inside-forwards of the calibre of Doug Lishman and Eddie Baily, restricted Alexander's opportunities in the following season to a single appearance, in which he scored in a 2-2 draw against Blackburn Rovers. A serious accident in training saw him out of action towards the end of the season, and in March 1958 he was transferred to Brighton & Hove Albion, along with a further three fringe players, Higham, E. Jones and Nicholson, all off loaded within the space of two days. Failing to get a first team outing with Brighton, Alexander took a final move in League football to Gateshead, where he completed 17 Division Four appearances and scored one goal in Gateshead's penultimate season as a Football League club - they were voted out after finishing in 22nd place in Division Four in 1959-60. In his first season with Ilkeston Town he made his debut against Forest 'A' on 22nd August 1959 and went on to score 23 goals in 54 appearances, assisting his team to reach the Derbyshire Cup Final.
Appearances: FL: 20 apps 4 gls Total: 20 apps 4 gls

ALLEN, Herbert Anthony 'Tanner'

Inside-forward
Born: Beeston, Nottingham, 27th October 1924
Died: Nottingham, 13th February 2014
CAREER: Cottesmore School. Nottingham Schoolboys. 17th Company Beeston Boys' Brigade. Beeston Boys' Club. **FOREST amateur 1st June 1944, professional 5th January 1946.** Notts. County August 1949. Corby Town July 1954. Grantham Town May 1956.
Debut v Watford, FAC Round 3 (h) 5.1.46, drawn 1-1 (scored)
A locally born Forest Reserve, who did rather better on crossing the Trent to join neighbours Notts County in August 1949. 'Tanner' Allen made 30 senior appearances for the Meadow Lane club, at wing-half and both full-back positions. In either role his thoughtful work was marked by unusual coolness. An industrial draughtsman by calling, he

played his football as a part-time professional. He was a welcome guest at Meadow Lane at the Shrewsbury Town match on 6th November 2004, when, to celebrate his 80th birthday, he was introduced onto the pitch and presented with a home jersey, squad number 80!
Appearances: FL 1 app 0 gls FAC: 3 apps 1 gl Total: 4 apps 1 gl

ANDERSON, John 'Johnny'

Half-back 5' 6½" 11st 12lbs
Born: Salford, 11th October 1921
Died: Manchester, 6th August 2006
CAREER: Salford Schoolboys. Lancashire Schoolboys. Adelphi Lads' Club. Brindle Heath Lads' Club. Manchester United amateur March 1938, professional December 1938 (Served in the Navy during WW2, and appeared as a guest player with Plymouth Argyle). **FOREST 3rd October 1949, fee £8,000**. Peterborough United August 1952, retired from playing in 1954 and appointed trainer-coach; caretaker-manager October to December 1962 and again February to April 1964.
Debut v Ipswich Town (a) 1.10.49, won 2-1
The son of a former Swinton Rugby League player who fathered eight children, Johnny Anderson was working as a clerk in a newspaper office when he joined Manchester United as a sixteen year-old amateur and collected a league medal with the 'A' Team just before leaving to join the Navy. Upon his return, the first season of post-war football saw him win a Central League medal, and in 1948 he became the first post-war footballer to receive an FA Cup winners' medal in the season of his League debut. At Wembley, he sealed United's splendid 4-2 victory against Blackpool with a 69th minute goal. Signed by Forest in October of the 1949-50 season, he immediately tightened up the defence and inspired the forwards with his fine constructive play. He was called upon less frequently in his second season, when promotion from Division Three South was achieved with Morley, Gager and Burkitt the regular selections in the middle line. In November 2016, his blue Manchester United number 4 shirt, worn in the 1948 FA Cup Final, was offered for sale by Graham Budd Auctions at Sotheby's, New Bond Street. It was offered along with a letter of authenticity from Anderson, written when he sold the shirt to a private collector in 1994. Estimated at £10,000-£15,000, it realised £10,000 at the hammer.
Appearances: FL: 40 apps 1 gl FAC: 2 apps 0 gls Total: 42 apps 1 gl
Honours: (Manchester United) FA Cup winners 1948

ANDERSON, Vivian 'Viv' Alexander M.B.E.
Full-back 6' 0½" 12st 4lbs
Born: Clifton, Nottingham, 29th July 1956
CAREER: Greencroft Middle School. Fairham Comprehensive. Nottingham Schoolboys. **FOREST apprentice 16th November 1972, professional 1st May 1974.** Arsenal July 1984, fee £250,000. Manchester United July 1987, fee £250,000. Sheffield Wednesday January 1991. Barnsley player-manager June 1993. Middlesbrough assistant manager May 1994 to July 2001.
Debut v Sheffield Wednesday (a) 21.9.74, won 3-2
Born in Nottingham of West Indian parents, Viv Anderson spent a school holiday at Manchester United's Old Trafford ground for coaching, but he was not taken on. After an apprenticeship with Forest, he became a full time professional in May 1974, and became the first black player to appear in League football for Forest, and in 1978 collected the first of 30 full caps for England. Always a supremely fit athlete, whose smooth overlaps often supported the attack, he appeared in ten seasons of League football with Forest. The tall and skilful defender was an outstanding figure in a decade of success, winning a League championship medal in 1978, European Cup

Viv Anderson in 1973

winners' medals in 1979 and 1980, Football League Cup winners' medals in 1978 and a finalists' medal in 1980. He was transferred to Arsenal for £250,000 in July 1984 where he made 120 League appearances for the Gunners and won a Football League Cup winners' medal in 1987. In July 1987 he was transferred to Manchester United, his £250,000 transfer fee fixed by a tribunal. Although passed 30, he came close to adding to his medal collection in his first season at Old Trafford when United were runners-up for the League championship. Limited first team opportunities eventually led to his free transfer to Sheffield Wednesday In January 1991, and he assisted them to win promotion to Division One in his first season at Hillsborough. In 1993 he was a finalist in the FL Cup and the FA Cup, Wednesday twice losing out to Arsenal who became the first club to win both competitions in the same season. After a year in charge at Barnsley, Viv Anderson renewed his Manchester United connections joining former team mate Bryan Robson as his number two at Middlesbrough. He was 38 years of age when he made his final two League appearances, as an emergency centre-half, in the1994-95 promotion campaign. Anderson was awarded the MBE on 31st December 1999, but left Middlesbrough, along with Bryan Robson, in January 2001, when Terry Venables was drafted in with the club in the lower reaches of Division One. In addition to the numerous honours listed above, Viv Anderson selected for the PFA Team of the Year in 1979, 1980 and 1987. He was also inducted into the National Hall of Fame in 2004.
Appearances: FL: 323/5 apps 15 gls FAC: 23 apps 1 gl FL Cup 39 apps 5 gls Other: 40 apps 1 gl Total: 425/5 apps 22 gls.
Honours: England International, 30 caps 1978-88. England 'B' International, 7 appearances. England Under-21 International, 1 appearance. **(FOREST)** European Cup winner 1979, 1980. FL champions 1978. FL Cup winner 1978, finalist 1980. UEFA Super Cup winner 1980. (Arsenal) FL Cup winner 1987. (Sheffield Wednesday) FA Cup finalist and FL Cup finalist 1993.

ARDRON, Walter 'Wally'

Centre-forward 5' 8½" 11st 9lbs
Born: Swinton-on-Dearne, Yorkshire, 19th September 1918
Died: Rotherham, February 1978
CAREER: Kilnhurst Colliery. L.N.E.R. Engine Department. Swinton Victoria. Denaby United. Rotherham United December 1938, fee £100. (Wartime guest player with Sheffield Wednesday, Accrington Stanley and Halifax Town. **FOREST 6th July 1949, fee £10,000 to May 1955.** Selby Town November 1955. Doncaster Rovers trainer-physiotherapist 1959 to 1963. Carlisle United scout 1963-68. Rawmarsh Welfare trainer 1968 to 1971.
Debut v Brighton & Hove Albion (a) 20.8.49, drawn 2-2 (scored one)
Forest fans were shocked when Jack Edwards and Gordon Lee were transferred but compensation came in the signing of Wally Ardron, the free-scoring Rotherham centre forward. It was said at the time that the cheque for £10,000, received from Southampton for the transfer of Jack Edwards, had hardly had time to clear through the banking system before Forest's manager, Billy Walker, paid the same amount to Rotherham United for Ardron's transfer. Forest were unlucky to go down in 1948-49 but they bounced back in 1950-51 with a club record 36 goals from Wally Ardron a key element in the successful campaign. One of the most coveted players in the immediate post war period, Ardron, a keen swimmer and boxer and railway fireman during the week, scored 40 goals for Rotherham United in 1946-47, and 98 in just 123 League matches before joining Forest. A strong, bustling type of leader, with few superiors in headwork, Wally was a firm favourite

with the City Ground fans, possessing the priceless assets of determination and never knowing when he was beaten. For the first time since joining the club he was not leading scorer in season 1954-55. He had a cartilage removed at the beginning of the season, and did not regain a first team place until half way through the campaign. A family connection occurred in October 1949, when Charlie Ardron, brother of Wally, had an unhappy debut when on trial with Forest Reserves against Scunthorpe United in a 2-3 defeat. He had plenty of dash, but was said to be on the small side. He did, however, score a goal near to the end. Later in the same season his exploits with Rawmarsh Welfare were revealed in the 'Sporting Mirror'. His four-goal blast against Grimethorpe was his tenth hat trick of the season, and he was tipped to be in League football shortly, but it didn't happen. Another brother, Ernest Ardron, managed Forest Juniors in their first season in the Mexborough & District Intermediate League for Under-18s. (1952-53). In 44 matches, 32 League and 12 Cup, they drew one and lost one, and scored 150 goals and conceded only 17. Walter, who scored his last goal for Forest in a 4-2 home win against Middlesbrough on 15th September 1954, announced his retirement at the end of the season. Moving back to Rotherham with his family, he took a job in a steel works, and his first week's wage was more than he had earned when playing football. His other jobs included that of a head messenger with the Nat West Bank, a part time business as a physiotherapist and chiropodist, and he ran the Swinton Manor Youth Club. A souvenir from his playing days was a mantle clock, awarded for his record 36 goals in season 1950-51.

Appearances: FL: 182 apps 123 gls FAC: 9 apps 1 gl Total: 191 apps 124 gls
Honours: **(FOREST)** FL Division 3 South champions 1951.

ARMSTRONG, John

Goalkeeper 5' 11" 12st 4lbs
Born: Airdrie, Scotland, 5th September 1936
CAREER: Armadale Thistle. Bellshill Athletic 1957. Barrow March 1958. **FOREST November 1958, fee £3,000**. Portsmouth February 1963. Southport August 1967, retired cs 1971. New Brighton manager 1972.
Debut v Leeds United (a) 22.4.59, lost 0-3

Barrow's goalkeeper in the early months of their first season in Division Four, John Armstrong took a large upward step in joining Forest of the First Division. It was a six-hour train journey through the fog that brought the Scottish goalkeeper to Nottingham, where his transfer was completed in the bedroom of manager Billy Walker, who was recovering from an attack of sciatica. In the season that Forest lifted the FA Cup, Armstrong was the fourth goalkeeper to appear in Division One, with 'Chic' Thomson the regular selection. Armstrong's debut, a matter of days before the Cup Final, also saw two others making their first appearance-Jimmy Martin and Bernie Kelly. Leeds United were three goals up with 39 minutes, but Armstrong had little chance with the three goals and punctuated his debut with considerable courage and no little skill. In the following season, when relegation from the top flight was narrowly avoided, Armstrong took over from Thomson for an eleven-match run, commencing with a welcome 2-1 win at Blackburn Rovers on 2nd January 1960. With Peter Grummitt 's successful introduction in the following term, Armstrong's opportunities were further restricted. Moving on, he subsequently enjoyed lengthy spells of first team football with Portsmouth (79 League matches) and Southport (86 matches) before a back injury enforced his retirement. He then worked for the Development Association of Southport FC until 1972. During his spell at Haig Avenue he coached the Manchester University team, and was later a representative with Hedges Frozen Foods for 14 years.

Appearances: FL: 20 apps 0 gls FAC: 1 app 0 gls FLC: 1 app 0 gls Total: 22 apps 0 gls

ASHMAN, George **Allan**

Centre-forward 5' 11" 11st 7lbs
Born: Herringthorpe, near Rotherham, 30th May 1928
Died: Walsall, 30th November 2002
CAREER: West Riding Schoolboys. Sheffield United amateur. **FOREST amateur 20th December 1945, professional 12th April 1946.** Carlisle United June 1951, fee £5,500, retired due to injury May 1958. Penrith FC manager. Carlisle United manager February 1963 to May 1967. West Bromwich Albion manager June 1967 to May 1971. Olympiakos (Greece) coach 1971-72. Carlisle United manager August 1972 to October 1975. Workington manager December 1975 to February 1977. Manchester United scout 1977-78. Walsall Manger December 1978 to February 1979. Derby County scout and later assistant manager 1979-82. Hereford United assistant manger 1983-87. Plymouth Argyle scout. Notts County scout, Mansfield Town scout. Telford United scout. Aston Villa scout to 2000.
Debut v Cardiff City (a) 5.2.49, lost 0-1
Great things were expected of the youthful Allan Ashman who, after playing with a representative team while serving in the army, returned to score a lot of goals for the Midland League side, his consistent form having much to do with the championship being won in consecutive seasons. He was recommended to the Forest manager by a relative, and first played for the Colts at the age of 16. His senior debut came in the 1948-49 relegation season, but the signing of Wally Ardron in the close season effectively ended Ashman's prospects at the City Ground. He certainly found more opportunities with Carlisle United, where he scored a hat trick on debut and netted over a century of League and Cup goals. Later again he enjoyed a successful managerial career that include two separate spells in charge at Brunton Park which included promotion from Division Three in 1965, and a third-place finish in Division Two in 1967. He then moved up to West Bromwich Albion and led them to an FA Cup Final win against Everton in 1968. In his second spell with Carlisle United he took them to their solitary season in Division One (1974-75). They shook the football world by beating Chelsea and Middlesbrough away, and Tottenham Hotspur at home in their first three matches, but eventually were relegated, along with Chelsea and Luton Town. During his spell in charge of Olympiakos he guided them to the runners-up position in the Greek League in 1972, they additionally won the Greater Greece Cup in the same season. Allan played in Minor Counties Cricket for Cumberland in 1956, and his elder brother, John Robert, was a slow left-arm bowler with Yorkshire, Worcestershire and the RAF.
Appearances: FL: 13 apps 3 gls Total: 13 apps 3 gls.

BAILY, Edward 'Eddie' Francis
Inside-forward 5' 8" 11st 0lbs
Born: Clapton, East London, 6th August 1925
Died: Welwyn Garden City, October 2010
CAREER: Hackney Schoolboys. Middlesex Schoolboys. Tottenham Juniors. Finchley. Tottenham Hotspur amateur. Chelsea amateur. Tottenham Hotspur amateur February 1946, professional October 1946. Port Vale January 1956, fee £6,000. **FOREST 8th October 1956, fee £5,000.** Leyton Orient December 1958, fee "about £3,000", appointed coach on retiring as a player in 1960. Tottenham Hotspur assistant manager October 1963. West Ham United scout September 1974. Chesham United coach. Chelsea scout 1974. West Ham United scout August 1976 to October 1977. Birmingham City assistant-manager October 1977, additionally England assistant-manager
Debut v Huddersfield Town (a) 6.10.56, lost 0-1

Born at Clapton, Eddie Baily began as a Hackney schoolboy and won honours with both Hackney Boys and Middlesex Boys. At the age of 14 he left school and joined Tottenham Juniors and after two seasons went on to Finchley, the amateur club. Then came the war and at the age of 18 he was called up. It was while with the BAOR that he played representative football against Polish, Czech, French and Swiss elevens. When he was demobbed in 1945 a strange thing happened. He found that his registration with Spurs had lapsed and he joined Chelsea. But when Chelsea found out that he had been a Spurs protégé they released him and he signed professional forms at White Hart Lane in 1946. In 1950 he played for England 'B' against Switzerland and also represented the Football League. Dubbed the 'Cheeky Chappie', it was a nickname that suited him on account of his personality that bubbled over with good humour. He was a member of the Spurs' side that carried off the championship of Divisions One and Two in consecutive seasons-1949-50 and 1950-51 and who were runners-up in Division One in 1951-52. A ball-artist who seldom wasted time working the ball across the field, and an expert at the first time, defence-splitting pass, he was the schemer of the Forest attack and although approaching the veteran stage in his City Ground days he remained one of the cleverest ball players in the side, an arch provider of openings for his colleagues. His signing in October 1956 paid immediate dividends as Forest won promotion from Division Two in the same season, and made a solid start in Division One in 1957-58, finishing in tenth place in the table. He was made captain for the day at White Hart Lane when on 5th October 1957 when Forest won 4-3 with John Quigley one of Forest's scorers on his first senior appearance. A London resident who worked part-time for a firm of coppersmiths in Stratford, Eddie Baily ended his senior career with Leyton Orient. His career aggregate figures were 419 League matches and 89 goals, of which 296 appearances and 64 goals were made with Tottenham Hotspur.

Appearances: FL: 68 apps 14 gls FAC: 8 apps 3 gls Total: 76 apps 17 gls

Honours: England International, 9 caps 1950 to 1952. England 'B' International, 3 caps. FL representative, 5 apps. (Tottenham Hotspur) FL Division 2 champions 1950, FL Division 1 champions 1951.

BAINES Stephen 'Steve' John

Half-back 6' 0" 12st 2lbs

Born: Newark, Notts. 23rd June 1954

CAREER: FOREST apprentice 30th July 1969, professional 3rd July 1972. Huddersfield Town July 1975. Bradford City March 1978, fee £18,000. Walsall July 1980, fee £50,000. Bury (loan) December 1981. Scunthorpe United player coach August 1982, fee £5,000. Chesterfield player-coach July 1983, fee £5,000. Matlock Town July 1987. Alfreton Town October 1987. Gainsborough Trinity November 1987. Burton Albion to retirement in January 1988. Subsequently

qualified as a Class One referee and was promoted to the Football League list in 1995, officiating in 204 matches between 1997 and 2004.
Debut v Preston North End (a) 21.4.73, lost 1-2
Steve Baines enjoyed a successful playing career and did similarly well when he qualified as a Class One referee and was promoted to the Football League list when his playing career ended after 441 League appearances and 42 goals for his seven League clubs. Chesterfield was his final League club and he had the satisfaction of captaining them to the Division Four championship in 1985. At the outset of his career, he played just twice, in the space of three days, for Forest in the season that Dave Mackay replaced Matt Gillies as manager. He remained in reserve through further managerial changes as Allan Brown and then Brian Clough took over, and it was not until he joined Huddersfield Town at 21 years of age that his career began in earnest.
Appearances: FL: 2 apps 0 gls Total: 2 apps 0 gls
Honours: (Chesterfield) FL Division 4 champions 1985

BAIRD, Dougald 'Doug' Francis Hogg

Full back 5' 10" 11st 4lbs
Born: Carron, near Falkirk, 26th November 1935
Died: Falkirk, December 2002
CAREER: Armadale Thistle. Partick Thistle December 1954. **FOREST 9th September 1960, fee £10,000, then loaned back to Partick Thistle until December 1960.** Plymouth Argyle October 1963. Tavistock Town 1968. Hamilton Academical first team coach, *circa* 1969-70. Dunipace Juniors coach 1971
Debut v Burnley, FLC round 3 (a) 10.1.61, lost 1-2
In six seasons at Firhill Park Doug Baird amassed 195 League appearances for the Scottish Division One side. He commenced his career with Armadale Thistle, a West Lothian junior club, initially as a wing-half, but his conversion to full-back by Partick Thistle proved the turning point of his career. A Scottish Under-23 and Scottish League representative, his style was described as 'rugged though stylish' and he impressed Forest's manager after a starring Thistle performance against Celtic, leading Billy Walker to make an immediate and successful approach for his services. Unfortunately, he did not settle too well into English First Division football, and his chances were further restricted when the Reds signed Joe Wilson from Workington in March 1962. Baird's best spell came towards the close of the 1962-63 season, both as an emergency wing-half and in his more familiar position at left full-back, but in October of the following season he was signed by Plymouth Argyle's caretaker-manager Andy Beattie, for whom he had played at the City Ground. He remained at Home Park for five seasons, making 157/1 League and Cup appearances, mainly at full-back but occasionally in the centre of defence. Argyle avoided relegation with a superior goal average of just 0.05 over Grimsby Town in his first season, and they generally struggled in Division Two until relegation finally arrived in 1967-68, at the close of which Doug Baird was released.
Appearances: FL: 32 apps 0 gls FAC: 1 app 0 gls FLC: 3 apps 0 gls Other: 1 app 0 gls Total: 37 apps 0 gls
Honours: Scottish League representative, 1 appearance 1959. Scotland Under-23 International, 1 appearance 1960.

BAKER, David Henry
Centre-half 6' 1" 12st 8lbs
Born: Penzance, Cornwall, 21st October 1928
Died: Nottingham, 3rd June 2008
CAREER: Mapperley Imperials. Wellington Town. Notts County amateur during WW2. Brush Sports F.C. (Loughborough). **FOREST October 1949.** Sutton Town 1952-53. Ilkeston Town July 1953. Ransome & Marles February 1962. Ilkeston Town reserve team trainer 1964.

Debut v Port Vale (a) 11.2.50, drawn 1-1
A part-time professional who worked in a solicitor's office, David Baker found few opportunities at the City Ground, with Gager, McKinlay and Rawson as strong competition for the centre-half spot. Ideally built for the position, Baker was described as: "A thoughtful type of pivot, who endeavours to part with the ball along the ground, and to the advantage of his own forwards." Placed on the transfer list, he moved into non-League circles, initially with Sutton Town during the 1952-53 season, moving quickly on to Ilkeston Town in July 1953. He remained with them for almost nine years, was ever-present in three seasons, and totalled 345 matches and 32 goals, 25 from the penalty spot. Ilkeston were Central Alliance champions in 1953-54 and 1954-55, and they won the Derbyshire Senior Cup in 1955-56 and 1957-58.
Appearances: FL: 3 apps 0 gls Total: 3 apps 0 gls

BAKER, Joseph 'Joe' Henry
Centre-forward 5' 7" 11st 9lbs
Born: Woolton, Liverpool, 7th July 1940
Died: Wishaw, 6th October 2003
CAREER: Park Street Primary School. St Joseph's High School. Motherwell and Wishaw Schoolboys. Motherwell Boys' Guild. Edinburgh Thistle. Coltness United. Armadale Thistle. Chelsea (one month's trial 1955). Hibernian June 1956. AC Torino (Italy) May 1961, fee £70,000. Arsenal July 1962, fee £67,500. **FOREST March 1966, fee £65,000**. Sunderland July 1969, fee £30,000. Hibernian January 1971, fee £12,000. Raith Rovers June 1972 to October 1974. Fauldhouse United manager-coach cs 1980. Albion Rovers manager July 1981 to February 1982 and again September 1984 to December 1984.
Debut v Burnley (h) 8.3.66, won 1-0
Joe Baker's family left Liverpool for Motherwell during the war to escape the air raids. Joe was then two years old. Oddly enough, his subsequent selection for Scotland Schoolboys took him back to Merseyside. The match, in which he scored both goals for Scotland in a 2-2 draw, was played on Everton's ground. His early days were spent in Scotland and is wasn't until he was 15 years old that he came back to England, actually to Chelsea where he spent a short time having trials with that club. He was unable to settle and returned home again to play for Scottish juniors, Armadale Thistle, and was spotted by Hibernian who quickly snapped him up. His career with them included 42 goals in season 1959-60, a club record. He also scored nine, and missed a penalty, in a Scottish Cup game against Peebles in February 1961. His outstanding overall record was 102 League games and 117 goals. In 1960 he played in five full international matches. Also with Hibs he played in six Under-23 internationals (scoring five goals), and was also in the Young England side v England in 1961. He was chosen as one of England's initial World Cup squad of 40 players in 1966, but didn't make the final party. Signed by Forest from Arsenal in March 1966 for a record fee of nearly £70,000, he was once described as a: "Wiry, highly skilled and quick as lightning striker." He was a most dangerous centre-forward who, in his first full season at the City Ground, linked up well with Ian Storey-Moore to form a successful scoring combination until a thigh injury in the sixth round FA Cup-tie at Everton put him out of action for the remainder of the season. The goals had dried up at the time of his transfer to Sunderland, who were relegated from the top flight in his first season at Roker. On leaving the game, Joe worked as a licensee in Wishaw, and as a hospitality host at Hibernian FC, later again in the building trade until 1993 when he suffered a heart attack. Earlier, he left Italy and Torino after needing life saving surgery when he crashed his Alfa Romeo Guelietta Sprint. Joe's elder brother, Gerry, was born in New York and made League appearances for four English clubs, most notably Manchester City for whom he scored 58 goals in 135 League appearances.
Appearances: FL: 117/1 apps 41 gls FAC: 8 apps 5 gls FLC: 5 apps 0 gls Other: 4 apps 3 gls Total: 134/1 apps 49 gls
Honours: England International, 8 caps 1959-66. England Under-23 International, 6 caps. Scottish Schoolboy International, 2 caps. (Hibernian) Scottish Cup finalists 1958.

Joe Baker in 1966

BALL, Geoffrey 'Geoff' Hudson

Full-back 5' 9" 10st 11lbs
Born: Nottingham, 2nd November 1944
CAREER: Ericssons Electric, Nottingham. **FOREST February 1963**. Notts County November 1967, fee £5,000. Ilkeston Town 1972, manager January 1973 to February 1975. Grantham Town March 1975 to August 1976.
Debut v Arsenal (a) 6.10.64, won 3-0
Fair-haired Geoff Ball was first spotted whilst playing for a Nottingham works' team, and it wasn't long before he gained a regular berth in the Football Combination team, where he created a good impression with his strong tackling and speedy recovery. However, due to the consistency of the more experienced full-backs on the books, he found few first team opportunities. His debut at Highbury was a surprise call-up, but he performed with great credit in the 3-0 victory, and held his place for the next match against Chelsea at the City Ground. On crossing over to Meadow Lane, he enjoyed more regular first team football (119/1 League and Cup appearances) before losing his place to Bill Brindley (q.v.) in season 1970-71. On leaving Meadow Lane at the close of the following season he moved into non-League circles, initially with Ilkeston Town. As player and then player-manager he appeared in 100/12 matches, scoring 12 goals. However, his managerial record was less impressive – just 29 wins in 97 games.
Appearances: FL: 3 apps 0 gls Total: 3 apps 0 gls

BANHAM, Roy

Centre half-back 5' 10½" 11st 6lbs
Born: Nottingham, 30th October 1936
CAREER: Hyson Green Boys' Club. **FOREST amateur, professional November 1953.** Sheffield United (trial). Peterborough United July 1958. Bedford Town 1962. March Town.
Debut v Leeds United (a) 8.10.55, lost 0-3
Roy Banham was still on Army service with the 7th Royal Tank Regiment at Catterick when he made his first team debut, along with Johnny Langford, another youngster making his senior bow. He had joined the Forest ground staff straight from school as an outstanding junior who had won International honours with the N.A.B.C. Signed by Peterborough United in July 1958, he won a Division Four championship medal as the 'Posh' won the title in their first League season, and additionally enjoyed a Cup run to round four at which point they lost 1-2 in a replay at Aston Villa, a match attended by 64,531 spectators.
Appearances: FL: 2 apps 0 gls Total: 2 apps 0 gls
Honours: (Peterborough United) FL Division 4 champions, 1961.

BARKS, Edwin 'Eddie'

Wing-half 5' 10½" 11st 5lbs
Born: Ilkeston, 1st September 1921
Died: Derby, 26th March 1989
CAREER: Heanor Town. **FOREST April 1939, re-registered 13th May 1946.** Mansfield Town January 1949 to his retirement in May 1955.
Debut v Watford, FAC Round 3 (h) 5.1.46, drawn 1-1
Eddie Barks, an apprentice plumber, was the first signing made by Forest manager, Billy Walker. With the war years intervening it was not until the 1945-46 season that he was able to appear regularly, and in the first two Football League seasons he alternated between right half-back and centre-forward, although the middle line proved to be his best position. He had played only twice in the 1948-49 season-that ended in relegation from Division Two, when he was transferred to Mansfield Town in mid term. Well built, strong, and possessing ability in both defensive and constructive work, he topped 200 appearances for the Stags in seven seasons, his total including 41 League and Cup outings in 1950-51 when the Stags were runners-up to Rotherham United for the Third Division North championship.
Appearances: FL: 66apps 5 gls FAC: 7 apps 3 gls Total: 73 apps 8 gls

BARNWELL, John

Midfield 5' 8" 12st 0lbs
Born: High Heaton, Newcastle-on-Tyne, 24th December 1938
CAREER: Newcastle Schoolboys. Whitely Bay. Bishop Auckland amateur. Arsenal amateur August 1955, professional November 1956. **FOREST March 1964, fee £30,000**. Sheffield United April 1970, fee £20,000, retired January 1972. Hereford United coach cs 1972. Peterborough United coach 1974, appointed manager May 1977 to November 1978. Wolverhampton Wanderers manager November 1978 to January 1982. Coaching in Saudi Arabia 1982 to 1983. AEK (Athens) manager August 1983 to January 1984. Notts County manager June 1987 to December 1988. Walsall manager January 1989 to March 1990. Northampton Town assistant manager December 1993 to 1994. Grantham Town manager and appointed CEO of the FL Managers Association in July 1996.
Debut v Sheffield Wednesday (h) 21.3.64, won 3-2
A Tynesider from High Heaton, near Newcastle, John Barnwell had seven years with Arsenal prior to joining Forest in March 1964. Most of his 138 FL games for the Gunners were at wing-half, though he

initially played most frequently in the attack with Forest. He played for England Under-23 v West Germany at White Hart Lane in March 1961 while at Highbury. A clever player and mainspring of many attacking moves, the midfield link of Barnwell and Newton was a key element in Forest's most successful campaign of 1966-67 when they were runners-up for the Division One championship, and additionally reached the semi-final of the FA Cup. In the following season he was constantly plagued by injuries and was restricted to just 17 appearances with newly signed Scottish International Jim Baxter his replacement. Transferred to Sheffield United, he played in only nine League matches before his contract was cancelled in January 1972. He then turned to coaching and management, the undoubted highlight being his League Cup Final success with the Wolves, who beat Forest in the final, in 1980. He also took Notts County to the Division Three Play-offs, but was dismissed after only eighteen months in the job.
Appearances: FL: 172/8 apps 22 gls FAC: 12/1 apps 2 gls FLC:5 apps 1 gl Other: 3 apps 0 gls Total: 192/9 apps 25 gls
Honours: England Youth and Under-23 International. (Wolverhampton Wanderers, FL Cup winners 1980.

BARRETT, James 'Jimmy' Guy

Forward 5' 8½" 10st 8lbs
Born: West Ham, London, 5th November 1930
Died: 21st October 2004
CAREER: West Ham United amateur June 1946, professional February 1949. **FOREST 25th December 1954, fee £5,900**. Birmingham City October 1959, fee £8,000. West Ham United player-manager of 'A' Team August 1960 to May 1968. Millwall coach 1968 to 1970.
Debut v Birmingham City (a) 25.12.54, won 1-0
Born on bonfire night just a stone's throw away from West Ham United's Boleyn Ground, Jimmy Barrett eventually followed in the footsteps of his illustrious father 'Big' Jim Barrett (469 League and Cup appearances and 53 goals for the Hammers between 1924-39). The youthful Jimmy Barrett commenced with the Hammers at 16 years of age, and had scored 25 goals in 87 League and Cup matches at the time of his Christmas Day transfer to the City Ground. A natural goal scorer and deadly from the penalty spot, Barrett peaked in season 1956-57 with 30 League and Cup goals despite missing ten matches through illness when he might well have broken Wally Ardron's record of 36 goals in season 1950-51. Barrett was leading the scoring lists with 12 in just 17 matches when he sustained a serious knee injury at Sunderland on 7th December 1957. After an operation for torn ligaments he returned to training in the final week of the season and continued throughout the summer in efforts to return to full fitness for the new campaign. Sadly, in the season that Forest lifted the FA Cup at Wembley, Jimmy Barratt played in only three League matches. After a short spell with Birmingham City (10 matches and four goals) he returned to his roots as player-manager of the Hammers 'A' Team, leaving to join another ex-West Ham United player, Benny Fenton, at Millwall. Later again he became a publican at the Napier Arms in Halstead, Essex, and was manager of a Haverhill Sports Centre in Suffolk.
Appearances: FL: 105 apps 64 gls FAC: 12 apps 5 gls Total: 117 apps 69 gls

BARRON, James 'Jim'
Goalkeeper 6' 0" 11st 10lbs
Born: Tantobie, County Durham, 19th October 1943
CAREER: West End Boys' Club (Newcastle). Newcastle West End. Wolverhampton Wanderers amateur June 1960, professional November 1961. Chelsea April 1965. Oxford United March 1966. **FOREST July 1970, fee £35,000**. Swindon Town August 1974. Connecticut Bi-Centennials player-coach March 1977. Peterborough United August 1977 to May 1981. Mansfield Town assistant-manager (briefly). Wolverhampton Wanderers coach and assistant-manager 1981 to

1983, then coach/caretaker-manager 1988-89. Cheltenham Town manager November 1989 to October 1990. Everton reserve team manager and goalkeeping coach 1991 to 1992. Aston Villa assistant manager/coach 1992 to 1993. Sheffield United assistant-manager 1996 to 1998. Birmingham City coach November 1998, joint caretaker-manager October 2001. Crystal Palace assistant-manager/coach 2002 to 2003. Wycombe Wanderers coach. Northampton Town coach June 2006.
Debut v Ipswich Town (a) 12.8.70, drawn 0-0
The son of a former Blackburn Rovers and Darlington goalkeeper, Jim Barron junior commenced with Newcastle West End and went on to record over 400 appearances with his six League clubs. He spent almost five years with the Wolves, making just eight League appearances. Transferred to Chelsea, he played once before joining Oxford United where he found regular first team football that included 35 appearances in 1967-68 when Oxford won the championship of Division Three. A starring display in Oxford's League Cup win at the City Ground in October 1969 had not gone unnoticed, and when a replacement for the injured Alan Hill was felt necessary, Jim Barron was signed for £35,000. Daring and confident, he missed just a handful of matches for four seasons prior to his transfer to Swindon Town in August 1974. A regular for two seasons at the County Ground, he made 93 League and Cup appearances before leaving for a brief stint in the United States, and a final spell with Peterborough United, managed by ex-Forest midfielder John Barnwell.
Appearances: FL: 155 apps 0 gls FAC: 15 apps 0 gls FLC: 8 apps 0 gls Other: 2 apps 0 gls Total: 180 apps 0 gls
Honours: (Oxford United) FL Division 3 champions 1968

BARTON, Anthony 'Tony' Edward

Winger 5' 9" 11st 2lbs
Born: Sutton, Surrey, 8th April 1937
Died: Southampton, 20th August 1993
CAREER: Sutton & Cheam Schoolboys. London Schoolboys. Sutton United. Fulham amateur June 1952, professional May 1954. **FOREST 2nd December 1959**. Portsmouth December 1961, fee £5,000, player/coach from May 1967. Aston Villa assistant-manager 1980, then manager February 1982 to May 1984. Northampton Town manager July 1984 to April 1985. Southampton assistant-manager September 1985 to May 1988, caretaker manager February to June 1991. Portsmouth assistant and then caretaler manager. Subsequent scouting appointments with Southampton and Bournemouth.
Debut v West Ham United (a) 5.12.59, lost 1-4
Tony Barton won an England Schoolboy cap against Scotland and appeared five times for England Youths. He was just past the age of 17 when he made his League debut for Fulham against Lincoln City in 1954. During National Service with the RAF he served in Malta, Gibralta and Cyprus and played in many inter-sevices competitions. He eventually arrived at the City Ground on the recommendation of his friend, Roy Dwight, a former playing colleague at Craven Cottage. Sadly, Tony Barton did not impress at the City Ground, the 'Post Guide' commenting that although a very neat ball player, his chief requirement was persistence and the abilty to stave off a tackle. If Barton's playing career at the highest level remained largely unfulfilled, he certainly enjoyed heady success in management, leading Aston Villa to victory in the European Cup Final, victory in the European Super Cup, and a place in the World Club Championship, where they were defeated by Penarol of Uruguay. He was out of football at the time of his early death from heart failure in August 1993 at the age of 56.
Appearances: FL: 22 apps 1 gl FAC: 1 app 0 gls FLC: 1 app 1 gl Total: 24 apps 2 gls
Honours: England Schoolboy International, 1 cap. England Youth International, 5 caps.

BAXTER, James 'Jim' Curran

Midfield 5' 10" 10st 6lbs
Born: Hill of Beath, Fife, 29th September 1939
Died: Glasgow, 14th April 2001
CAREER: Crossgates Primrose. Raith Rovers April 1957, fee £200. Glasgow Rangers June 1960, fee £18,000. Sunderland May 1965, fee £72,500. **FOREST 15th December 1967, fee £105,000**. Glasgow Rangers May 1969, retired November 1970.
Debut v Sheffield United (h) 16.12.67, won 1-0
Jim Baxter was one of those cavalier characters touched by genius, much talked about and much relished, whose inate ball skills and other idiosyncrasies are recalled decades after they have left the scene. 'Slim Jim' as he was known, entranced crowds, possessed a left foot described as a magic wand, and a talent for improvisation best summed up as devastating. A master at reading the game, ever cool and at times appearing almost lethargic, he was the perfect link man between defence and attack. A maverick entertainer, Baxter was revered by Scots for his breathtaking Wembley display as World Champions England were beaten 3-2 in April 1967. He originally worked as a carpenter then as a miner before joining the Black Watch for his National Service. During his football career, he appeared in more than 400 games in Scotland and England, but on retiring from the game he became a licensee and, through a drink problem, became seriously ill, undergoing two major operations, leading to his early demise at the age of 61.
Appearances: FL: 47/1 apps 3 gls FAC: 2 apps 0 gls Total: 49/1 apps 3 gls
Honours: Scotland International, 34 caps. Scotland Under-23 International 1 cap. Scottish League representative, 5 apps. (Glasgow Rangers) Scottish League champions 1961, 1963, 1964. Scottish Cup winner 1962 1963, 1964. Scottish League Cup winner 1961, 1962, 1964, 1965.

BAXTER, William 'Bill' Amelius

Centre half-back 5' 8" 11st 0lbs
Born: Basford, Nottingham, 6th September 1917
Died: Nottingham, 21st February 1992
Debut v Burnley (a) 11.9.37, drawn 0-0
CAREER: Berridge Road School. Nottingham Schoolboys. Willson's F.C. Vernon Athletic. Berridge Road Institute. **FOREST amateur July, professional December 1936**. (Wartime guest player with Notts County, Derby County, Leicester City and Mansfield Town). Notts County October 1946, fee £2,500. Grantham Town May 1954 to March 1955.
Fair-haired Bill Baxter, one of a family of ten children, joined Forest as a youngster. Strong in the air and with any amount of stylish touches on the ball, he was nevertheless unfortunate to sustain cartilage trouble early in his career, the injury requiring surgery and keeping him sidelined for much of season 1937-38. During military service during the war, further knee trouble developed and he was invalided out-on crutches. It was thought that he would never play football again, yet he returned to the game and moved across the Trent to join Notts County for the first post war season. At either centre-half or

on the flank he appeared in 153 League and Cup matches for the Magpies, assisting them to promotion in 1950, and later captained their Reserve team.
Appearances: FL: 15 apps 0 gls FAC: 3 apps 0 gls Total: 18 apps 0 gls
Honours: Notts County, FL Division 3 South champions 1950

BLACKMAN, Ronald 'Ronnie' Henry

Centre-forward 6' 0" 11st 9lbs
Born: Cosham, Portsmouth, 2nd April 1925
Died: Fareham, Portsmouth, 16th February 2016
CAREER: Gosport Borough. Reading March 1947. **FOREST 15th June 1954, fee £6,600.** Ipswich Town July 1955, fee £2,800. Tonbridge July 1958. Reading scout 1960s.
Debut v Luton Town (a) 21.8.54, lost 0-3
93 goals for Gosport Borough led to Ron Blackman's move to Reading, after his hometown club, Portsmouth, had tried and rejected him. He left the Portsmouth dockyards, where he worked as an electrical fitter, to move to Elm Park for an intial wage of £5. 10 shilling per week. After a first season spent mainly in reserve, a hat trick in the opening fixture of the 1948-49 season ensured his first team place. A centre-forward with all the necessary attributes, he was particularly deadly in the air, 96 of his 167 Reading goals being scored with his head. He was the leading scorer in the Third Division South in 1951-52 with 39 goals, and twice scored five goals in a match. His 158 League goals for Reading beat the previous record of 154 by Trevor Senior. Sadly, he failed to shine at the City Ground. After leading the attack in the first five matches of the season-all lost with a goal average of one scored and eleven conceded, he lost his first team place and never fully regained it. Three seasons with Ipswich Town followed, but a series of injuries restricted his appearances to 27 League matches in which he scored 12 goals. After leaving the game, Blackman worked as a telephone engineer, retiring as an office manager. To mark his death, a minute's applause preceded Reading's FA Cup-tie against West Bromwich Albion on 19th February 2016.
Appearances: FL: 11 apps 3 gls Total: 11 apps 3 gls

BLAGG, Edward 'Ted' Arthur

Centre-half 6' 0½" 13st 12lbs
Born: Shireoaks, Worksop, 9th February 1918
Died: Shireoaks, Worksop, 28th October 1976
CAREER: Netherton United. Wood End F.C. **FOREST amateur December 1937, professional March 1938. Re-registered 14th May 1946.** Southport November 1948, fee £3,000. Worksop Town cs 1949 to 1952.
Debut v Watford, FAC Round 3 (h) 5.1.46, drawn 1-1
Ted Blagg was unfortunate to lose his first team place when a broken nose injury forced Forest to enter the transfer market for cover for the centre-half role. Horace Gager was recruited from Luton Town, and he played so well that Blagg was unable to regain his first team place. By far the biggest player on the books at a fraction over six feet and a weight approaching 14 stones, he was signed by manager Billy Walker on his demob from the Army, and played regularly from season 1942-43 to midway through season 1947-48, replacing Wales wartime international Bob Davies in the first season of Second Division football after the war. Southport paid Forest what was, at that time, a hefty fee for a Northern Section club, but he failed to meet expectations at Haig Avenue, appearing in just 11 first team matches. A fine cricketer – a right-hand batsman and right-arm fast medium bowler, he was a member of the Nottinghamshire C.C.C. ground staff and appeared in one first class

match for the County against Leicestershire in June 1948. Unfortunately, rain ruined the match and no decision was reached. Ted Blagg did not bat and bowled only four overs that cost 20 runs. He did rather better in five Minor Counties matches for Notts 2nd X1, and in four games for the Club & Ground, his best bowling figures were 5 wickets for 19 runs against Leicestershire Club & Ground in May 1948.
Appearances: FL: 54 apps 0 gls FAC: 7 apps 0 gls Total: 61 apps 0 gls

BOOTH, Colin

Inside-forward 5' 8" 11st 0lbs
Born: Middleton, Lancs. 30th December 1934
CAREER: Newton Heath Technical College. Manchester Schoolboys. Wolverhampton Wanderers amateur 1949, professional January 1952. **FOREST 31st October 1959, fee £20,000**. Doncaster Rovers August 1962. Oxford United July 1964 to May 1966, fee £7,500. Cambridge United. Cheltenham Town.
Debut v Chelsea (h) 31.10.59, won 3-1
Darkly handsome Colin Booth caused a sensation when playing for Manchester Schoolboys against Swansea Schoolboys in the English Shield final. As a boy he alternated between Maine Road and Old Trafford as a spectator, and both Manchester clubs were included in the eighteen clubs who sought his services, but it was the Wolves who were successful in obtaining his signature. He went on to win one England Under-23 cap while at Molineux, where, despite the strong competition for a first team place, he made the most of his limited opportunities, scoring 26 goals in 78 League appearances. In October 1959 he became the most expensive player on Forest's books, and eight goals in 24 games in his first season assisted Forest to avoid relegation. He then heading the scoring lists in the following two campaigns, being particularly effective in 1960-61 with 19 goals in 35 League matches. On leaving Forest to join Doncaster Rovers he gave Division Four defenders a lot of trouble for two seasons, netting 57 goals in 88 matches. Oxford United paid their then record fee to obtain his services and he enjoyed an outstanding first season, missing only one match, scoring 23 goals to assist his team to promotion from Division Four. Sadly, he played only three more matches before a cruciate knee injury required an operation, and he was forced to retire at the end of the 1966-67 season. He received a fee of £1,000 from the Football League in compensation, and dropped into the Southern League. He later worked in healthcare and retired to Dorset.
Appearances: FL: 87 apps 39 gls FAC: 5 apps 1 gl FLC: 4 apps 1 gl Other: 2 apps 0 gls Total: 98 apps 41 gls
Honours: England Under-23 international, 1 cap.

BOWYER, Ian

Midfield 5' 10" 11st 11lbs
Born: Little Sutton, Cheshire, 6th June 1951
CAREER: Manchester City apprentice June 1966, professional August 1968. Leyton Orient June 1971, fee £25,000. **FOREST 19th October 1973, fee £40,000**. Sunderland January 1981, fee £50,000. **FOREST January 1982, fee £50,000**. Hereford United July 1987, player-manager from October 1987 to May 1990. Grantham Town 1990. Cheltenham Town coach February 1991. Plymouth Argyle assistant-manager 1994 to 1995. Rotherham United coach September 1996. Birmingham City coach 1997 to 2001. **FOREST coach July 2002 to 2005.** Rushden & Diamonds assistant manager to October 2006. Portsmouth scout. Blackburn Rovers scout. Blackpool scout.
Debut v Blackpool (a) 20.10.73, drawn 2-2 (scored one goal)

Ian Bowyer first came into the limelight as a goalscoring teenager with Manchester City in 1969-70. He faded from the scene in the following term and moved to Leyton Orient where he finished as their leading goal scorer in 1971-72. In his first spell at the City Ground he made an immediate impact, scoring on his debut, and netting twice against his former side, Manchester City in a 4-1 FA Cup win. He blossomed following the arrival of Brian Clough into one of the game's outstanding midfielders with the priceless knack of scoring vital goals during Forest's greatest era. He joined Sunderland in January 1981, but suffered a knee injury just two months later and failed to impress in a poor team battling against relegation. After just twelve months at Roker Park he returned to Forest and clocked up another double-century of League appearances before ending his playing career in the colours of Hereford United in season 1989-90. His career aggregate of League appearances totalled 590/38 and he scored 102 goals. Son Gary, also a midfield player, appeared in League football with Hereford United and Rotherham United, and was also on Forest's books without making a League appearance. He is currently the manager of Blackpool.
Appearances: FL: 425/20 apps 68 gls FAC: 34 apps 7 gls FLC: 45/2 apps 13 gls Other: 37/1 apps 8 gls Total: 539/23 apps 97 gls
Honours: (Manchester City) FL Cup winners 1970. European Cup Winners' Cup winners 1970. **(FOREST)** FL Division 1 champions 1978. FL Cup winners 1978, 1979, finalists 1980. European Cup winners 1979, 1980. European Super Cup finalists. Anglo-Scottish Cup winners 1977.

BRIDGETT, Raymond 'Ray' Alwyne

Full-back 5' 10½" 11st 8lbs
Born: Nottingham, 5th April 1947
Died: Walsall, October quarter 1997
CAREER: Walsall Youth. **FOREST amateur July 1962, professional 6th May 1964 to April 1970.**
Debut as sub v Southampton (a) 30.9.67, lost 1-2
Ray Bridgett was playing in junior football in the Walsall district when first recommended to Forest in 1962. He eventually became the mainstay of the Forest Intermediate League defence, who were runners-up in both league and cup competitions in 1966. Compaired in build and style to John Winfield, he nevertheless failed to establish a position in the League side owing to the consistency of the first team full-backs. He was rarely absent from Central League duty, but had a long wait for a first team call, initially from the bench at Southampton and Fulham before a first starting appearance, as deputy for John Winfield, in a 0-2 defeat at Leeds United on 25th November 1967. His second, and final first team appearance came at Burnley in a 0-5 defeat on 21st February 1970.
Appearances: FL: 2/2 apps 0 gls Total: 2/2 apps 0 gls

BRIGHAM, Harold 'Harry'

Full-back 5'8½" 12st 0lbs
Born: Selby, Yorkshire, 19th November 1914
Died: Hull, 14th March 1978
CAREER: South Milford FC. Bolton Wanderers amateur. Frickley Colliery September 1934. Stoke City May 1936. (Wartime guest player with Derby County, Chester and Wrexham). **FOREST 8th November 1946, fee £3,580**. York City July 1948. Gainsborough Trinity June 1950. Selby Town.
Debut v Millwall (h) 9.11.46, lost 1-2
Once described as: "A sturdy defender with a good turn of speed," Harry Brigham, a miner in early days, became an amateur with Bolton Wanderers before he developed into one of the stars of Frickley Colliery's Midland

League side. Stoke City signed him in May 1936, at the age of 21, and he quickly established himself, appearing in 107 League and Cup match before the outbreak of WW2. He continued to assist Stoke throughout the war years, but applied for a transfer in November 1946 and was almost immediately signed by Forest for a fee approaching £4,000. Having lost his first team place in his second season, Brigham was transfer listed in October 1947, but remained at the City Ground until the following season when he joined York City. In two seasons at Bootham Crescent he made 60 League and Cup appearances and scored six goals in his role as penalty kick expert.
Appearances: FL: 35 apps 2 gls FAC: 4 apps 0 gls Total: 39 apps 2 gls

BRINDLEY, John Charles 'Bill'

Full-back 5' 9" 10st 11lbs
Born: Nottingham, 29th January 1947
Died: Nottingham, 6th April 2007
CAREER: Nottingham People's College. Nottingham Schoolboys (Cobbin Cup winners 1962). North Midlands Schoolboys. **FOREST from school, professional February 1964**. Notts County May 1970, fee £5,000. Gillingham July 1976. Grantham Town July 1977. Burton Albion 1979-80. Boston F.C. manager. Heanor Town manager. Ilkeston Town manager 1995. Arnold Town assistant-manager June 1996. Arnold Town manager during season 2003-04, resigned May 2005.
Debut v Stoke City (a) 29.9.65, lost 0-1
Bill Brindley won England Schoolboy caps against Wales and Scotland in 1961, and joined the ground staff at Forest on leaving school. In April 1965 he appeared in the final of the International Youth Tournament, dubbed 'The Little World Cup' in West Germany. He was also a finalist with the Forest Youth team in two International Youth Tournaments in France and Holland in the 1965-66 season. Despite his undoubted pedigree, Brindley had to cross the Trent in search of regular first team football. He was immediately successful at Meadow Lane, two promotions in his first three seasons lifting the Magpies into Division Two. Aside from absences through injury, he was a fixture at right full-back for five consecutive seasons, (appearing in exactly 250 senior matches) and a tremendous stumbling block to any "Fancy Dan" (his own words) wingman who crossed his path!
Appearances: FL: 7/7 apps 1 gl FAC: 1 app 0 gls Total: 8/7 apps 1 gl
Honours: England Schoolboy International, 2 caps 1961-62. England Youth International, 1 app v Ireland 1963-64, and 5 apps in the International Youth Tournament, held in West Germany April 1965. (England reached the final but lost 2-3 to East Germany). (Notts County) FL Division 4 champions 1971.

BROWN, Gordon Steele
Half-back 5' 9" 11st 0lbs
Born: Church Warsop, Notts, 21st March 1929
Died: Nottingham, 15th August 2010
CAREER: Worksop junior football. **FOREST amateur 1st June 1944. Registered again as amateur 15th May 1945, professional 25th December 1946**. York City June 1950. Sutton United July 1958. Shirebrook Miners' Welfare
Debut v Sheffield Wednesday (a) 12.4.47, lost 0-2
Associated with Forest from the tender age of 15, and a professional at 17, Gordon Brown lacked opportunities at the City Ground and was tranfer listed in May 1950. In the following month he was signed by York City, and after a disappointing start, a 2-7 defeat at Tranmere Rovers on his debut, Brown was destined to remain at Bootham Cresent for eight seasons. Initially fielded at inside-forward, he was successfully switched to wing-half and remained a regular first team

player throughout, appearing in 351 League and Cup matches, scoring 25 goals. He appeared in all eight of the FA Cup-ties in season 1954-55 as York City's players became national heroes in an amazing run to the semi-final of the competition, only losing after a replay to Newcastle United, the eventual winners of the trophy. Their 'scalps' along the way included Blackpool, Tottenham Hotspur and Notts County.
Appearances: FL: 1 app 0 gls Total: 1 app 0 gls

BROWN, Robert Albert John 'Sailor'

Inside-forward 5' 8" 10st 5lbs
Born: Great Yarmouth, 7th November 1915
Died: Forres, 27th December 2008
CAREER: St Peter's School. Gorleston Juniors. Gorleston F.C. Charlton Athletic August 1934. (Wartime guest player with Newcastle United, West Ham United, Millwall, York City, Leicester City, Manchester City, Wolverhampton Wanderers and East Fife). **FOREST 11th May 1946, fee £6,750.** Aston Villa October 1947 to retirement in June 1949, fee £9,000. Gorleston player-coach June, player-manager August 1949 to cs 1954. Aston Villa scout 1954 to 1956.
Debut v Barnsley (a) 31.8.46, lost 2-3 (scored one goal)
Known throughout as 'Sailor' Brown, not for any particular association with the sea, but because of a distinctly rolling gait. His overall Football League record – 47 goals in 122 matches – was severely curtailed by the war years, although he was far from inactive during the hostilities, appearing as a guest player for several clubs, representing the RAF and appearing in six wartime internationals for England, in which he scored four goals. Shortly after appearing in the FA Cup Final of 1946 he joined Forest for a then substantial transfer fee of £6,750. He led the scoring list with 16 goals in 41 League matches in his first season, but was in and out of the team at the start of the following term, as Forest lost six of their first seven matches. On November 3rd he was placed on the transfer list, and less than a fortnight later was transferred to Aston Villa, who paid one of the highest fees ever received by Forest at that time. He scored nine goals in 30 League matches for the Villa before being forced to retire due to injury. Outside of the game he worked as a motor mechanic.
Appearances: FL: 45 apps 17 gls FAC: 4 apps 0 gls Total: 49 apps 17 gls
Honours: FA Tour to South Africa 1939. England Wartime International, 6 apps. (Charlton Athletic) FL Cup South finalist 1943, winner 1944. (Millwall) FL Cup South finalist 1945. (Charlton Athletic) FA Cup finalists 1946.

BUCKLEY Alan Peter

Forward 5' 6" 10st 3lbs.
Born: Eastwood, 20th April 1951
CAREER: FOREST apprentice 15th August 1967, professional 24th April 1968. Walsall August 1973. Birmingham City October 1978. Walsall July 1979, including spells as player, player-manager June 1979 to July 1986, fee £175,000. Stourbridge September 1986. Tamworth October 1986. Kettering Town manager November 1986. Grimsby Town manager June 1988. West Bromwich Albion manager Autumn1994. Lincoln City manager cs 1997. Lincoln City manager February 2001 to May 2002. Rochdale manager June to December 2003. Grimsby Town manager November 2006 to September 2008. Grimsby Town Youth Coach June 2012. Debut as sub v Tottenham Hotspur (a) 23.10.71, lost 1-6
Alan Buckley joined Forest straight from school and was signed as a

professional on reaching his 17th birthday. Despite his small stature, he was a frequent scorer for the Colts and in the Intermediate League sides, but on reaching League level he found less success. His career blossomed with Walsall, on either side of a ten-month spell with Birmingham City. The blond-haired striker's overall record for the Saddlers was an impressive one, 205 goals in all competitions in 461/22 appearances. His first brief taste of management came as caretaker following Dave Mackay's departure in 1978, but he led the Saddlers to promotion from Division Four in his first season in charge. Later with Grimsby Town he led them to promotion from Division Four in 1990 and from Division Three in the following year, in all, he achieved three promotions with the Mariners and passed the managerial milestone of overseeing over 1,000 competative matches. At the age of 61 he returned to Grimsby as coach to the Youth Team. Alan's brother, Steve, was a full-back with Luton Town, Derby County and Lincoln City, appearing in 482 League matches, scoring 32 goals. Family traditon continued with Alan's son, Adam, appearing as a midfielder with Grimsby Town and Lincoln City
Appearances: FL: 16/2 apps 1 gl FLC: 0/1 app 0 gls Total: 16/3 apps 1 gl

BURKITT, John 'Jack' Orgill
Wing-half 5' 9½" 11st 9lbs
Born: Wednesbury, Staffordshire, 19th January 1926
Died: Brighouse, Yorkshire, 12th September 2003
CAREER: Darlaston F.C. **FOREST 14th May 1946, fee £500, to retirement in May 1962, when appointed reserve team trainer; later first team trainer from cs 1964.** Notts County manager March 1966 to February 1967. Derby County trainer September 1967 to May 1969.
Debut v Coventry City (a) 30.10.48, won 2-1
Dubbed by many judges as the best uncapped half-back in the country, like manager Billy Walker, Jack Burkitt hailed from Wednesbury, and came to the City Ground as a centre-half from Darlaston FC. Commencing as a member of the 'A' Team in 1946-47, he won the Central Alliance Cup and League medal that season. His first team debut came in 1948 as a wing-half and maintained a high level of performance as a determined and tireless worker, noted for his 100% effort and 90 minites graft. He made a great recovery from a serious knee injury in 1951-52, and hardly missed a match for the next eight seasons, eventually breaking the club's appearance record. He became club captain in 1954-55, and was a member of the team relegated from Division 2 in 1949-50, promoted as champions in 1950-51 and from Division 2 as runners-up in 1956-57. His proudest moment in a long career was, when as captain, he led Forest to a hard-won victory over Luton Town in the Wembley Final of 1958-59. In November 1961 a testimonial game was played against Malmoe as a tribute to Jack Burkitt, whose overall senior appearances for the club had reached the 500 mark on 25th March 1961. He retired from playing in May 1962 to take up a position with the club's coaching and training staff. He was next appointed manager of Notts County in March 1966 but stayed for less than a year, later joining Brian Clough and Peter Taylor as trainer to Derby County. He was subsequently employed as a sub postmaster on Oakdale Road in Nottingham.
Appearances: FL: 463 apps 14 gls FAC: 37 apps 1 gl FLC: 2 apps 0 gls Total: 502 apps 15 gls
Honours: **(FOREST)** FL Division 3 South champions 1951. FA Cup winners 1959.

Jack Burkitt, 1959

BURTON, Bruce **Brian**
Outside-left 5' 9" 10st 10lbs
Born: Nottingham, 28th December 1932
CAREER: Basford Boys' Club. **FOREST apprentice 1949, professional 3rd July 1951 to May 1955.** Grantham Town 1956 to 1961.
Debut v Blackburn Rovers, FAC Round 3 (h) 12.1.52, drawn 2-2
Brian Burton was a N.A.B.C. international who toured Germany and on his return signed professional forms. Described as: "A natural footballer with a deceptive body swerve", like many of his generation his progress was halted by the call of National Service. Promising enough to warrant a first team debut at the age of 19, he nevertheless found his opportunities at a premium with experienced wingmen of the calibre of Collin Collindridge, Hugh McLaren and Peter Small barring his progress.
Appearances: FL: 1 app 0 gls FAC: 2 apps 0 gls Total: 3 apps 0 gls

BUTLIN, Barry Desmond

Forward 5' 11½" 11st 7lbs
Born: Rosliston, Derbyshire, 9th November 1949
CAREER: Granville County Grammar School.Derby County January 1967. Notts County (loan) January to October 1969. Luton Town November 1972, fee £50,000. **FOREST 1st October 1974, fee £122,000**. Brighton & Hove Albion (loan) September 1975. Reading (loan) January 1977. Peterborough United August 1977, fee £20,000. Sheffield United August 1979 to July 1981.
Debut v Aston Villa (a) 2.10.74, lost 0-3
Barry Butlin's early experience of League football came during an extended loan with Notts County. There was the possibility of an extension, but when the Magpies were given the option to take him on a permanent basis they were unable to match the £50,000 fee offered by Luton Town. In season 1973-74 he headed the Hatters' scoring list with 17 when they finished as runners-up in Division Two. A regular with Forest for two seasons, but after playing in ten of the opening twelve matches of 1976-77 he was replaced by Tony Woodcock, loaned to Reading in mid season, and then transferred to Peterborough United in the close season. Forest meanwhile finished third in Division Two and were promoted, Barry Butlin's contribution to the successful campaign being 10/2 League appearances and three goals. In a career spanning eight different League clubs his aggregate figures were 284/4 appearances and 81 goals. A career in finance followed, latterly as financial advisor and mortgage manager with C. Alexander & Partners Ltd. Between July 2000 and October 2010, Barry was also secretary & treasurer of the Derby County Former Players Association.
Appearances: FL: 71/3 apps 17 gls FAC: 7 apps 0 gls FLC: 2 apps 0 gls Other: 5 apps 3 gls Total: 85/3 apps 20 gls

CANNING, Leslie **Daniel 'Danny'**
Goalkeeper 5' 10" 12st 4lbs
Born: Penrhiwceiber, 21st February 1926
Died: Saundersfoot, Pembrokeshire, 30th June 2014
CAREER: Abercynon. Cardiff City July 1945. Swansea Town January 1949. **FOREST 18th July 1951, fee £1,750**. Yarmouth Town August 1952. Newport County August 1955 to April 1956.
Debut v Birmingham City (a) 1.9.51, won 2-0
In Forest's first season back in Division Two following their championship of the Third Division South in 1950-51, Harry Walker continued to dominate the first team goalkeeping position, leaving Danny Canning few opportunities. The fair-haired Welshman was a more than competent reserve, having appeared in 80 League matches for Cardiff City, and 47 for Swansea

Town, including 18 in 1948-49 when the Third Division South championship was won. After leaving Forest, he spent three seasons with Yarmouth Town and followed with a final term as reserve goalkeeper with Newport County. Outside of the game, his occupations included a spell as an apprentice toolmaker, and later an electronics engineer designing military equipment.
Appearances: FL: 5 apps 0 gls Total: 5 apps 0 gls
Honours: (Swansea Town) FL Division 3 South champions 1949. Welsh Cup finalists 1949, winners 1950.

CAPEL, Thomas Arthur 'Tommy')

Inside-forward 5' 10½" 11st 6lbs
Born: Chorlton-on-Medlock, 27th June 1922
Died: Basford, Nottingham, 5th October 2009
CAREER: Manchester Schoolboys. Rusholme F.C. Goslings F.C.. Droylsden F.C. Manchester City November 1941. Chesterfield October 1947. Birmingham City June 1949. **FOREST 4th November 1949, fee £13,500,** Coventry City June 1954, along with Colin Collindridge for a combined fee of £10,500. Halifax Town October 1955. Heanor Town July 1956 to 1962.
Debut v Crystal Palace (h) 5.11.49, won 2-0
Most of Tommy Capel's early football was played in the Manchester area. He played for Manchester Boys, Rusholme and the Goslings and was still in junior circles when he joined the Marines in 1942. In India and Ceylon, they discovered his talent, and he was soon playing in Service Representative matches. Back at home several clubs sought his signature, but being Manchester born, City was his choice. Bob Brocklebank, then manager of Chesterfield then sought his transfer. City demanded Billy Linacre in part exchange. So manager Brocklebank made his shrewdest move-Linacre for Capel and Peter Robinson. As an interesting aside, Capel and Robinson, both Manchester born, were then dubbed the 'twins' of football. Apart from the war they had been inseparable since their schooldays. They played together for Manchester Boys and signed amateur forms with Manchester City on the same day. Two years later, at the age of eighteen, they enlisted on the same day. Capel joined the Royal Marines and Robinson the Army. They were demobbed on the same day, and joined Chesterfield on the same day. Their paths diverged when manager Brocklebank moved to Birmingham City, he signed Capel for the second time in 20 months, on this occasion paying £10,000 for his transfer. His subsequent move to Forest came as no surprise, as since joining Birmingham he was just not able to recapture the brilliant form that made him the talk of Chesterfield. Forest's manager Billy Walker evidently had no doubts about his great ability for he paid £14,000 for his transfer-at that time the highest Forest had ever paid for a player. An early match report suggested that the record signing was money well spent: "Forest were inspired by the wizardry of Capel whose electric bursts and corkscrew dribbles made him the outstanding forward." In Forest's Third Division South championship season he scored 23 goals in 35 matches, and it was suggested at the time that if his right foot had been as effective as his left he would have surely been an England international. His career aggregate figures, for six different League clubs, were certainly impressive-120 goals in 276 matches. His younger brother, Fred was a full-back with Chesterfield from 1948 to 1957, appearing in 285 League matches, scoring 16 goals.
Appearances: FL: 154 apps 69 gls FAC: 8 apps 3 gls Total: 162 apps 72 gls
Honours: **(FOREST**) FL Division 3 South champions 1951

CARGILL, James 'Jimmy' Gordon
Goalkeeper 5' 9" 11st 1lb
Born: Alyth, Dundee, 22nd September 1945
CAREER: Dundee Schoolboys. Dundee North End. **FOREST apprentice October 1961, professional September 1962.** Notts County July 1966 to April 1967.

Debut v Arsenal (a) 6.10.64, won 3-0

Jimmy Cargill joined Forest from Scottish schools football. He was capped by Scotland schools in 1961 and in1963 represented Scotland in the International Youth Tournament at Wembley. As deputy to Peter Grummitt, he kept a good goal on his League debut, a 3-0 win at Highbury. A more than useful reserve, he was nevertheless unable to break Grummitt's monopoly of the position. Crossing the Trent to Meadow Lane for a season in Division Four he shared first team duties with George Smith and Mike Rose, making 10 League appearances. He was released from his contract in April 1967, having taken up employment, outside of the game, in Nottingham.

Appearances: FL: 2 apps 0 gls FAC: 1 app 0 gls Total: 3 apps 0 gls

Honours: Scotland Schoolboy International, 4 caps 1961. Scotland Youth International, 1 app. 1963.

CHAPMAN, Robert Dennis 'Sammy'

Central defender 5' 10" 11st 8lbs

Born: Walsall, 18th August 1946

CAREER: Staffordshire junior football. **FOREST amateur March 1962, professional August 1963**. Notts County August 1977, fee £7,500. Shrewsbury Town July 1978, Tulsa Roughnecks USA March to August 1979. Burton Albion until April 1981. Keyworth United (there January 1985). Selective Travel (there May 1985, when he helped them to win the Notts FA Thursday League Cup.)

Debut v Stoke City (h) 18.1.64, drawn 0-0

Spotted by a Forest scout when playing in Staffordshire youth football and, after trials at the City Ground, Sammy Chapman signed professional forms on his 17th birthday. He became the youngest forward ever to appear for the club at senior level when he made his debut against Stoke City in January 1964. He also captained Forest's Youth Team in the European International Tournaments in France and Holland in the summer of 1965. Chapman eventually succeeded Frank Wignall as attack leader in 1967-68, but it was not until his conversion to a defender that he found his regular place in the side. Having assisted Forest to promotion from Division Two in 1977, he was allowed to move across the Trent to join Notts County, following the signing of his replacement, Kenny Burns. Despite appearing in all but one of the season's League and Cup matches during his spell at Meadow Lane, he moved on to Shrewsbury Town in the close season. He played in 24/1 League matches and scored four goals in a successful season for the Shrews who won the championship of Division Three, additionally reaching Round Six of the FA Cup before losing to Wolverhampton Wanderers after a replay. Sammy is currently employed with his wife Hazel in a family business, Rushcliffe Fencing Ltd of Gotham.

Appearances: FL: 347/12 apps 17 gls FAC: 30/2 apps 2 gls FLC: 19/1 apps 1 gls Other: 11/1 apps 3 gls Total: 407/15 apps 23 gls

Honours: (Shrewsbury Town) FL Division 3 champions 1979

CLARKE, James 'Jim'

Full-back 5' 9½" 11st 1lb

Born: Wednesbury, Staffordshire, 7th December 1923

Died: 12th December 2014

CAREER: FOREST junior *circa* 1944, professional 14th May 1946 to May 1954. Boston United 1955.

Debut v Newcastle United (h) 27.3.48, drawn 0-0

A full-back who believed in making the ball do the work, Jim Clarke had many admirers as a studious type of player who tried to use the ball to the best advantage. A part-time dental

mechanic, and for many seasons the backbone of the Midland League side, he just seemed to lack that extra 'bite' in his play to seriously challenge players of the calibre of Whare, Thomas and Hutchinson.
Appearances: FL: 18 apps 0 gls FAC: 2 apps 0 gls Total: 20 apps 0 gls

CLUROE, Malcolm
Inside-forward 5' 9" 11st 2 lbs
Born: Nottingham, 6th February 1935
Died: Nottingham, 26th September 2006
CAREER: Oakwell Rangers. **FOREST amateur July 1952, professional 24th November 1954.**
Debut v Luton Town (h) 18.12.54, lost 1-5
A National Association of Boys' Clubs international whose progress was not maintained after he had scored 15 goals in 23 matches for the Midland League side in season 1955-56. He was expected to develop when free of National Service duties with the RAF, but then failed to show the anticipated progress on returning to civilian life. His one senior appearance resulted in the heaviest home defeat of the season.
Appearances: FL: 1 app 0 gls Total: 1 app 0 gls

COBB, Walter **William 'Billy'**

Forward/Midfield 5' 8" 10st 5lbs
Born: Newark, Notts. 29th September 1940
CAREER: Ransome & Marles. **FOREST amateur October 1958, professional 21st September 1959 (#).** Plymouth Argyle October 1963. Brentford October 1964, fee £5,000. Lincoln City November 1966. Boston United July 1968 to May 1971.
Debut v Preston North End (a) 26.12.60, won 1-0
Signed as an amateur from the Newark works of Ransome & Marles, Billy Cobb began in Forest's Youth Team and signed professional forms in September 1959. Considered an inside-left of considerable promise he developed into the ultimate utility man, appearing in no fewer than seven different positions in 1962-63, as diverse as outside-left and right half-back. In the previous season he became Forest's first scorer in the Inter-Cities Fairs Cup-tie against Valencia CF in October 1961. When former Forest manager Andy Beattie took over as caretaker-manager to the relegation-threatened Plymouth Argyle side, he signed Billy Cobb and Dougie Baird from his old club and, by the narrowest of margins, relegation from Division Two was averted. Moving on to Brentford, Cobb was leading scorer in his first season with 18 goals, and later commenced with a bang at Lincoln City, scoring a hat trick on his debut in an 8-1 win against Luton Town. His career aggregate figures for four different League clubs were 197/2 appearances and 38 goals. Latterly employed locally as licensee of the Sherwood Inn and as manager of bars at the Nottingham Ice Stadium.
Appearances: FL: 30 apps 5 gls FAC: 4 apps 0 gls FLC: 1 app 1 gl Other: 1 app 1 gl Total: 36 apps 7 gls

COLLIER, Graham Ronald
Centre-forward 6' 0" 11st 5lbs
Born: Lenton, Nottingham, 12th September 1951
CAREER: Nottingham Schoolboys. FOREST apprentice 3rd May 1967, professional 26th March 1969. Scunthorpe United July 1972. Barnsley August 1977, fee £5,000. Buxton cs 1978. York City September-November 1978. Grantham Town. Boston United 1980 to 1982. Burton Town. Ilkeston Town assistant-manager June 1994.
Debut v Wolverhampton Wanderers (a) 6.9.69, drawn 3-3

Graham Collier graduated through the Colts and Intermediates, and was a member of the team that won the Swiss Shield. A tall youngster who played mainly at centre-forward in the reserves, he lacked opportunities at the City Ground, but his career took off when he joined Scunthorpe United. Settling in a midfield role he clocked up 155/6 League appearances and 19 goals for the Iron before taking his career total to over the 200 mark in final spells with Barnsley and York City.
Appearances: FL: 13/2 apps 2 gls FAC: 2/2 apps 2 gls Total: 15/4 apps 4 gls

COLLINDRIDGE, Colin

Outside-left 5' 10" 11st 6lbs
Born: Barugh Green, Barnsley, 15th November 1920
Died: 14th April 2019
CAREER: Wombwell Main. (Trials with Rotherham United and Forest). Barugh Green FC. Wolverhampton Wanderes amateur. Sheffield United January 1939. **FOREST 17th August 1950, fee £12,500**. Coventry City June 1954, along with Tommy Capel for a combined fee of £10,500. Bath City July 1956. Arnold St. Mary's.
Debut v Newport County (a) 18.8.50 (scored one goal)
Rotherham United signed Colin Collindridge for trials on his 17th birthday, but released him a few weeks later. Forest stepped in and gave him a series of trials but considered that he would never be strong enough for League football. A very bad decision as things turned out, as the prematurely balding wingman eventually proved to be one of the most valuable acquisitions ever signed by the club. Collindridge gave Sheffield United excellent service, dividing his appearances for the Blades almost equally between leading the attack, and playing on the left-wing. When he asked for a transfer, he stated that he felt he could do better at outside-left (his real position) instead of centre-forward. He certainly was a speedy wingman with a terrific left-foot shot and was extremely popular with players and spectators alike at the City Ground. In his first season, Forest scored 110 League goals and conceded just 40 to take the Third Division South title with a six-point margin over runners-up, Norwich City. One of four ever-presents during the campaign, Collindridge netted 16 goals. Unfortunately, through injury, he missed most of the games in the second half of the following season. During his absence the forward line lacked finish and it was widely felt that the loss of his services had cost Forest a return to the top flight, as they finished fourth in Division Two, when an additional three points would have seen them promoted. After again missing out on promotion by finishing fourth in season 1953-54, wholesale changes in the playing staff saw the departure of both Collindridge and Capel, Forest's regular left-wing pairing, to Coventry City. Two seasons in the Third Division South wound up Collindridge's senior career in which he netted 103 League goals in 327 matches. He was, however, still enjoying his football while turning out with Arnold St Mary's in the early 1960s.
Appearances: FL: 151 apps 45 gls FAC: 5 apps 2 gls Total: 156 apps 47 gls
Honours: **(FOREST)** FL Division 3 South champions 1951

CORMACK, Peter Barr

Midfield 5' 9" 10st 12lbs
Born: Granton, Edinburgh, 17th July 1946
CAREER: Tynecastle Boys' Club. Heart of Midlothian groundstaff. Hibernian August 1962. **FOREST 27th March 1970, fee £80,000**. Liverpool July 1972, fee £110,000. Toronto City (guest) 1967. Bristol City November 1976, fee £50,000. Hibernian February 1980. Partick Thistle manager December 1980 to May 1984. Anorthosis FC, Famagusta (Cyprus) manager 1984-85. Botswana national team coach 1986. Hibernian assistant-manager November 1986. Morton assistant manager July 1994. Anorthosis (Cyprus) manager 1985 to 1986. Cowdenbeath manager December 2000. Morton manager July 2001 to March 2002.
Debut v West Bromwich Albion (a) 4.4.70, lost 0-4

Signed by Forest as an inside-forward, in which position he had scored 76 goals in 182/1 Scottish League matches for Hibernian. Peter Cormack's transition to a midfield role occurred during his spell at the City Ground and he struggled to adapt in his changed role in a poor Forest side of 1971-72 who won only six matches at home, and two on foreign soil. As Forest were relegated, Cormack joined Liverpool, having been recommended to their manager, Bill Shanky, by his brother Bob. It was success all the way for the attacking midfielder who collected FL Championship and UEFA Cup medals in his first season at Anfield, following with an FA Cup winners' award and a second FL Championship. In four seasons he accumulated 168/9 League and Cup appearances and scored 26 goals, and it was surprising that he did not add to his collection of Scottish caps during such a successful spell with the Anfield Reds. He did appear in Scottish squads for five different managers. A spell with Bristol City ended in their Division One relegation season 1979-80 and a brief return to his first club, Hibernian, preceded his move into management, initially with Partick Thistle where he replaced Bertie Auld. Goals were in short supply, but an improved defensive record kept the Jags in the Premier League in his first season. They were relegated in the following term and were still in Division One when he took his first overseas appointment. In the 1990s he had a painting and decorating business that employed thirty people. In 2017 he was inducted into the Hibernian FC Hall of Fame.

Appearances: FL: 74 apps 15 gls FAC: 6 apps 1 gl FLC: 4 apps 2 gls Other: 2 apps 2 gls Total: 86 apps 20 gls

Honours: Scotland Amateur and Full International, 9 caps. Scotland Under-23 International, 5 caps. Scottish League representative 6 apps. (Hibernian) Scottish League Cup finalists 1969. (Liverpool). UEFA Cup winners 1973. FL Division 1 champions 1973, 1976. FA Cup winners 1974.

COTTAM, John Edward

Central defender 6' 0" 13st 0lbs
Born: Worksop, 5th June 1950
CAREER: FOREST apprentice 5th August 1966, professional 24th April 1968. Mansfield Town (loan) November 1972. Lincoln City (loan) March 1973. Chesterfield August 1976, fee £7,000. Chester July 1979, fee £15,000. Scarborough July 1982, player-manager from June to October 1984. Burton Albion 1984. Bridlington Town December 1985.

John Cottam captained the Forest Colts team that won the Swiss Shield by defeating the County Police in the final at the City Ground. During the 1967-68 season he became established in the Central League side in the centre-half position. He had some time to wait for a first team place, but this came when Liam O'Kane was injured in December 1971. A dominant figure whose physical presence alone did much to inspire confidence in his fellow defenders, Cottam played under five different managers in his

decade at the City Ground, his longest spell of first team action coming in 1973-74 when Forest finished in seventh place in Division Two. He subsequently gave excellent service to both Chesterfield (120 League matches and seven goals) and Chester (117/3 League matches and one goal).
Debut v Sheffield United (a) 18.12.71, lost 1-2
Appearances: FL: 92/3 apps 4 gls FAC: 7/1 apps 0 gls FLC: 5 apps 0 gls Total: 104/4 apps 4 gls

COYLE, Francis 'Fay'
Centre-forward 5' 10" 11st 3lbs
Born: Londonderry, N. Ireland, 1st April 1933
Died: Londonderry, N. Ireland, 30th February 2007
CAREER: Coleraine 1953. **FOREST 6th March 1958, fee £250.**
Debut v Chelsea (a) 4.4.58, drawn 0-0
A much decorated Irish international, Fay Coyle made several appearances for the Irish League X1 and represented his country against England and Scotland in 1955, and against Portugal and Argentine in World Cup matches. The latter appearance made when he was on Forest's books. In three outings for the Reds in late season 1957-58 he showed some nice touches on the ball, but found the pace of English football "slightly disconcerning" according to the 'Post Guide' for season 1958-59.
Appearances: FL: 3 apps 0 gls Total: 3 apps 0 gls
Honours: Northern Ireland Amateur and full International, 4 caps 1955-58. Irish League representative 4 apps.

CROWE, Christopher 'Chris'

Inside-forward 5' 7" 11st 5lbs
Born: Newcastle-on-Tyne, 11th June 1939
Died: Bristol, May 2003
CAREER: Edinburgh Schoolboys. Leeds United amateur October 1954, professional June 1956. Blackburn Rovers March 1960, fee £25,000. Wolverhampton Wanderers February 1962, fee £28,000. **FOREST 22nd August 1964, fee £45,000**. Bristol City January 1967. Walsall September 1969. Auburn F.C., Australia May 1970. Bath City February to May 1971.
Debut v Birmingham City (h) 22.8.64, won 4-3
Although born at Newcastle-upon-Tyne, Chris Crowe was living in Edinburgh when he won Scottish Schoolboy honours. He joined Leeds United from school and remained there until March 1960 when he was transferred to Blackburn Rovers. Despite winning two England Under-23 caps while at Ewood he failed to meet expectations and had lost his first team place at the time of his move to Wolverhampton Wanderers in February 1962. A return to his best form at Molineux earned him his England cap against France in 1963 and he cost Forest a club record fee when signed by manager Johnny Carey in August 1964. Fielded mainly on the right wing during his stay at the City Ground, his hat trick against Manchester United in a 4-2 win on 1st October 1966 was a personal highlight, but the signing of Barry Lyons in the following month effectively ended Chris Crowe's involvement at senior level and he departed to Bristol City in mid season where he linked effectively with ex-Forest star Johnny Quigley, appearing in 66/1 League matches and scoring 13 goals. Walsall was his final League club, where he took his overall career figures to 378/4 League matches and 83 goals.
Appearances: FL: 73 apps 12 gls FAC: 3 apps 2 gls FLC: 2 apps 1 gl Total: 78 apps 15 gls
Honours: Scotland Schoolboy International. England Youth international. England Under-23 International, 4 apps. England international, 1 cap v France 1963

DAVIES, Robert Griffith
Centre half-back
Born: Blaenau Ffestiniog, North Wales, 19th October 1913
Died: Nottingham, 10th May 1978
Debut v Bradford Park Avenue (h) 6.3.37, won 3-2
CAREER: Blaenau Ffestiniog F.C. July 1932. **FOREST amateur 21st July, professional 2nd December 1936, fee £55 plus the proceeds of a match**. (Wartime guest player with Notts County, Blackpool, Leicester City. Rochdale and Wrexham). **FOREST Reserve team coach 1947-54. Later physiotherapist to 1974.** Walsall physiotherapist to his death
A central defender with few frills in his play, Bob Davies was a strapping figure who kicked like a horse – according to the' Post Football Guide' – who also considered that he should; "Lie further up the field, the third back game can be carried to excess." Despite operating in the shadow of star centre-half Tommy Graham, Davies proved a sound deputy, able to occupy both wing-half berths as required. He volunteered for the RAF when war broke out, where he studied physiotherapy and became a qualified masseur. He was one of several Forest unfortunates who succumbed to cartilage problems, an operation restricting his activities in his final season, 1946-47. This was far from the end of the story, however, as he remained at the City Ground for a further twenty-plus years, memorably as trainer to the successful Midland League side. In September 1963 the Sportsmen's Club made a presentation to Forest's popular and long-serving masseur, at a dance at the Commodore Ballroom. He was also working during summer months as masseur to the Nottinghamshire County Cricket Club. In the summer of 1974, in preperation for his first full season as Forest's manager, Allan Brown created surprise when he sacked Bob Davies. Ironically, he was sacked himself just 13 months later.
Appearances: FL: 55 apps 0 gls FAC: 4 apps 0 gls Total: 59 apps 0 gls
Honours: Wales Wartime International, 6 apps.

DENNEHY, Jeremiah 'Miah'
Outside-left 5' 6" 10st 4lbs
Born: Cork, Ireland, 29th March 1950
CAREER: Cork Hibernian. **FOREST February 1973, fee £20,000**. Shamrock Rovers (loan). Walsall July 1975. Bristol Rovers July 1978. Trowbridge Town August 1980. Cork United. Waterford 1981-82. Limerick United 1982-83. Drogheda United 1985. Newcastle West End 1985.
Debut v Preston North End (a) 21.4.73, lost 1-2
Miah Dennehy joined Forest from League of Ireland club Cork Hibernian. Ironically, his best season at the City Ground was his last, although he played little following the appointment of Brian Clough as manager in January 1975. Despite his exceptional skills on the ball, the lightly built Irishman failed to hold down a first team place in his first full season, but he continued to find favour with the Irish selectors, winning seven of his eleven caps while on Forest's books. He was certainly more at home in Division Three with Walsall, missing very few matches in a stay of three seasons, scoring 22 goals in 128 League matches. He followed with 52 appearances and six goals for Bristol Rovers before stepping down, initially into non-League football and later an Irish sojourn. In August 2007 Miah was serious assaulted in a pub in Mayfield and spent several weeks in hospital in a coma having sustained brain damage. His attacker was jailed for six years.
Appearances: FL: 37/4 apps 4 gls FAC: 2/2 apps 0 gls FLC: 2 apps 0 gls Total: 41/6 apps 4 gls
Honours: Ireland International, 11 caps. Ireland Under-23 International 1 cap.

DWIGHT, Royston 'Roy' Edward

Outside-right 5' 8" 11st 7lbs
Born: Belvedere, Kent, 9th January 1933
Died: Woolwich, London, 9th April 2002
CAREER: Erith Technical School. North Kent schoolboys. Kent County schoolboys. Hastings United Reserves. Slades Green Athletic. Fulham amateur 1949, professional June 1950. **FOREST 21st July 1958, fee £7,000.** Gravesend & Northfleet February 1961. Coventry City January 1962. Millwall January 1964, youth team manager September 1964. Dartford player-coach August 1965. Erith & Belvedere manager January to August 1968. Detroit Cougars (NASL) coach August 1968. Erith & Belvedere manager January 1969. Tooting & Mitcham manager December 1971 to 1976. Dartford manager May 1976 to February 1978. Tilbury manager February 1978.
Debut v Wolverhampton Wanderers (a) 23.8.59, lost 1-5 (scored)
A star in school's football, and a Charlton Athletic fan as a youngster, Roy Dwight was spotted by a Fulham scout when playing for Slades Green Athletic on Dartford Heath. Invited for a trial at Craven Cottage, he was then signed on amateur forms at the age of sixteen. Two appearances for England's Youth team followed, played against the youth teams of Switzerland and Luxembourg in Vienna. National Service in the R.A.M.C. interrupted his progress, and it was not until March 1955 that he made his League debut against Birmingham City at Craven Cottage, scoring in a 2-3 defeat. Occasional first team games followed, but his big chance came in unfortunate circumstances, when Bedford Jezzard's career was prematurely ended by an ankle injury sustained on the FA's tour of South Africa in 1956. In the two seasons prior to joining Forest, Roy Dwight scored 26 goals in 1956-57 and 24 in 1957-58. Although fielded out of position on his Forest debut, he scored against the Wolves and was quickly switched to the right wing with Billy Gray moving over to inside-left. With all the necessary attributes of pace and footwork for his position, Dwight also packed a terrific shot that netted him 26 goals in League and Cup in his debut season. Sadly, after scoring the opening goal in the FA Cup Final win against Luton Town he suffered a broken leg. He was out until March of the following year, scored on his return, but managed to play in only three matches. His bad luck continued early in the following season with a broken arm suffered in a reserve team match against Birmingham City Reserves, and yet another set back came in the form of Achilles trouble. Departing into non-League football with Gravesend & Northfleet, it appeared that his senior career was at an end but he returned to League football with Coventry City (31 matches and eight goals) and finally Millwall (seven matches and two goals). Roy was the uncle of singer Elton John, who acted as a pageboy at Roy's wedding.
Appearances: FL: 44 apps 21 gls FAC: 9 apps 6 gls Total: 53 apps 27 gls
Honours: England Youth International. (**FOREST**) FA Cup winners 1959

EDWARDS, John 'Jack'

Inside-forward 5' 10" 10st 7lbs
Born: Salford, 23rd February 1924
Died: Nottingham, December 1978
CAREER: Adelphi Lads' Club. Long Eaton United. **FOREST 3rd May 1944**. Southampton June 1949, fee £10,000. Kidderminster Harriers (loan) June 1952. Notts County November 1952, in exchange for Alex Simpson. Kings Lynn cs 1954. Great Yarmouth Town player-manager August 1955 to January 1956.
Debut v Newcastle United (h) 5.9.46, lost 0-2
Born within walking distance of Manchester United's ground, Jack Edwards played for Adelphi Lads' Club from the age of 15. During the war he served in the Navy, and it was while playing for a Navy team he was spotted by a Navy Commander who happened to be a keen

supporter of the Forest. On his recommendation, manager Billy Walker gave Edwards a trial and signed him immediately. At this stage Edwards was outstanding for his shooting power and clever ball control, and when Forest visited Liverpool in a 1947-48 FA Cup-tie, the Merseysidde club made a big offer for his transfer after the game. Forest refused to let him go, and during the following campaign turned down three more offers, reported to be in the region of £15,000. When Forest were relegated, however, Edwards was one of three players who requested a transfer, and Southampton stepped in with a successful offer. He joined a former Forest colleague, Roland Wheatley, who was transferred to Southampton in the previous season. The 'Notts Journal' commented that while Edwards was a brilliant ball player when on form, he had failed to do himself justice in the team that was relegated from Division Two. In three years at the Dell he appeared in 85 matches and scored 16 goals, but he was out on loan at Kidderminster Harriers when Notts County signed him in an exchange deal that took Alex Simpson to the Dell. After appearing regularly in his first season at Meadow Lane, he did not feature after the appointment of new manager George Poyser on 22nd October 1953. Jack Edwards was later to lose his life in a street mugging in Nottingham in December 1978.
Appearances: FL: 77 apps 20 gls FAC: 4 apps 1 gl Total: 81 apps 21 gls

ELLIOTT, Bernard 'Bryn' Harry
Wing-half 5' 7" 9st 12lbs
Born: Beeston, Notts. 3rd May 1925
CAREER: Beeston Fields Senior School. Beeston Lads' Club. **FOREST October 1942**. Boston United August 1948. Southampton October 1949, fee £1,050. Poole Town July 1969 to May 1960.
Debut v Birmingham City (a) 3.4.48, lost 1-2
A Forest wartime discovery with 34 appearances in the Football League North, and five goals, all from the penalty spot in 1944-45, a total that included two in one match against Notts County in April 1945. When normal League football resumed after the hostilities, Elliott's only run in the first team came in the relegation season 1948-49. Before leaving the City Ground in October 1949 he had spent some months with Boston United when Southampton brought him back into League football, and his lengthy spell with the Saints brought regular first team football for the first time in his career, spanning 251 League and Cup matches and two goals. He later ran an off-licence in Freemantle (Southampton) for over forty years.
Appearances: FL: 10 apps 0 gls Total: 10 apps 0 gls

FARMER, Ronald 'Ron' James

Wing-half 5' 8½" 12st 3lbs
Born: Guernsey, Channel Islands, 6th March 1936
CAREER: North Athletic Club. **FOREST 20th May 1953**. Coventry City November 1958, with Arthur Lightening (q.v.) for a combined fee of £6,000. Notts County October 1967, fee £12,000. Grantham Town July 1969, retired 1970. Coventry City youth-team coach.
Debut v Gillingham, FAC 3, (h) 4.1.57, won 2-0
Captain of Forest's Youth team, Ron Farmer became the third member of the playing staff to hail from the Channel Islands when he joined the club as an amateur in 1951, on the recommendation of his brother, Bill, Forest's goalkeeper. In the latter part of his National Service with the RAF he had a cartilage operation but made an excellent recovery. Failing to establish a first team place at the City ground, he moved on to Coventry City and became an important element in the Sky Blues' meteoric elevation from Division Four to Division One, appearing in over 300 matches as an attacking wing-half, scoring 52 goals in nine seasons at Highfield Road. Two seasons with Notts County followed in which he missed very few matches, making 71 League and Cup appearances, scoring five goals.
Appearances: FL: 9 apps 0 gls FAC: 1 app 0 gls Total: 10 apps 0 gls
Honours: (Coventry City) FL Division 3 champions 1964. FL Division 2 champions 1967.

FARMER, William 'Bill' Henry

Goalkeeper 6' 1" 11st 4lbs
Born: Guernsey, Channel Islands, 24th November 1927
Died: Corby, 12th July 2014
CAREER: St. Martin's F.C. (Guernsey). **FOREST May 1951**. Brush Sports (Loughborough) June 1957. Oldham Athletic July 1957, fee £350. Worcester City July 1968. Coventry City (trial) August-September 1959. Corby Town October 1959 to cs 1962.
Debut v Hull City (h) 16.9.53, won 2-0
Goalkeeper Bill Farmer was recommended to the club by Ted Malpas, a former playing colleague of Forest's manager, Billy Walker. Several League clubs were interested, but Farmer decided to join his fellow Channel-Islander, Bill Whare, at the City Ground. Understudy to the consistent Harry Walker for two seasons, his chance came in 1953-54 but he was injured after making twelve appearances. He took over for a lengthy run of 28 League matches in the following term, but was back in reserve in 1955-56 with Harry Nicholson, the ex-Grimsby Town 'keeper the main man throughout the promotion season. Placed on the transfer list in April 1957, Bradford Park Avenue expressed an interest, but while they hesitated, Brush Sports stepped in. Farmer became a Brush Sports player for one month, but he never played for the Birmingham League club. In late July Oldham Athletic paid Forest £400 for his transfer. Sadly, the Latics made a dreadful start to the season 1957-58 and Bill Farmer lost his place after conceding 13 goals in his five appearances. In a 1956 interview, Farmer stated that he intended to return to his old trade of painting and decorating when his playing days ended. He kept his hand in with odd jobs, and in another string to his bow, each summer he took a job as a carpet salesman.
Appearances: FL: 52 apps 0 gls FAC: 6 apps 0 gls Total: 58 apps 0 gls

FRASER, Douglas 'Doug' Michael
Defender 5' 8" 11st 4lbs
Born: Busby, Renfrewshire, 8th December 1941
CAREER: Rolls Royce F.C. Eaglesham Amateurs. Blantyre Celtic 1956. Trials with Celtic and Leeds United. Aberdeen amateur April 1958, professional December 1959. West Bromwich Albion September 1963, fee £ 23,000. **FOREST January 1971, fee £ 35,000**. Walsall July 1973, player-manager January 1974 to March 1977, fee £8,000.
Debut v Newcastle United (h) 16.1.71, won 2-1
Doug Fraser began his senior career with Aberdeen, making his debut against Ayr United in a 2-0 home win on 30th April 1960. He went on to accumulate 88 Scottish League and Cup appearances and scored two goals before joining West Bromwich Albion in September 1963. A stylish and hard-working wing half or full-back, he appeared in over 300 League and Cup matches, appeared in three League Cup Finals and was an FA Cup winner in 1968 against Everton. He won his two Scottish caps while on Albion's books, his debut coming in a 0-0 draw against Holland in Amsterdam in May 1968, and his second cap in a 5-0 win against Cyprus in Nicosia in December of the same year. Forest were lifted by his arrival in January 1971, but they were relegated in the following season and finished in a disappointing 14th place in Division Two in 1972-73. In this season he met up again with his former team, West Bromwich Albion, when four matches were required to determine the outcome of the Fourth Round FA Cup-tie, eventually decided after two replays when Albion progressed with a 3-1 win at Filbert Street, Leicester. Fraser's playing career wound up with Walsall (26/1 League appearances) and he then left the game to work as a prison officer in Nottingham.
Appearances: FL: 85 apps 3 gls FAC: 7 apps 0 gls Other: 3 apps 1 gl Total: 95 apps 4 gls

Honours: Scotland International, 2 caps 1968-69. (West Bromwich Albion) FL Cup winner 1966, finalists 1957, 1970. FA Cup winner 1966.

FRASER, William 'Willie' Alexander

Goalkeeper 6' 0" 11st 13lbs
Born: Brighton, Victoria, Australia, 24th February 1929
Died: Kirkcaldy, 7th March 1966
CAREER: Cowie F.C. Stirling Juniors. Third Lanark 1947. Sunderland March 1954, fee £5,000. **FOREST 29th December 1958 to 1959, fee £5,000.**
Debut v Birmingham City (h) 7.3.59, lost 1-7
Willie Fraser qualified for Scotland by reason of Scottish parentage: his mother was born in Stirling, his father in Inverness. Willie had arrived in Scotland from Australia at the age of six and lived in Stirling from then on. He first played in 105 games for Airdrie before joining Sunderland for whom he made 143 League and Cup appearances, highlights being his appearances in the FA Cup semi-finals of both 1955 and 1956. Both of his Scottish caps were earned while at Roker Park, in season 1954-55 against Wales and Northern Ireland. He became the twelfth Scot on Forest's books when signed, and the third international from that country, joining Joe McDonald and Stewart Imlach. Signed to strengthen reserve ranks, with Chic Thomson the regular first team goalkeeper, he was summoned from Sunderland, where he did his training, as stand in for 'flu victim Thomson, for the fifth round FA Cup-tie at Birmingham. In the event, Thomson recovered and Fraser's debut, against the same opponents but in a Division One match, featured a much-changed Forest line-up who were hammered 7-1 in the worst display of a season when Forest went on to lift the FA Cup.
Appearances: FL: 2 apps 0 gls Total: 2 apps 0 gls
Honours: Scotland International, 2 caps 1954-55

FRENCH, John 'Jackie' William

Wing-half 6' 0" 12st 0lbs
Born: Stockton-on-Tees, 19th January 1925
Died: Ipswich, 9th March 2002
CAREER: Middlesbrough October 1943. Southend United February 1947. **FOREST 3rd November 1952, fee £7,500.** Southend United July 1956, fee £450. Folkestone Town June 1957. Basildon player-manager.
Debut v Rotherham United (a) 1.11.52, won 3-2
Jackie French was a nephew of John Proctor French, also known as Jackie, a full-back with Middlesbrough, Southend United and Brentford in the 1920s and 1930s. Their careers had some similarities, as both commenced with Middlesborough before moving to Southend in search of regular first team football. J P French made 174 appearances and scored two goals, while Jackie made 182 and scored 19 goals. Jackie was a strong, attacking half-back who, on joining Forest, was ever present until he sustained a severe ankle injury at Rotherham United in January 1954. The injury was slow to mend, and it was not until February of the following year that he was finally back, and he scored Forest's only goal in a 4-1 defeat against Notts County at Meadow Lane. In his final season, stiff competition from Bill Morley limited his appearances to 13 Division Two matches. In the summer he returned to Southend United for another season but made only five appearances before dropping into non-League football. In April 1948, Jackie French was captaining the Royal Armoured Corps in an Army Cup Final replay at Aldershot when two players were tragically killed by a lightening strike.
Appearances: FL: 80 apps 8 gls FAC: 6 apps 0 gls Total: 86 apps 8 gls

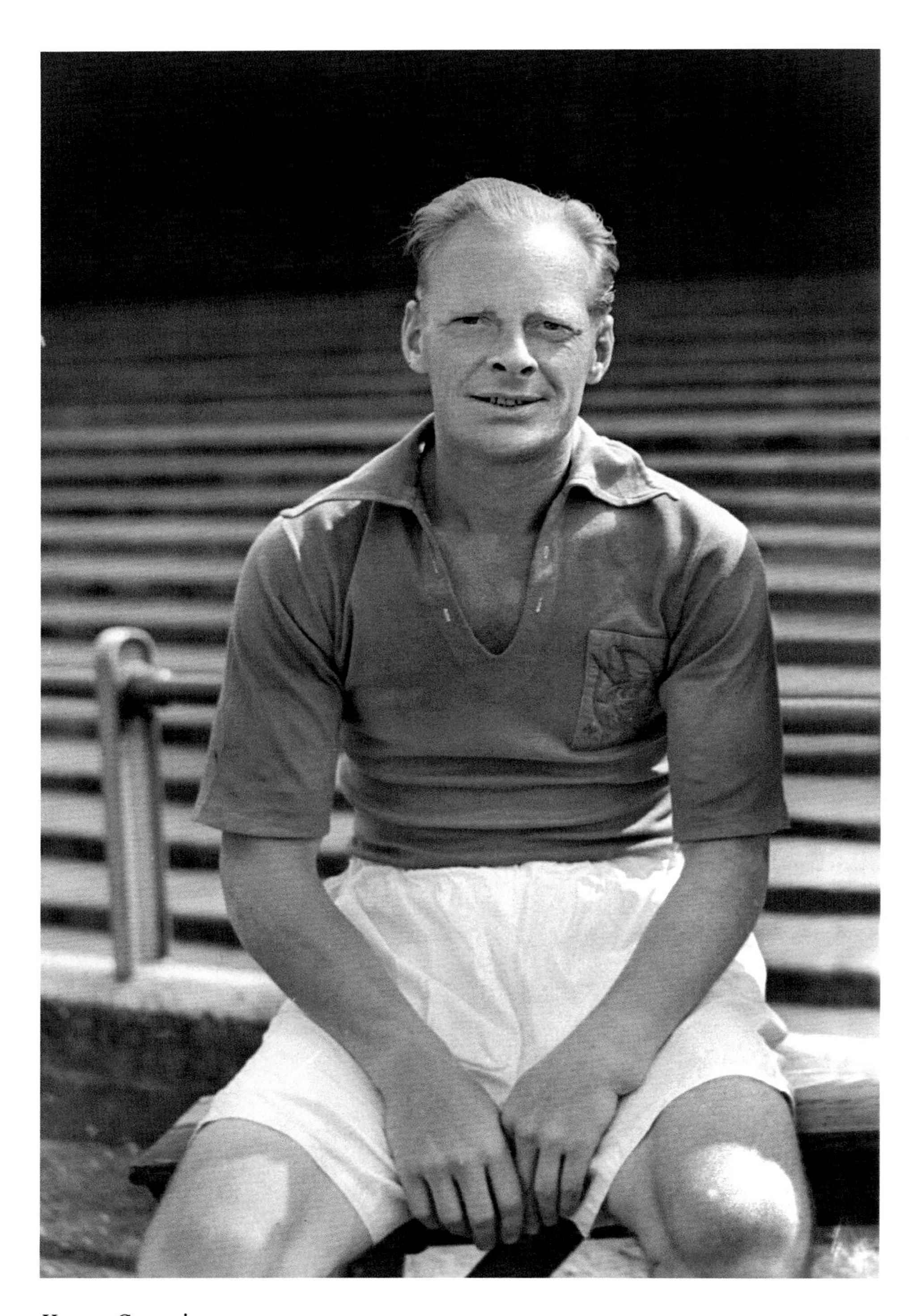

Horace Gager in 1950

GAGER, Horace Edwin
Centre-half 5' 10½" 11st 10lbs
Born: Leyton, London, 25th January 1917
Died: Bingham, Notts. March 1984
CAREER: St Matthew's School (Luton). Sundale F.C. Vauxhall Motors F.C. Luton Town November 1937. (Wartime guest player with Glentoran). **FOREST 27th February 1948, fee £8,000 to May 1955.**
Debut v Leicester City (h) 28.2.48, won 1-0
Born in London, Horace Gager moved to Luton as a boy and played his early football in local junior circles and later with Vauxhall Motors F.C. before joining Luton Town in November 1937. Originally a forward, he first appeared for the Hatters at inside-left, but in the season prior to his move to Forest he was spoken of as one of the best centre-halves in Division Two. By no means a youngster, he had spent ten seasons with Luton Town, but he remained a regular choice with Forest for seven seasons, maintaining an amazing standard of fitness and accuracy until well into the veteran stage. Appointed captain in succession to Bob McCall, he was a dominating factor in the Club's promotion to Division Two in 1951. He remained a regular until early in 1953-54 when, at the age of 37, he lost his place to Forest's next great centre-half, Bob McKinley. In September 1956 Horace Gager was lying seriously ill in hospital, and not expected to be up and about for some time. The Club were quick to assist their old skipper, but supporters also rallied to the cause, a collection at the City Ground in the match against Port Vale on 22nd September raised over £205, and was presented along with a "get well soon" message.
Appearances: FL: 258 apps 11 gls FAC: 10 apps 0 gls Total: 268 apps 11 gls
Honours: **(FOREST) FL Division 3 South champions 1951.** (Glentoran) Irish League representative, 2 appearances.

GALLEY, John Edward
Inside or Centre-forward 6' 0" 12st 3lbs
Born: Clowne, near Chesterfield, 7th May 1944
CAREER: North East Derbyshire Schoolboys. Wath-on-Dearne. Wolverhampton Wanderers June 1959, professional May 1961. Rotherham United December 1964, fee £10,000. Bristol City December 1967. fee £29,000. **FOREST 14th December 1972, fee £30,000**. Peterborough United (loan) October 1974. Hereford United December 1974 to May 1977. Telford United. Atherstone Town to 1979. Keyworth United youth coach. Forest scout and ran their Academy Youth Hostel.
Debut v Fulham (a) 16.12.72, lost 1-3 (scored)
Free-scoring centre or inside-forward John Galley left Wolves in search of first team football, and made a big impact with both Rotherham United and Bristol City, scoring a hat trick on his debut for both clubs. Unfortunately, he was unable to maintain his record on joining recently relegated Forest in a £30,000 transfer from Bristol City. Signed by manager Dave Mackay, Galley found little favour under new manager Allan Brown, and he dropped down a Division to join Hereford United, managed by former Bristol City team mate, John Sillett. In his second season he collected a Third Division championship medal as the Hereford United club moved into Division Two for the first time in its history. Despite operating in a central defensive role in later seasons, John Galley scored 149 League goals in 400/9 appearances for his six senior clubs. Two of John's elder brothers played in the Football League. Gordon with Darlington and Maurice with Chesterfield.
Appearances: FL: 31/6 apps 6 gls FAC: 3 apps 2 gls FLC 2/1 apps 0 gls Total: 36/7 apps 8 gls
Honours: (Hereford United) FL Division 3 champions 1976

GEMMELL, Thomas 'Tommy'

Full-back 6' 2" 13st 0lbs
Born: Motherwell, 16th October 1943
Died: 2nd March 2017
CAREER: Meadow Thistle Amateurs 1957. Coltness United October 1961. Celtic October 1961. **FOREST 22nd December 1971, fee £40,000**. Miami Toros 1973. Dundee July 1973 to December 1976, manager June 1977 to April 1980. Bannockburn F.C. manager October 1984. Albion Rovers manager January 1986 to December 1988. Albion Rovers manager again April 1993 to January 1994.
Debut v Arsenal (h) 27.12.71, drawn 1-1
Dubbed "The best full-back in the world" by Celtic's legendary manager Jock Stein. Equally good in defence and attack, he was renowned for his speedy forays down the flank, and outstanding, too, for his long range shooting that had the power to surprise many a goalkeeper. Amongst his 64 goals for Celtic, were memorable strikes in two European Cup Finals. He was appointed club captain on arrival at the City Ground, but despite his five goals in the final 18 matches of 1971-72, it proved insufficient to drag Forest to safety, and they were relegated from Division One. Despite a bright opening to the following season in Division Two, Forest then won just one of nine matches, leading to the dismissal of manager Matt Gillies. Injured in an accident involving a lawnmower, Tommy Gemmell played in only half of the season's League matches. After spending the summer in the USA with Miami Toros he returned to Scotland to join Dundee, and was a Scottish League Cup winner against his old team Celtic in December 1973. He was later appointed manager of the Dark Blues and followed with two separate spells as manager of Albion Rovers. Later employed as a hotelier and as a manager with the Sunlife Assurance Company. He was inducted into the Scottish Football Hall of Fame at Hampden Park in 2006. ***Note:*** *On 26th October 1994, at Christie's Auction Rooms in Glasgow, a collection of 31 lots awarded to Tommy Gemmell were sold. The star item was his 1967 European Cup Winner's medal that sold for £12,000 at the hammer. His runners-up medal from the 1970 European Cup Final realised £1,800. At the lower end of the scale, his Scottish FL medal for the match against the Football League in 1966-67 realised £200.*
Appearances: FL: 39 apps 6 gls FAC: 1 app 0 gls FLC: 1 app 0 gls Total: 41 apps 6 gls
Honours: Scotland International, 18 caps. Scottish League representative, 5 apps. (Celtic) European Cup winners 1967, finalist 1970. Scottish League Champions 1966, 1967, 1968, 1969, 1970, 1971. Scottish Cup winner 1965, 1967, 1969, finalist 1966, 1970. Scottish League Cup winner 1966. 1967, 1968, 1969, finalist 1965. (Dundee) Scottish League Cup winner 1974.

GRANT, Brian Patrick

Left full-back 5' 8" 10st 5lbs
Born: Coatbridge, 10th May 1943
CAREER: Belshill Athletic. **FOREST amateur 1959, signing professional 11th May 1960.** Hartlepool United January 1966. Bradford City (non-contract) 1967. Cambridge United *circa* 1968, and still with them when they joined the FL in 1970. Kettering. Bishop Stortford manager.
Debut v Leicester City (h) 22.4.61, drawn 2-2
Said to have been the youngest Forest player to appear in the senior side when he made his debut at the age of 17, Brian Grant had played regularly in the Reserves at 16, and was righty considered a very bright prospect. In the event, eight appearances in season 1961-62 proved to be his best return in terms of senior action. He subsequently made 35 League appearances for Hartlepools United and 14 for Cambridge United, having assisted them to Football League status in 1970. He subsequently worked as a painter and decorator.
Appearances: FL: 18 apps 0 gls FAC: 1 app 0 gls FLC: 3 apps 0 gls Total: 22 apps 0 gls

GRAY, William 'Billy' Patrick

Forward, later full-back 5' 7" 11st 0lbs
Born: Dinnington, County Durham, 24th May 1927
Died: Apsley, Nottingham, 11th April 2011
CAREER: Dinnington Colliery. (Wolverhampton Wanderers and Gateshead during WW2). Leyton Orient May 1947. Chelsea March 1949. Burnley August 1953, fee £ 16,000. **FOREST 26th June 1957, fee £4,250.** Millwall player-manager November 1963 to May 1966. Brentford manager July 1966 to September 1967. Notts County manager March 1967 to September 1968. Fulham coach January 1969. **FOREST** groundsman 1970.
Debut v Preston North End (h) 24.8.57, (scored one goal)
Billy Gray began in junior football with Dinnington when working as a miner. Just after the war, his team won the Newcastle Welfare League championship, the knockout shield and the Headon Holmes Cup, and the scouts came calling. He first appeared in League football with Leyton Orient, and whilst with them he was selected to play for the London FA against Berlin. He was later capped by England 'B' against Switzerland in 1950, while on Chelsea's books. He moved to Burnley in 1953 as a replacement for England left-winger Billy Elliott who had moved to Sunderland. He joined Forest for their return to Division One following promotion in 1956-57 and was immediately impressive, scoring on his debut and assisting in a wonderful start to life in the top flight, the Reds winning eight of their first eleven matches. A member of the 1959 FA Cup winning side, he moved from the wing to inside-forward and later again to left full-back, and was equally effective in each role. He was honoured towards the end of the 1961-62 season when he was handed the captaincy when Bobby McKinley asked to be relieved of the position. In his final season he made fewer first team appearances but he proved invaluable for his guidance and coaching of younger players in the Football Combination side. Moving on to Millwall as player-manager he led the Lions to two promotions, but was less successful at Brentford and Notts County, who were at the foot of Division Four when he resigned in September 1968. A keen golfer and tennis player, Billy Gray held coaching certificates for both football and tennis, and ran a grocery business on Wollaton Road in Nottingham in the 1960s. During his career he amassed a fine record of 506 League appearances and 73 goals for his five clubs.
Appearances: FL: 201 apps 29 gls FAC: 17 apps 5 gls FLC: 2 apps 0 gls Other: 3 apps 0 gls Total: 223 apps 34 gls
Honours: England 'B' International, 1 cap v Switzerland at Hillsborough 1950. **(FOREST)** FA Cup winner 1959

GREENWOOD, Patrick 'Paddy' George
Defender 6' 0" 11st 6lbs
Born: Hull, 17th October 1946
CAREER: Hull Schoolboys. Hull City July 1961, professional October 1964. Barnsley November 1971, fee £12,000. Boston Minutemen, USA, (loan) May 1974. **FOREST 4th October 1974 to January 1976, fee £10,000**. Boston Minutemen player-coach May 1976. Bridlington Trinity, as a player, December 1977.
Debut v Southampton (a) 5.10.74, won 1-0
In either defence or midfield, Paddy Greenwood was a solid performer for both Hull City and Barnsley with over a century of appearances for each club. He was less fortunate on joining Forest, having made just 19 first team appearances when a broken leg injury ended his senior career. He returned for a second spell with Boston Minutemen but made only five appearances, later returning to England to assist Bridlington Trinity.
Appearances: FL: 15 apps 0 gls FAC: 4 apps 0 gls Total: 19 apps 0 gls

GRUMMITT, Peter Malcolm

Goalkeeper 5' 10" 10st 11lbs
Born: Bourne, Lincs. 19th August 1942
CAREER: Bourne Secondary Modern School. Bourne Town August 1957. (Trials with Birmingham City and Notts County). **FOREST amateur January, professional 12th May 1960**. Sheffield Wednesday January 1970, fee £35,000. Brighton & Hove Albion (loan) December 1973, permanent January 1974, fee £6,000. Dover 1978. Worthing Town 1979.
Debut v Bolton Wanderers (h) 12.11.60, drawn 2-2
A goalkeeper from the age of eleven with his school, Bourne Secondary Modern, Peter Grummitt was signed for Bourne Town, by ex-Forest stalwart, Sid Ottewell. Before becoming a First Division goalkeeper he was an electrician's mate in his native Bourne. He became Forest's youngest-ever goalkeeper to play for the first team at the age of 18, and despite a nervy debut, when a pass back from Jim Iley resulted in an own goal, Peter Grummitt became Forest's first choice goalkeeper for nine seasons, winning Under-23 and Football League honours along the way. He made good recoveries after two separate broken arm injuries, at Bolton Wanderers in October 1962, and against Leeds United at Elland Road in the FA Cup-tie in February *1968. On recovering from the latter, he was unable to regain his number one spot that had been taken over by Alan Hill. Moving on to Sheffield Wednesday he contested the number one jersey with Peter Springett, adding a further 121 League appearances to his total before a loan move to Brighton & Hove Albion was quickly made permanent. In four seasons at the Goldstone Ground he remained first-choice goalkeeper until a knee injury sustained in March 1977 enforced his retirement. He did, however, play in his own benefit match in the following*

May, the proceeds enabling him to buy a newsagent's and tobacconists shop in the town. One of the best un-capped goalkeepers in the game, Grummitt appeared in 570 League appearances for his three clubs.
Appearances: FL: 313 apps 0 gls FAC: 26 apps 0 gls FLC: 7 apps 0 gls Other: 6 apps 0 gls Total: 352 apps 0 gls
Honours: England Under 23 International, 3 caps. FL representative. FA Tour to Australia 1971.

GUNN, Alfred 'Alfie' Herman
Centre-forward 5' 9½" 12st 0lbs
Born: Essen, Germany, 11th July 1924
Died: Brighton, March 1982
CAREER: Southwick Wednesday. Brighton & Hove Albion (debut) October 1940. **FOREST 22nd February 1947 to June 1947.**
Debut v Manchester City (a) 29.3.47, lost 1-2
Alfie Gunn was a member of the Brighton & Hove Albion junior X1, winners of the Sussex County Wartime League Cup in season 1942-43. Military service in Italy curtailed much of his football career, with odd appearances over three seasons amounting to 15 matches and four goals. On joining Forest in February 1947, he was promoted after scoring a hat trick for Forest Reserves at Bradford and, one week later, made his senior debut against the Division Two champions elect, Manchester City at Maine Road. He retained his place for the trip to Tottenham Hotspur in the following week, but the 2-0 defeat proved to be his last at senior level, and he was released on a free transfer in the close season.
Appearances: FL: 2 apps 0 gls Total: 2 apps 0 gls

HALL, Colin Thomas

Inside-forward 5' 8" 10st 11lbs
Born: Wolverhampton, 2nd February 1948
CAREER: FOREST April 1964, professional 3rd March 1966. Bradford City June 1970. Bristol City July 1972. Hereford United September 1972 to May 1973. Bath City. Gloucester City 1978.
Debut v Fulham (a) 18.11.67, lost 0-2
Colin Hall received a private education, and soccer was not on the curriculum. However, whilst playing for a Youth Club he was recommended to Forest in the summer of 1964 as a 16 year-old. He won three England Youth caps in the 1965-66 season as an amateur and immediately after his last honour joined the professional staff in March 1966. He was top scorer in the Midland Intermediate League with 20 goals (Runners-up in both League and Cup), and second highest scorer with the Reserves in 1967-68 with 11 goals in 31 matches. Lacking first team opportunities, he moved on to Bradford City where he enjoyed the best spell of his career, making 65/1 appearances, scoring seven goals. He played in little first team football for his two subsequent League clubs, his career aggregate figures being 97/11 League matches and nine goals.
Appearances: FL: 27/9 apps 2 gls FAC: 1 app 0 gls FLC: 0/1 apps 0 gls Total: 28/10 apps 2 gls
Honours: England Youth International

HARBY, Michael 'Mick' John
Goalkeeper
Born: Bulwell, Nottingham, 7th November 1948
CAREER: FOREST amateur May 1963, professional 27th July 1966 to May 1968.
Debut v Sunderland (h) 30.3.68, lost 0-3

As a regular performer in the Central League side, Mick Harby proved himself a very efficient and competent goalkeeper who was safe rather than spectacular. Injuries to both Grummitt and Williamson caused Mick to be unexpectedly plunged into the first team towards the end of season 1967-68 when the club were going through a poor spell. Unhappily, he was beaten 15 times in his three Division One outings, with a final 6-1 defeat against Liverpool at Anfield, ending Forest's dreadful run in, in which they won only one of their last ten League fixtures.
Appearances: FL: 3 apps 0 gls Total: 3 apps 0 gls

HARRIS, Leonard 'Len' James
Right full-back 5' 9" 11st 0lbs
Born: Nuneaton, 29th May 1949
CAREER: Nuneaton junior football**. FOREST amateur April, professional 9th June 1966 to May 1971**. Doncaster Rovers (loan) September 1970.
Debut v Tottenham Hotspur (h) 12.4.69, lost 0-2
Len Harris was spotted whist playing in minor soccer in Nuneaton and recommended for trials. He came to the City Ground in April 1966, played in a few games and showed sufficient promise to be then recruited to the professional staff. An adaptable player who performed equally well at full-back, wing-half or inside-forward, he was captain of the Youth team that travelled to Amsterdam to play in the Youth Tournament, losing to Rotherham United in the Final. Despite his Football League debut at the age of 19 he was restricted to just two senior outings with Forest, and four while on loan with Doncaster Rovers, in their relegation season from Division Three, 1970-71.
Appearances: FL: 2 apps 0 gls Total: 2 apps 0 gls

HENNESEY, William Terrance 'Terry'

Wing half-back/defender 6' 0" 11st 5lbs
Born: Llay, Mid-Wales, 1st September 1942
CAREER: Grove Park Grammar School. Wrexham & District Schoolboys. Birmingham City June 1957, professional September 1959. **FOREST 20th November 1965, fee £ 45,000**. Derby County February 1970, fee £110,000. Tamworth F.C. manager April 1974. Kimberley Town coach 1977, Tulsa Roughnecks (NASL) assistant coach cs 1978. Shepshed Charterhouse coach 1978 to October 1980. Tulsa Roughnecks (NASL) assistant-coach November 1980, chief coach 1981-83. Vancouver Whitecaps (NASL) assistant-coach then manager. Toronto coach/manager. Melbourne Croatia coach-manager 1986. Heidelberg F.C., Australia, coach/manager 1987-88.
Debut v Blackpool (h) 20.11.65, won 2-1
Terry Hennesey was a top class wing-half with a telling tackle, constructive approach and the ability to carry the ball out of defence to set up attacks. He began with Birmingham City and appeared in 178 League matches and was a FL Cup winner against local rivals Aston Villa in 1963. On joining Forest he was elected captain at the start of the 1966-67 season and led his team to the runners-up position in Division One, and to the semi-final of the FA Cup. In five seasons at the City Ground, whether operating in the back four or midfield, he was an automatic choice for both club and country (15 of his Wales caps awarded when on Forest's books.) An

operation for appendicitis proved to be the forerunner of Hennesey's sale to fierce rivals Derby County in February 1970. With the emerging Liam O'Kane successfully stepping into the breach, Hennesey became the Rams first £100,000 signing. Sadly, his time at the Baseball Ground was blighted by ankle and Achilles injuries but he did play in enough games to qualify for a Division One championship medal in 1971-72, and in all eight matches in the Texaco Cup competition in the same season, won against Airdrieonians with an aggregate score of 2-1. In subsequent coaching appointments, the undoubted highlight was his winning of the Soccer Bowl with his team, Tulsa Roughnecks, who beat Toronto Blizzard 2-0 in Vancouver on 1st October 1983.
Appearances: FL: 159 apps 5 gls FAC: 12 apps 1 gl FLC: 8 apps 0 gls Other: 4 apps 0 gls Total: 183 apps 6 gls
Honours: Wales Schoolboy and Youth International; Under-23 International, 6 caps. Full International, 39 caps (First v Ireland in 1962). (Birmingham City) Inter Cities Fairs Cup finalist 1961, FL Cup winner 1963. (Derby County) FL Division One champions and Texaco Cup winners 1972.

HIGHAM, Peter

Centre-forward/Outside-right 5' 11" 12st 3 lbs
Born: Wigan, 8th November 1930
CAREER: Wigan Grammar School. Wigan Athletic August 1946. Portsmouth amateur July 1948, professional November 1949. Bolton Wanderers November 1950. Preston North End May 1952. **FOREST 17th August 1955, along with E. Jones (signed in the following month) for a combined fee of £5,600.** Doncaster Rovers March 1958, fee £4,500, to May 1959. Mossley. Buxton Town. Stalybridge Celtic. Altrincham. Morecambe. Rhyl. Chorley player-coach. Subsequently held coaching appointments in Zambia, South Africa, and for ten summers in Virginia (USA).
Debut v Liverpool (h) 20.8.55, lost 1-3 (scored)
While serving with the Royal Marines Peter Higham made a single League appearance for Portsmouth while on amateur forms. He was offered but declined a professional engagement to return north with Bolton Wanderers. Without appearing at senior level, despite scoring 93 goals for the Reserves and 'A' Team, he was transferred to Preston North End. Again he was mainly in reserve and scored 60 goals in 81 Central League matches, but he attracted Forest's attention after scoring 10 goals in 14 first team appearances in 1954-55, including a hat trick against Sheffield Wednesday. A dashing, hard-working leader, he netted 16 goals in 39 matches in his first season, but in the following term, when promotion from Division Two was secured, he was switched onto the right wing due to Peter Small's loss of form. When Billy Gray was signed for the return to the top flight, Peter Higham lost his place in the side but continued to score heavily for the Reserves. He was linked with a move to Torquay United after he was transfer listed, but moved instead to Doncaster Rovers, along with Eric Jones (q.v.) Peter held a full FA coaching badge and taught PE in Bootle and Magull. His brother, Ted, played Rugby League football with Warrington and was an AAA coach.
Appearances: FL: 61 apps 20 gls FAC: 6 apps 1 gl Total: 67 apps 21 gls

HILL, Alan

Goalkeeper 6' 0" 12st 6lbs
Born: Barnsley, 3rd November 1943
CAREER: Barnsley & Yorkshire Schoolboys. Barnsley 1959, professional April 1961. Rotherham United June 1960. **FOREST 13th March 1969, fee £12,000; retired June 1970. Later appointed youth team coach.** Derby County youth team coach October 1973. **Forest youth development officer and scout December 1975.**
Debut v West Bromwich Albion (a) 22.3.69, won 3-0
A first team debut at the age of 17 suggested that Barnsley's goalkeeper Alan Hill was destined for a bright future in the game. Unfortunately his career was blighted by injuries. He was a regular for two seasons at Oakwell but totalled only 133 League appearances in six seasons before being transferred to Rotherham Unted. 82 appearances in three seasons at Millmoor was a better return, and it preceded his arrival at the City Ground. Taking over from Peter Grummitt, who had suffered a broken arm in a 2-0 defeat by Leeds United, Hill proved a worthy successor until he was injured himself a year later in the home draw against Everton on 28th February 1970. After several attempts at a comeback, his fractured arm and elbow remained troublesome and he was forced to admit defeat and was obliged to retire. Aided by a testimonial, he purchased a small hotel in Nottingham, and later moved out of the city as licensee of the Rangcliffe Arms Hotel in the village of Bunny.
Appearances: FL: 40 apps 0 gls FAC: 2 apps 0 gls FLC: 3 apps 0 gls Total: 45 apps 0 gls

HILLEY, David 'Dave'

Inside-forward 5' 9" 11st 2lbs
Born: Glasgow, 20th December 1938
CAREER: Muirend Amateurs. Jordanhill F.C. Pollok Juniors. Third Lanark June 1958. Newcastle United August 1962, with Stewart Mitchell for a combined fee of £40,000. **FOREST 5th December 1967, fee £25,000**. Highlands Park F.C., (South Africa), November 1970. Hellenic F.C. (South Africa) 1973. Scarborough F.C. October 1975. South Shields July 1976. Bedlington Terriers July 1977 to May 1978.
Debut v Sheffield United (h) 16.12.67, won 1-0 (scored)
Scottish schoolboy international Dave Hilley represented three well-known Scottish amateur teams before joining Third Lanark in June 1958. He was a PE student at Jordanhill Training College at that time, and progress with the Thirds was hampered when he suffered a broken collarbone while playing rugby at the college. Otherwise, he enjoyed a successful four-year spell at Cathkin that included an appearance in the Scottish Cup Final against Hearts in 1959, and in 1960-61 he was ever-present when Thirds finished, appropriately, in third place in Division One, scoring exactly 100 goals in the 34-match tournament. On joining Newcastle United, he missed very few matches in a stay approaching five years, in all competitions scoring 33 goals in 209 matches and winning a Division Two championship medal in 1965. Forest were in the midst of an injury crisis when Dave Hilley arrived at the City Ground. In the same month, Scottish international Jim Baxter was signed from Sunderland and the pair introduced some much needed flair and scheming ability to take Forest to the safety of a mid-table finish. As Forest replaced outgoing manager Johnny Carey with Matt Gillies in January 1969, Hilley continued to command a regular starting berth in the side until early in 1970-71, when he had started on the bench, and in November departed to play in South Africa. He was later a schoolteacher in Newcastle, and a feature writer for the Sunday Post newspaper. He was the author of a book 'What Game' that revealed details of illegal football matches played in by Scottish footballers, including himself, held on the Costa Bravo, Spain, between 1959 and 1962.)

Appearances: FL: 72/16 apps 14 gls FAC: 3 apps 1 gl FLC: 5 apps 0 gls Other: 2 apps 1 gl Total: 82/16 apps 16 gls
Honours: Scotland Under-23 International, 2 caps 1961. Scottish League representative, 1 app 1960. (Third Lanark) Scottish Cup finalists 1960. (Newcastle United) FL Division 2 champions 1965.

HINCHCLIFFE, Tom

Inside-forward 5' 10" 10st 10lbs
Born Denaby, near Doncaster 6th December 1913
Died West Bridgford, Nottingham, January quarter 1978
CAREER: Conisburgh Welfare. Denaby United August 1933. Grimsby Town October 1933, fee £300. Huddersfield Town February 1938. Derby County November 1938 (Wartime guest player with **Forest,** Notts County, Reading, Aldershot, Bournemouth & Boscombe Athletic and Chelsea). **FOREST 30th May 1946.** Gainsborough Trinity Sept 1946. Denaby United Aug 1948.
Debut v Barnsley (a) 31.8.46, lost 2-3
Tom Hinchcliffe had a lengthy wait for a first team opportunity with Grimsby Town, first appearing in Division One at Sheffield Wednesday in a 2-0 defeat on 7th November 1936 – a little over three years after first signing for the Mariners from Denaby United. He made only five League appearances in his first season, but played regularly in the following campaign (22 appearances and four goals) before he joined Huddersfield Town in an exchange deal that took Jack Beattie to Blundell Park. After scoring on his debut in a 4-1 win at Wolverhampton Wanderers, that ended a winless run of seven matches, he made infrequent appearances thereafter and moved on to Derby County in the final season of peacetime football. He made just six appearances for the Rams and scored one goal. After assisting a variety of clubs in wartime football, he signed with Forest in May 1946, but played only once before dropping into non-League football. At the time of the 1939 Census, Tom was living with wife Mary at Highbury Road, Bingham. His employment (or lack of same) was given as: "A footballer seeking employment." He would not have been alone in that predicament of course, with World War Two disrupting football across the board.
Appearances: FL: 1 app 0 gls Total: 1 app 0 gls

HINDLEY, Peter

Half-back 5' 10" 11st 10lbs
Born: Worksop, 19th May 1944
CAREER: Worksop junior football. **FOREST amateur October 1960, professional June 1961**. Coventry City January 1974, fee £35,000. Peterborough United July 1976. Burton Albion July 1979.
Debut v West Bromwich Albion, FAC 4, (a) 6.3.63, drawn 0-0
Peter Hindley followed his father, Frank, a Forest centre-forward in pre-war days, when he joined the City Ground staff in 1960. Like his father, Peter joined as a centre-forward but later starred in both wing-half positions before a further successful switch took him to full-back. He made a great impression on his debut, playing a key role in a 4-2-4 system that earned a goalless draw at the Hawthorns. In the following month a broken collarbone at Manchester City brought his season to a premature end. As a reward for a fine season in 1966-67, came selection to tour the Balkans with the England Under-23 side and a cap against Greece in Athens. During the

entire 1967-68 season he missed only two League games, and his full-back partner, John Winfield, missed only one. A feature of their play was strong runs down the wing and powerful crosses. Hindley was also noted for his tremendously strong tackling, which earned him the nickname of the 'The Tank'. In his final season, having lost his first team place to Liam O'Kane, a transfer to Coventry City took him back to Division One for 33 League appearances before a final move to Peterborough United, who suffered relegation to Division Four in Hindley's last season, after he had completed 112 League appearances.
Appearances: FL: 366 apps 10 gls FAC: 30 apps 1 gl FLC: 14 apps 0 gls Other: 6 apps 0 gls Total: 416 apps 11 gls
Honours: England Under-23 International, 1 cap

HINTON, Alan Thomas

Outside-left 5' 10" 11st 5lbs
Born: Wednesbury, Staffs. 6th October 1942
CAREER: South-East Staffordshire Schoolboys. Wolverhampton Wanderers July 1957, professional October 1959. **FOREST January 1964.** Derby County September 1967, fee £30,000. Borrowash Victoria player-manager August 1976. Dallas Tornado, (NASL) March 1977. Tulsa Roughnecks (NASL) October 1968. Vancouver Whitecaps (NASL) 1978. Seattle Sounders (NASL) player-coach November 1979 to January 1983. Vancouver Whitecaps (NASL) coach 1984. Tacoma Stars (MISL) player coach 1985 to 1990. Crossfire Sounders coach 1992 to 1997.
Debut v Bolton Wanderers (a) 1.2.64, won 3-2
Alan Hinton was a creative wingman with a blistering left foot shot, and a great exponent of any dead-ball situation with his accurate corner and free kicks. He began with the Wolves, straight from school, and made 75 League appearances, scoring 29 goals, before arriving at the City Ground in an exchange deal that took 'Flip' Le Flem in the opposite direction. Hinton's ability to cross the ball accurately from the wing was quickly in evidence, with Frank Wignall taking full advantage when he notched his first senior hat trick, two scored from crosses by Hinton who was making his debut. During his spell at the City Ground, Hinton won two England caps, to add to the one that he had won with the Wolves. Additionally, he won four of his seven England Under-23 caps as a Forest player. He enjoyed his best season at the City Ground in 1964-65 when he missed just one first team match, scoring 13 goals in 44 League and Cup appearances. At the time of his transfer to Derby County he had lost his first team place, but his £30,000 move to Derby County certainly gave the Rams a lift under Brian Clough and Peter Taylor, winning Second and First Division titles. Hinton later had a successful career in the North American Soccer League, moving to play and coach in the Major Indoor Soccer League following the collapse of the NASL. In terms of English League football, his career figures were 423/17 matches and 117 goals. He moved to the USA in 1976 and was an estate agent, with his wife Joy, in Seattle.
Appearances: FL: 108/4 apps 24 gls FAC: 7/1 apps 0 gls FLC: 0/1 app Other: 1 app 0 gls Total: 116/6 apps 24 gls
Honours: England Youth, Under-23 (7 caps) and Full International, 3 caps. (Derby County) FL Division 2 champions 1969; FL Division 1 champions 1971, 1972.

HOCKEY, Trevor

Midfield 5' 5" 10st 0lbs
Born: Keighley, Yorkshire, 1st May 1943
Died: Keighley, Yorkshire, 1st April 1987
CAREER: Eastwood School (Keighley). Keighley Schoolboys. Yorkshire Schoolboys. West Riding Under-19s. Keighley Central Youth Club 1958. Bradford City apprentice June 1958, professional May 1960. **FOREST November 1961, fee £15,000**. Newcastle United November 1963, fee £25,000. Birmingham City November 1965, fee £22,500. Sheffield United January 1971, fee £35,000. Norwich City February 1973. Aston Villa June 1973, fee £38,000. Bradford City June 1974. Athlone Town player-manager March 1976. San Diego Jaws (NASL) April 1976. Las Vegas Quicksilver (NASL) March 1977. San Jose Eartquakes (NASL) June 1977. Stalybridge Celtic manager August 1977. Ashton United. Keighley Town.
Debut v Bolton Wanderers (h) 25.11.61, lost 0-1
Trevor's father, Albert, was a Rugby Union player with Abertillery and later coached Keighley Rugby League Club. Lightweight wingman Trevor had already played in 53 Third and Fourth Division League matches for Bradford City when he joined Forest at the tender age of 18. A fast and tricky winger, able to occupy either flank, he took the step up to Division One in his stride, scoring his first goal against Manchester United at Old Trafford on Boxing Day on his sixth appearance. After two years at the City ground he made the first of his many subsequent moves to Newcastle United, whom he assisted to the championship of Division Two, and later helped take Sheffield United into the top flight as runners-up to Leicester City for the Second Division title in 1970-71. Along the way, both his role and appearance changed to a marked degree, evolving as an all-action midfield ball winner with long hair and a luxuriant beard, (known as the Blade without a razor in his Sheffield United days), he was good enough to win nine caps for his adoptive country, Wales. In terms of League matches alone, his career figures for his seven different clubs totalled 521/2 matches and 28 goals. He was just 43 years old when he sadly died of a heart attack after playing in a five-a-side football match.
Appearances: FL: 73 apps 6 gls FAC: 6 apps 2 gls Total: 79 apps 8 gls
Honours: Wales International, 9 caps 1972-74. (Newcastle United) Division 2 champions 1965.

HOLDER, Alan Maurice
Wing half-back 5' 11" 10st 11lbs
Born: Oxford, 10th December 1931
Died: Kidlington, near Oxford, 19th June 2013
CAREER: Army football (R.A.O.C.) **FOREST amateur October 1951, professional 9th April 1952**. Lincoln City July 1955, fee £1,150. Tranmere Rovers December 1956. Headington United July 1958 to June 1959.
Debut v Plymouth Argyle (a) 23.10.54, won 2-1
Alan Holder joined the Reds immediately after completing his National Service, during which he had played a big part in the successful 6th Battalion RAOC eleven. A cartilage operation in 1953-54 sidelined him for some months, but he recovered to make his senior bow in the following season. In four matches during the campaign he was never on the losing side, but he was transferred to Lincoln City in the close season. He played only once at senior level for the Imps, but did rather better with a struggling Tranmere Rovers who finished 23rd in Division Three North and had to apply for re-election. Holder played in 13 League matches and celebrated New Year's Day 1957 by registering his first and only League goal in a 3-0 victory against Crewe Alexandra at Prenton Park.
Appearances: FL: 3 apps 0 gls FAC: 1 app 0 gls Total: 4 apps 0 gls

HOLLINS, David 'Dave' Michael
Goalkeeper 6' 0" 11st 5lbs
Born: Bangor, Wales, 4th February 1938
CAREER: Merrow FC. (Guildford). Brighton & Hove Albion amateur October 1956, professional November 1955. Newcastle United March 1961, fee £12,000. Mansfield Town February 1967, fee £2,500. **FOREST (loan) 2nd March to May 1970.** Aldershot July 1970. Romford F.C. May 1971 to 1972.
Debut v Chelsea (a) 7.3.70, drawn 1-1
Dave Hollins had a lengthy wait for a first team outing with Brighton & Hove Albion, before deputising for the experienced Eric Gill (247 consecutive matches) in three matches in the Division Three championship-winning season 1957-58. Life in Division Two began with a visit to Middlesbrough and a record League defeat for the Seagulls by 9-0 with a certain Brian Clough scoring five of the goals. Despite the severe baptism, Hollins took over as first team goalkeeper in the same season and won his first Wales Under-23 cap. After appearing in 73 League and Cup matches for the Goldstone club, he was transferred to Newcastle United in March 1961. Four weeks after his arrival at St James Park, Newcastle were relegated from Division One, Chelsea having scored six goals against him on his home debut. Eventually replaced by Gordon Marshall-another goalkeeper with Forest connections-Hollins was transferred to Mansfield Town after almost six years on Tyneside in which he made 121 League and Cup appearances and won his eleven Welsh caps. A member of the Stags successful FA Cup side who reached round six for the first time in the club's history, he recorded 126 League and Cup appearances before rounding off his career with 16 appearances for Aldershot. In the final months of season 1969-70 Hollins was loaned to Forest following the injury that was to end Alan Hill's career. His swansong in Division One proved unrewarding as Forest won only one of the nine matches in which he appeared, conceding 22 goals and scoring nine. It was odd that brothers Dave and John, a midfielder with Chelsea, QPR and Arsenal, won international caps for different countries. John, who was born in Guildford, played for England.
Appearances: FL: 9 apps 0 gls Total: 9 apps 0 gls
Honours: Wales Under-23 International, 2 caps; Wales full International 11 caps.

HUDDLESTONE, Edward 'Ted' Thomas
Centre-forward 5' 11" 11st 1lb
Born: Nottingham, 29th September 1935
CAREER: Meadow Rangers FC. Blackpool amateur September 1951. Meadow Rangers FC. **FOREST amateur 1952, professional 1st December 1956 to February 1957.** Ilkeston Town. Long Eaton United.
Debut v Grimsby Town (a) 1.12.56, drawn 0-0
A former Nottinghamshire AAA junior sprint champion, Ted Huddlestone signed his first amateur form with Forest at 17 years of age and played in a number of games including FA Youth Cup matches, before being called up for RAF National Service. He played in several representative games whist stationed in Germany. Demobbed in May 1956 he played in seven matches for the 'A' Team, in which he scored nine goals. Promoted to the Reserves he scored three goals in two matches. Signed as a professional in December 1956, he made his senior debut on the same day as deputy for Jim Barrett in a goalless draw at Plymouth Argyle. Lacking opportunities in the side that won promotion from Division Two, he dropped into non-League football before the end of the season. It was a disappointing outcome for the trainee-salesman who, in earliest days, appeared capable of making his mark in the football world.
Appearances: FL: 1 app 0 gls Total: 1 app 0 gls

HULLETT, William 'Bill' Alexander

Centre-forward 5'11" 11st 0lbs
Born: West Derby, Liverpool, 19th November 1915
Died: Whitchurch, Cardiff, 6th September 1982
Debut v West Ham United (h) 4.12.48, won 3-0 (scored one goal)
CAREER: Everton amateur September, professional December 1935. New Brighton (loan) January 1937. Everton May 1937. Plymouth Argyle October 1937. Manchester United March 1939. (Wartime guest player with Runcorn, Southport, **Forest,** Lincoln City, Barnsley, Tranmere Rovers, Grimsby Town, Burnley & Aldershot). Merthyr Tydfil. Cardiff City February 1948, fee £6,000. **FOREST 27th November 1948, fee £6,000.** Merthyr Tydfil player-manager June 1949, fee £1,250, manager from February 1950. Worcester City (trial) October 1953. Treharris Athletic November 1953.

Everton reserve Bill Hullett was loaned to New Brighton in January 1937 and was immediately impressive, scoring seven goals in his first seven appearances. His season was ended by injury in early April, but he was the Rakers' second-highest goalscorer for the season, despite having made only 14 appearances. Said to "Take a lot of shaking off the ball" and with a terrific volley, he proved a consistent goalscorer throughout his career, although his best years were spent with a variety of clubs during wartime football. He joined Forest after ten months with Cardiff City, and although his debut against Tottenham Hotspur lasted for only seventeen and a half minutes before the game was abandoned, manager Billy Walker was said to be enthusiastic about his capture. In the event, Hullett struggled in a poor side heading for relegation from Division Two and departed after seven months when offered the post of player-manager to Merthyr Tydfil.
Appearances: FL: 13 apps 2 gls FAC: 2 qpps 0 gls Total: 15 apps 2 gls

HULME, Eric Martin
Goalkeeper 5' 10" 11st 4lbs
Born: Houghton-le-Spring, 14th January 1949
CAREER: Spennymoor United 1956. **FOREST 2nd February 1970**. Lincoln City (loan) September 1972, signing permanently October 1972, fee £4,000. Gainsborough Trinity (loan) January 1973. Worksop Town July 1974.
Debut v Liverpool (h) 16.10.71, lost 2-3
As deputy for Jim Barron in the 1971-72 relegation season, Eric Hulme was kept busy in a run of five consecutive matches spanning October and November. His sojourn in the seniors included a rare away victory – 1-0 at Huddersfield Town, but it also included a 6-1 defeat at Tottenham Hotspur. In the following season, a loan spell to Lincoln City was quickly made permanent, but he was in turn loaned out to Gainsborough Trinity when his place in goal was taken by the Imps' long serving schoolteacher-goalkeeper, John Kennedy. Hulme had completed 23 Division 4 outings at the time of his release on a free transfer.
Appearances: FL: 5 apps 0 gls FLC: 1 app 0 gls Total: 6 apps 0 gls

HUTCHINSON, John 'Jack' Arthur

Full-back 5' 9½" 11st 2lbs
Born: Heanor, Derbyshire, 1st June 1921
Died: Nottingham, 27th November 2004
CAREER: Loscoe Colliery FC. (Wartime guest player with Notts County.) **FOREST August 1943. Professional 26th September 1946.** Ilkeston Town player-coach cs 1959.
Debut v Millwall (h) 9.11.46, lost 1-2

In sixteen years of service with the Forest, Jack Hutchinson saw them progress from the Third Division South to the First Division and a Cup Final triumph. As a youngster he was always a Notts County supporter but while playing for Loscoe Colliery FC as an inside forwrd he was recommended to Forest's manager, Billy Walker, and signed as an amateur. In 1943 he was called in to RAF and posted to Newark, but managed to get away to play in Forest wartime games. He was then posted to India and played for representative teams captained by Eric Hayward (Blackpool) and Tommy Walker (Hearts). Jack Hutchinson made appearances in 13 seasons of postwar football for the Reds having developed into a stylish full-back who placed the emphasis on intelligent positional play. Having started life as a forward, his powers of speedy recovery would often catch a fugitive wingman by surprise. A quiet and unassumining character and an outstanding servant to the club, he received two benefits, one of £750 and one of £1,000. Having spent much of his last two seasons in reserve, he decided to retire in the month of Forest's FA Cup Final win against Luton Town.On moving to Ilkeston Town as player-coach, he played in just two matches before accepting the fact that, at 38 years of age, his playing career was over.

Appearances: FL: 241 apps 0 gls FAC: 13 apps 0 gls Total: 254 apps 0 gls

ILEY, James 'Jim'

Wing half-back 5' 10" 11st 3lbs
Born: South Kirkby, near Pontefract, Yorkshire, 15th December 1935
CAREER: South Elmsall Schoolboys. Pontefract F.C. Moorthorpe St Joseph's Boys'Club. Sheffield United amateur March 1951, professional June 1953. Tottenham Hotspur August 1957, fee £16,000. **FOREST August 1959, fee £16,000**. Newcastle United September 1962, fee £17,000. Peterborough United player-manger January 1969 to September 1972. Cambridge United scout October 1972 to March 1973. Barnsley manager April 1973. Blackburn Rovers manager April 1978. Luton Town scout October 1978. Bury manager July 1980 to February 1984. Exeter City manager June 1984 to April 1985, Charlton Athletic scout. Luton Town scout.
Debut v Manchester City (a) 22.8.59, lost 1-2 (scored)

At the age of 16 Jim Iley first appeared at the City Ground in a North of England Schoolboys trial, and in 1953 he figured in a Wembley Cup Final for the NABC X1 that met the Air Training Corps at the stadium. He commenced with Sheffield United as a strong, left footed wing-half and made 99 League appearances, scoring 13 goals, and received his first senior representative honour while at Bramall Lane in April 1956 when he played for the Football League against the Irish League. After spending two seasons with Tottenham Hotspur, where he won his England Under-23 cap, he joined Forest for a then record fee of £16,000. A strong, attacking player with good distribution, he occupied a variety of roles in his first season, with Whitefoot and Burkitt's consistent form preventing him from a regular place in his accepted position. With Jack Burkitt's fine career drawing towards its close, Iley became first choice at left-half under new manager Andy Beattie, apart from an enforced absence of some five months due to a cartilage operation in 1960-61. Moving on to Newcastle United he enjoyed the best spell of his career, winning promotion from Division Two as champions in 1964-65 (when Northampton Town were runners-up) and appearing in 243 League and Cup matches, scoring 16 goals. Two seasons as player-manager of Peterborough United, prior to hanging up his boots, took his overall record to 536/9 League appearances and 31 goals. He had less success in management despite a promising start with Barnsley. Sacked when just 172 days into a two-year contract with Blackburn Rovers, he was unlucky in his next post, Bury missing out on promotion from Division Four on the final day of season 1982-83. His final appointment with Exeter City lasted less than a season when he was asked to resign after ten months in charge. He refused and was sacked, but he had the sympathy of many Grecians' supporters who produced a 1,000-name petition deploring his dismissal. Bitter about his sacking, Iley called a public meeting in a church hall to air his grievances, and even offered to buy a controlling share interest in the club in order to remain in charge. All to no avail, but he remained in the game with scouting appointments at Charlton Athletic and Luton Town. Jim Iley was the brother-in-law of Colin Grainger, the England international wingman.

Appearances: FL: 93 apps 4 gls FAC: 4 apps 1 gl FLC: 3 apps 0 gls Other: 3 apps 0 gls Total: 103 apps 5 gls

Honours: England Under-23 International v Wales, 1 cap. Football League representative v Irish and Scottish Leagues. (Newcastle United) FL Division 2 champions 1965.

IMLACH, James John **Stewart**

Outside-left 5' 6" 10st 9lbs

Born: Lossiemouth, 6th January 1932

Died: Formby, 3rd October 2001

Debut v Leyton Orient (a) 18.8.56, won 4-1

CAREER: Lossiemouth. Bury October 1952. Derby County May 1954, in exchange for Cecil Law and Norman Nielson. **FOREST 26th July 1955, fee £5,875**. Luton Town June 1960, fee £8,000. Coventry City October 1960, fee £8,000. Crystal Palace July 1962 to December 1964. Dover January 1965. Chelmsford City player-coach February 1965. Crystal Palace player-coach February 1966. Notts County Youth coach March 1967. Everton assistant coach May 1969, first team trainer July 1972 to January 1976. Blackpool coach June 1976 to August 1977. Bury coach June 1978 to October 1979.

Stewart Imlach commenced with Bury at 20 years of age, and with nine months remaining on a joinery apprenticeship. The lightweight and speedy wingman was promoted to the first team almost immediately. He had appeared in 71 League matches and scored 14 goals for the Shakers at the time of his move to Derby County, but the Rams were relegated from Division Two in his only season at the Baseball Ground and he made the short trip to the City Ground in the close season. He appeared on both wings in his first season before settling in at outside-left, in which position he helped the Reds to promotion to the First Division in 1957, and the FA Cup win of 1959. Between times he won four Scotland caps, the final two gained in the 1958 World Cup Finals in Sweden. Skilful and fast and possessing a strong shot in either foot, his ability as a marksman came to the fore in seasons 1956-57, when he scored 14 in League and Cup, and in the following term he netted 16. Sadly, his form dipped in 1959-60, and he was out of the first team in the final month of the season, in which relegation from Division One was only narrowly avoided. Luton Town finished at the foot of the table, but their signing of Imlach in the close season did not have the desired effect, and he was on the move after just eight matches. Dropping into Division Three with Coventry City, he

was rarely absent, appearing in 73 League matches, scoring 11 goals. His senior career ended with Crystal Palace, in two separate spells he made 51 League appearances and scored 3 goals, taking his overall career figures to 423 matches and 73 goals. A lengthy spell in coaching terminated back at Gigg Lane where, after being appointed to succeed Billy Rudd, he departed in October of the following season, swiftly followed by Bury's player-manager, Dave Hatton.
Appearances: FL: 184 apps 43 gls FAC: 19 apps 5 gls Other: 1 app 0 gls Total: 204 apps 48 gls
Honours: Scotland International, 4 caps 1957-58. **(Forest)** FA Cup winners 1959

INGRAM, Alexander David
Centre-forward
Born: Edinburgh, 2nd January 1945
CAREER: Queen's Park FC. August 1963. Ayr United 1966. **FOREST 22nd December 1969**. Ayr United February 1971.
Debut v Arsenal (h) 26.12.69, drawn 1-1
Commencing with the famous amateurs, Queen's Park, Alex Ingram moved on to Ayr United after scoring 12 goals in 25 Scottish League Division Two matches in 1965-66. His first spell at Somerton Park included relegation and promotion, his impressive contribution to the 1968-69 runners-up success being 25 goals. He had netted seven in 16 matches in the following campaign when Forest signed him in mid season. At the City Ground he took over from his fellow Scot, Dave Hilley, as attack leader, and if a return of three goals in 16 matches was a little disappointing, he failed to find the net in 12 matches from the start of the following season. He then lost his place in the side and returned to Ayr United following Forest's signing of Neil Martin from Coventry City. Back at Somerton Park he added a further 32 goals in 152/16 matches in seven seasons of top flight Scottish football.
Appearances: FL: 28 apps 3 gls FLC: 2 apps 0 gls Other: 1 app 0 gls Total: 31 apps 3 gls
Honours: Scotland Amateur International. Scottish League representative v Irish League, 19th November 1969 at Ibrox Park.

JACKSON, Thomas A 'Tommy'

Midfield 5' 7" 11st 4lbs
Born: Belfast, 3rd November 1946
CAREER: Glentoran. Everton February 1968, fee £10,000. **FOREST October 1970, in exchange deal taking Henry Newton to Goodison Park**. Manchester United June 1975, fee £75,000. Waterford July 1978. Ballymena manager.
Debut v Coventry City (a) 17.10.70, lost 0-2
Tommy Jackson was an Irish Cup finalist with Glentoran in 1967, and in the following year left The Oval, shortly after the Irish League championship had been clinched, to join Everton in a £10,000 transfer. His second appearance was made in the semi-final of the FA Cup against Leeds United. Everton won with the only goal of the gane, but Jackson did not get a place in the final, won 1-0 by West Bromwich Albion. He did, however, win a League championship medal, appearing in 15/1 matches as Everton took the title by the margin of nine points over Leeds United. He joined Forest in the following season in a £150,000-rated player exchange deal that took Henry Newton to Goodison Park. In five years at the City Ground, Jackson played under four different managers and experienced relegation for the first time in his career when Forest finished in 21st position in Division One in season 1971-72. Signed by Manchester United's manager, Tommy Docherty, with the intention of captaining the Central League team, he actually began in the first team, but lost his place when Gordon Hill was signed from Millwall. Tommy Jackson won Northern Ireland Under-23 honours and made his full international debut against Israel in September 1968. He won a total of 35 caps for his country,

19 of them while on Forest's books. He later worked as an upholsterer with Bannon & Co (Belfast).
Appearances: FL: 73/8 apps 6 gls FAC: 8 apps 0 gls FLC: 6 apps 0 gls Total: 87/8 apps 6 gls
Honours: N.Ireland International 35 caps, 1968-?. N.Ireland Under-23 International, 1 app. (Everton) FL Division 1 champions 1970 (Glentoran) Irish League champions 1968. Irish Cup finalist 1967.

JOHNSON, Thomas 'Tom'/'Tucker' Dobson.

Inside-forward 5' 8" 11st 13lbs
Born: Gateshead, 21st September 1921
Died: Poole, Dorset, 8th March 1999
CAREER: Boldon Juniors. Boldon Villa. Gateshead September 1941. **FOREST, 11th May 1946, retired May 1952.**
Debut v Grimsby Town (h) 1.9.48, drawn 0-0
Rejoicing in the unusual nickname of 'Tucker', Johnson was a wartime discovery by the Gateshead club for whom he appeared in five seasons with marked success. He was particularly effective in 1943-44, netting 20 goals in 35 matches. The former apprentice fitter went on to record 60 goals in 147 War League matches, and he earned Gateshead a then record fee of £7,000 when he moved to the City Ground, on the strong recommendation of Fred Scott (q.v.) Not particularly tall, but strongly built and with an eye for goal, he was extremely unlucky with injuries, spending long spells of inactivity due to a persistent groin strain, and he later suffered a broken leg in the opening game of the 1950-51 season after scoring the second goal in Forest's 2-0 win at Newport County. He made a remarkably quick recovery, however, and his scoring feats in the final two months of the season, which included a hat trick at Exeter City, had much to do with Forest holding off Norwich City in the promotion race. The unfortunate 'Tucker' was again hospitalised at the mid point of the following season for the removal of a cartilage. At that point he had scored five goals in 11 matches and his presence was much missed in the brave, but ultimately unsuccessful, bid for a second consecutive promotion that ended just two points adrift of runners-up Cardiff City.
Appearances: FL: 68 apps 27 gls FAC: 4 apps 3 gls Total: 72 apps 30 gls
Honours: **(FOREST**) FL Division 3 South champions 1951

JOHNSTON, Thomas 'Tom' Deans

Outside-left/Left half-back 5' 9" 11st 4lbs
Born: Glendale, 30th December 1918
Died: Stapleford, Nottingham, 27th November 1994
CAREER: Berwickshire High School, Duns. Peterborough United 1939. **FOREST May 1944, fee £50**. Notts County 7th August 1948, fee £8,500. Valkeakoski Harka, (Finland) coach June to August 1957. Birmingham City coach September 1957. Heanor Town player-manager July 1958. Rotherham United manager November 1958. Grimsby Town manager July 1962. Huddersfield Town manager October 1964 to May 1968. York City manager October 1968. Huddersfield Town general manager and manager January 1975 to August 1978.
Debut v Watford, FAC 3 (h) 5.1.46, drawn 1-1
A speedy and opportunist wingman who, although a Scot, played all of his football with English clubs. He was playing for Berwickshire High School when Peterborough United's manager Sam Haden moved in swiftly to sign him. The war broke out shortly afterwards but Johnston remained in the Midlands. Joining Forest for a

mere £50 in May 1944 he netted 35 goals in two wartime seasons, with hat tricks from the wing against Fulham and Newport Count in 1945-46. In similar vein, he scored 14 in 32 matches in 1946-47, a season in which he played for 90 minutes as emergency goalkeeper at Luton Town. The signing of George Lee for the following season saw Tom Johnston appear in all forward positions but mainly at centre-forward. A move across the Trent to Notts County saw him back in his favoured outside-left position, and he responded with 26 goals in League and Cup in 45 matches in his first season. In later seasons he developed into a fine left half-back, but it was in his favoured number eleven jersey that he made his final appearance aginst Grimsby Town at Meadow Lane on 22nd December 1956, just eight days away from his 38th birthday. His outstanding record with the Magpies was 286 League and Cup matches and 92 goals. A qualified FA Coach, he spent several summers working in Finland, and he joined the coaching staff at Birmingham City on leaving Meadow Lane. Highlights in his subsequent managerial career included taking Rotherham United to the FL Cup Final against Aston Villa in 1961, and York City from Division Four to Division Two.
Appearances: FL: 64 apps 26 gls FAC: 5 apps 0 gls Total: 69 apps 26 gls
Honours: (Notts County) FL Division 3 South champions 1950

JONES, Charles **Wilson**
Centre-forward
Born: Pentre, Broughton near Wrexham, 29th April 1914
Died: Birmingham, 9th January 1986
CAREER: Brymbo Chums. Brybmo Green F.C. August 1930. Oswestry Town 1931. (Trials with Blackburn Rovers and Bolton Wanderers).Wrexham amateur May 1932, professional August 1932. Birmingham September 1934. Solihull Town November 1939. (Wartime guest player with Mansfield Town, Southampton, Birmingham, Blackpool, Huddersfield Town, West Bromwich Albion and Wrexham). **FOREST 8th September 1947, fee £1,500**. Kidderminster Harriers July 1948. Redditch United August 1949; retired May 1950.
Debut v Chesterfield (h) 6.9.47, lost 1-3 (scored)
Despite severely limited opportunities with Wrexham, due to the outstanding form of centre-forward Tommy Bamford, Birmingham obviously saw something in Wilson Jones, the youthful, red-haired attack leader who had scored lots of goals in Wrexham's reserve team. He was an immediate success at St Andrew's scoring 17 goals in his first season and 20 in his second, but he was well into the veteran stage when he joined Forest but managed to score five goals-three from the penalty spot-in just seven matches.
Appearances: FL: 7 apps 5 gls Total: 7 apps 5 gls
Honours: Wales International, 2 caps 1935-39. (Birmingham) Wartime FL South champions 1946.

JONES, David Edward
Central defender 6' 1" 12st 8lbs
Born: Gosport, Hampshire, 11th February 1952
CAREER: Portsmouth associate schoolboy. Gosport Borough. Fareham Town. Bournemouth apprentice June 1968, professional January 1970. **FOREST 16th August 1974, fee £80,000**. Norwich City September 1975 to April 1980, fee £55,000. Wroxham August 1982 to October 1985. Bournemouth coach. Lymington coach. New Milton coach. Bashley assistant manager June 2001.
Debut v Bristol City (h) 17.8.74, drawn 0-0
David Jones was a promotion winner with Bournemouth (as runners-up to Notts County) from Division Four in 1970-71, and was unfortunate in the following season not to win a second promotion when his team finished third in Division Three. He had appeared in 128/6 League matches and scored five goals for the Cherries when he moved to the City Ground. He joined a poor Forest side who finished 16th in Division Two and parted company in mid season with manager Allan Brown, who was quickly replaced at the helm by Brian Clough. As Clough set about reshaping the side, Jones was one of the casualties, joining Norwich City, and his old

Bournemouth manager, John Bond, at Carrow Road. In the best spell of his career, Jones was capped eight times by Wales but in his final appearance, against England at the Racecourse in 1980 he aggravated a previous knee injury that brought his senior career to a close. He did, however, play for five more seasons with Wroxham in the Anglian Combination League. Later working in the printing trade and as a delivery driver, he also coached Bournemouth's Under-15s for a spell.
Appearances: FL: 36 apps 1 gl FAC: 3 apps 1 gl FLC: 2 apps 0 gls Total: 41 apps 2 gls
Honours: Wales International, 8 caps. Wales Under-23 International 4 caps.

JONES, Eric

Winger 5' 9½" 10st 5lbs
Born: Ulverston, 23rd June 1931
CAREER: Christ Church School. Blackburn Rovers amateur. **FOREST amateur.** Notts County amateur 1950. Preston North End professional January 1952. **FOREST September 1955, for a joint fee of £5,600, also covering the earlier signing of P. Higham**. Doncaster Rovers March 1958, fee £350. Accrington Stanley July 1959. Southport July 1960. Lancaster City August 1962.
Debut v Stoke City (h) 3.9.55, lost 2-3

Eric Jones played as an amateur for both Forest and Notts County while serving in the RAF in the Nottingham area. A neat ball player with a good shot in either foot, Jones was a club colleague of Peter Higham (q.v.) at Preston North End, and it was Higham who recommended Jones to Forest's manager, Billy Walker. Due to unfortunate injuries, his chances were restricted, and he spent much of his time at the City Ground in the Midland League side, with Stewart Imlach the regular choice at outside-left. Subsequent moves brought mixed fortunes, with his best spell coming with Southport, his final League club. In 1960-61 he appeared in 45 League matches and scored 12 goals, and added a further 31 appearances and six goals in 1961-62. Off the field, Eric Jones was employed in the motor trade.
Appearances: FL: 18 apps 3 gls Total: 18 apps 3 gls

JOYCE, Christopher ' Chris'

Inside-forward 5' 8" 10st 9lbs
Born: Dumbarton, 19th April 1933
Died: Nuneaton, 20th December 2002
CAREER: Vale of Leven. **FOREST 29th September 1956, fee £250**. Notts County July 1959. Nuneaton Borough July 1962.
Debut v Sunderland (h) 7.12.57, won 2-0
Chris Joyce joined the City Ground professional staff from his native Scotland, where he played for Vale of Leven FC in his native Dumbarton. Following a two-week trial period when the 1956-57 season opened, he quickly proved his worth, and after a brief return home to complete his apprenticeship in the shipyards, he signed the necessary forms. After appearing in ten First Division matches in his first season, the signing of Eddie Baily effectively ended his involvement with the seniors. He had scored six goals in 29 Football Combination matches in 1958-59 before being released on a free transfer. He took the short trip to Meadow Lane and made an immediate impact, ten goals in 22 matches in his first season assisted his new team to promotion from Division Four. In the Third Division campaign that followed he lost his place at inside-right but later returned to first team status on the wing.
Appearances: FL: 10 apps 0 gls Total: 10 apps 0 gls

JULIANS, Leonard 'Len' Bruce

Centre-forward 5' 10" 12st 0lbs
Born: Tottenham, 19th June 1933
Died: Canvey Island, Essex, 17th December 1993
CAREER: Tottenham Schoolboys. Harris Lebus Y.C. Walthamstow Avenue. Leytonstone. Walthamstow Avenue. Leyton Orient June 1955. Arsenal December 1958, fee £12,000. **FOREST 23rd June 1960, fee £10,000.** Millwall January 1964. Detroit Cougars (USA) coach 1968. Gormahia (Kenya) manager
Debut v Manchester City (h) 20.8.60, drawn 2-2 (scored one)

35 goals in 66 League matches for Leyton Orient earned Len Julians his move to Highbury, but despite netting seven goals in 18 League matches he was largely a reserve team player, his record at that level 17 goals in 27 matches. On joining Forest he scored on his debut, but a leg injury limited his appearances to just seven in his first season. Having asked for a transfer, he did not get a chance in the first team until midway through the following season, but he then scored eight goals in 18 appearances as attack leader. Then followed his most productive season, 14 goals in 29 League matches helping Forest to finish ninth in Division One, and to the sixth round of the FA Cup. During his spell at the City Ground, Len Julians, who was a qualified FA coach, worked three evenings a week with players from the Russell Youth Club and Calverton Colts, and the freshmen of Loughborough College. Signed by Millwall's new player-manager Billy Gray (q.v.) in January 1964, Julians' arrival was unable to save his new team from relegation from Division Three. They very quickly bounced back, however, achieving successive promotions from Division Four, as runners-up to Brighton & Hove Albion, and to Division Two, again as runners up to Hull City. He then led the scoring list with 17 in 39 matches as Millwall made a solid start to life in Division Two, finishing in eighth place in the table. He then spent an unrewarding spell as coach to Detroit Cougars, being replaced by Andre Nagy, the Cougars finishing at the foot of the Lakes Division of the Eastern Conference. Later with Gormahia (Kenya) he won four league titles in 1983, 1984, 1985 and 1991.

Appearances: FL: 58 apps 24 gls FAC: 3 apps 1 gl Total: 61 apps 25 gls

KAILE, Gordon Walter

Winger 5' 6" 10st 8lbs
Born: Pimperne, Blandford Forum, Dorset, 7th December 1924
Died: Pimperne, Blandford Forum, 28th February 1988
CAREER: R.A.O.C. Chilwell. **FOREST 25th May 1945.** Preston North End July 1951, fee £5,250. Exeter City August 1954. St. Luke's College, player-coach. Grantham Town.
Debut v Leeds United (h) 18.10.47, won 1-0

Gordon Kaile was spotted by Forest while playing in army football in the Notts Amateur League during the Second World War period. A versatile forward, able to fill any position in an emergency, he signed a professional form just before being posted to India. The presence of George Lee kept him out of the first team for much of season 1948-49, but when Lee left to join West Bromwich Albion in July 1949, Kaile seized his opportunity, enjoying his best season at the City Ground, appearing in 40 League matches and scoring six goals. His goal against Millwall, scored on New Year's Eve 1949 at the City Ground, was timed at 30 seconds from the kick off. Trying his luck from a very narrow angle, his shot took a slight deflection past Millwall's goalkeeper Ted Hinton. Sadly, a slow recovery from a cartilage operation subsequently robbed him of his true form, and he moved on to Preston North End in July 1951. He played in little first team football subsequently, with just

seven appearances and one goal for Preston North End, and six matches and one goal for Exeter City
Appearances: FL: 65 apps 8 gls FAC: 2 apps 1 gl Total: 67 apps 9 gls

KEAR. Michael 'Mike' Philip

Outside-right 5' 8" 10st 7lbs
Born: Coleford, Gloucs. 27th May 1943
CAREER: Cinderford Town. Newport County amateur, signing professional August 1963. **FOREST 13th December 1963, fee £7,000.** Middlesbrough September 1967, fee £20,000. Barnsley August-September 1970. Berchem Sport (Belgium) cs 1971. Cheltenham Town January 1977.
Debut v Tottenham Hotspur (h) 21.12.63, lost 1-2
As an amateur Mike Kear first attracted Newport County and was quickly signed as a professional by the Fourth Division club in August 1963. Despite having appeared in only six League matches his wing play interested several clubs but it was Forest who paid £7,000 for his signature on 13th December 1963. In almost four years at the City Ground his role was that of a valuable reserve team player, after appearing in 11 matches in his debut season, when he contested the outside-right position with David Pleat and Ian Storey-Moor. In the run-in to Forest's second place finish in Division One in 1966-67, Mick Kear starred in the 4-1 home win in the Easter match against Burnley, scoring two of his side's goals. Early in the following season he departed to Middlesbrough, finding more opportunities, he made 56/2 League appearances and scored seven goals. A six-year spell in Belgium followed, with a final move to Cheltenham Town in January 1977.
Appearances: FL: 26/1 apps 5 gls Total: 26/1 apps 5 gls

KELLY, Bernard 'Bernie'
Inside-forward 5' 10" 11st 10lbs
Born: Carfin, Scotland, 21st October 1932
Died: Detroit, USA, 8th October 2004
CAREER: Dunipace F.C. Law Hearts F.C. Muirkirk Juniors 1951. Raith Rovers October 1951. Leicester City July 1958. **FOREST 18th April 1959**. Aberdeen July 1959. Raith Rovers August 1960. Cowdenbeath 1961. Vale of Leithen. Cumbernauld United manager 1965.
Debut v Leeds United (h) 22.4.59, lost 0-3
Bernie Kelly was a Scottish 'B' and Scottish League representative with an impressive record of 92 League and Cup goals in 207 matches in seven seasons with Raith Rovers. He continued to find the net on crossing the border to join Leicester City (15 League and Cup goals in 27 appearances) but he moved quickly on to Forest having failed to settle at Filbert Street. A match report of his Forest debut against Leeds United diplomatically suggested that he could have had a happier debut: "Some of his wing bound balls had class about them, but he seemed less than match fit and too rarely worked hard to get possession." After the briefest of stays at the City Ground, Kelly returned homewards but his earlier form in the Scottish League had seemingly deserted him, as he added just a further 20 appearances and three goals for his three different clubs.
Appearances: FL: 2 apps 0 gls Other: 1 app 0 gls Total: 3 apps 0 gls.
Honours: Scotland 'B' International. Scottish League representative, 1 appearance.

KELLY, Noel
Inside-forward 5' 7" 10st 10lbs
Born: Dublin, 28th December 1921
Died: Poulton-le-Fylde, 11th August 1991
CAREER: Dublin Bohemians amateur. Shamrock Rovers. Glentoran. Arsenal September 1947, fee £650. Crystal Palace March 1950, fee £8,000. **FOREST 21st August 1951, fee £6,250.** Tranmere Rovers 30th July 1955, fee £1,000, player-manager from September 1955 to October 1957. Ellesmere Port Town player-manager 1957. Northwich Victoria manager April 1968 to January 1969. Holyhead Town manager.
Debut v Birmingham City (a) 1.9.51, won 2-0
Noel was the father of John Kelly, the Bebington-born midfielder, who represented six different League clubs and made 399/37 League appearances and scored 63 goals between 1979-93. Kelly senior's record was modest by comparison- 143 League appearances and 23 goals for his four clubs, but he was good enough to be capped by his country while at the City Ground, where he played some of the best football of his career. On his day, Noel Kelly was a brilliant ball player whose speciality was the defence-splitting cross-field pass. In October and November of the 1954-55 season he hit the target in four consecutive matches and netted seven goals in the space of six outings. He scored seven goals in 52 Third Division North matches for Tranmere Rovers, but his tenure as player-manager ended in November of his second season, his team having won only two of the opening 18 matches of the season.
Appearances: FL: 48 apps 11 gls FAC: 3 apps 1 gl Total: 51 apps 12 gls
Honours: Irish International, 1 cap 1954. League of Ireland representative.

KNIGHT, Frank
Left half-back 5' 7" 11st 2lbs
Born: Hucknall, Notts. 26th October 1921
Died: Nottingham, 18th December 1993
CAREER: Hucknall Town. Mansfield Town July 1939. **FOREST wartime guest, signing professional 13th August 1946, retired May 1950.** Re-registered on 18th August 1950 and joined the training staff, and appointed assistant-trainer in 1951. In 1966 took over temporary duties as first team trainer when Jack Burkitt left to join Notts County as their manager.
Debut v Bradford Park Avenue (a) 16.11.46, won 1-0
A Forest wartime signing, Frank Knight played in much services football in India during the hostilities, including international matches, and was a regular member of Tommy Walker's X1, captained by the famous Scottish international forward. Returning after the war, he made his 'home' debut (and second Football League appearance) against Manchester City on 23rd November 1946. With the City Ground flooded and no play possible, neighbours Notts County loaned the Meadow Lane ground so that the game could go ahead. Forest lost 0-1 to the eventual champions of Division Two. It was Forest's first 'home' game on a foreign enclosure, and the crowd numbered 32,194. A regular first team player in his first season Knight later captained the Reserves on the occasion that they won the Midland League X1 for the first time. For the 1951-52 season, he was rewarded for his long service by a role on the training staff, while continuing to play for the 'A' Team. He remained at the City Ground until the early 1970s when, in the midst of several managerial changes in quick succession finally brought his extremely loyal service to the club to an end in December 1972.
Appearances: FL: 48 apps 1 gl FAC: 5 apps 0 gls Total: 53 apps 1 gl

KNIGHT, Peter Robert
Outside-right
Born: Ilford, Essex, 26th December 1937
CAREER: Southend United June 1958. **FOREST 11th August 1959**. Oxford United July 1960. Reading November 1964, fee £3,500. Guildford City cs 1966.
Debut as sub v Wolverhampton Wanderers, FA Charity Shield, (a) 18.8.59, lost 1-3
After being released on a free transfer by Southend United, having failed to make a first team appearance, the Third Division cast-off was propelled into the limelight when he appeared as a second half substitute for FA Cup winners Forest in the Charity Shield Final against Wolverhampton Wanderers. Peter Knight was originally signed for a month's trial at the City Ground, but was signed as a professional four days after his Charity Shield debut and was then given his Football League debut at Manchester City, replacing Billy Gray on the right wing. Released after making just four first team appearances, he joined Oxford United, members of the Southern League Premier Division. It was success all the way for two seasons, when consecutive championships were won, Knight's outstanding contribution being 21 goals in 83 league matches. Elected to Division Four of the Football League in 1962, he added a further 106 League and Cup appearances and twelve goals before moving on to Reading in November 1964. After appearing in 32 League and Cup matches and scoring three goals, he joined Guidford City in the summer of 1966, and was a Southern League Cup winner with them in his first season.
Appearances: FL: 4 apps 0 gls Other: 0/1 apps 0 gls Total: 4/1 apps 0 gls

LANGFORD, John William

Outside-left 5' 9" 10st 8lbs
Born: Kirkby-in-Ashfield, 4th August 1937
CAREER: Leicester City amateur. **FOREST amateur, signing professional 17th August 1955**. Notts County August 1958, fee £600. Bourne Town. Long Eaton January 1961. Spalding United cs 1962. Ilkeston Town December 1962. Loughborough United. Arnold St Mary's. Alfreton Town. Belper Town. Sutton United.
Debut v Leeds United (a) 8.10.55, lost 0-3
In his first season as a part-time professional (he worked as an underground electrician at the East Kirkby Colliery) John Langford scored 17 goals in 37 Midland League matches for Forest Reserves. Additionally, he had a run of four matches in the first team. He was unable to capitalise on his bright start, however, Stewart Imlach very successfully dominating the outside-left position. After moving across the Trent to join neighbours Notts County, he appeared in the first 14 Division Three fixtures – only one of which was won – he then lost his place, the mid-term signing of Alan Withers ending Langford's involvement at senior level. Currently living at Sutton-in-Coldfield, and enjoying watching his grandson, Nick, who is on Mansfield Town's books.
Appearances: FL: 4 apps 0 gls Total: 4 apps 0 gls

LAY, Peter John
Left full-back 6' 0½" 11st 7lbs
Born: Stratford, Essex, 4th December 1931
CAREER: R.A.F. Watnall. **FOREST professional 27th April 1953**. Queens Park Rangers July 1956, fee £500. King's Lynn cs 1957.
Debut v Bristol Rovers (a) 16.4.55, lost 1-2
One of two young players to sign professional forms in April 1953, both recommended to the club by supporter Danny Long, for whose RAF team they played in the Canal Zone. Peter Lay was ideally built for his role at left full-back, but despite showing early promise he failed to make the

grade, and was similarly unsuccessful on moving to Queens Park Rangers, for whom he made a single first team appearance.
Appearances: FL: 1 app 0 gls Total: 1 app 0 gls

LEE, George Thomas

Outside-left 5' 10" 11st 4lbs
Born: York, 4th June 1919
Died: Eaton, Norwich, 1st April 1991
CAREER: Knavesmire School. York and Yorkshire Schoolboys. Acomb F.C. Scarborough F.C. February 1935. York City amateur June 1936, professional July 1937. (Wartime guest player with Bradford Park Avenue, Lincoln City and Chester.) **FOREST 15th August 1947, fee £7,500**. West Bromwich Albion July 1949, fee £12,000. Lockheed Lemington June 1958. Vauxhall Motors January 1959. West Bromwich Albion trainer-coach 1959 to November 1962. Norwich City trainer-coach and kit man May 1963 to May 1987.
Debut v Bury (h) 23.8.47, won 2-1 (scored one)
When George Lee was signed from York City it was revealed that Forest's manager, Billy Walker, then in charge at Sheffield Wednesday, had offered York City £1,750 and the proceeds of a match for his transfer. It was a substantial offer for a relatively inexperienced player, whose career was put on hold by the outbreak of the Second World War. During military service, Lee won the BAOR titles for the 100 and 880 yards track events, and made several representative appearances for the Combined Services X1, several times being partnered by the Scottish international, Billy Steel. Immediately after his demobilisation he moved on from York City, following two of his friends, Fred Scott and Bert 'Sailor' Brown to the City Ground. He fought two relegation battles in successive seasons in a poor Forest side that finished 19th in Division Two in his first season, and 21st (and relegated) in 1948-49. At this point, West Bromwich Albion manager Jack Smith approached Forest for both Lee and Edwards, the left wing pairing who had so nearly saved Forest from relegation. Southampton stepped in and signed Edwards for £10,000, but George Lee did move to the Hawthorns and enjoyed great success, winning an FA Cup medal in 1954, and helping his team to finish runners-up to the Wolves for the Division One championship in the same season. The strong running, hard shooting wingman appeared in 271 League matches and scored 59 goals for the Baggies before dropping into non-League football at the age of 39.
Appearances: FL: 76 apps 20 gls FAC: 3 apps 0 gls Total: 79 apps 20 gls
Honours: (West Bromwich Albion) FA Cup winners 1954

LE FLEM, Richard Peter 'Flip'

Outside-left 5' 9" 11st 0lbs
Born: Bradford-on-Avon, 12th July 1942
CAREER: Guernsey football. **FOREST amateur August 1959, professional 11th May 1960**. Wolverhampton Wanderers January 1964, in exchange for Alan Hinton. Middlesbrough February 1965, fee £10,000. Leyton Orient March 1966 to cs 1967, fee £2,000.
Debut v Cardiff City (a) 10.9.60, won 3-1
After just 55 League matches, 'Flip' Le Flem was awarded an England Under-23 cap against Holland in Rotterdam in November 1961. Signed by Forest in the face of competition from several other top-flight clubs, he made his League debut at 18 years of age. Fast and tricky and essentially an artistic performer, he replaced Tony Barton for his debut at Cardiff City and remained first choice outside-left throughout, despite

a tendency to perform erratically he could be a match winner when on top form. His move Wolverhampton Wanderers lasted for just over a year, and he made little impact with either Middlesbrough or Leyton Orient. With the latter club, a change of manager did not help his cause, as when Dick Graham took over Le Flem was quickly dropped, became disenchanted with reserve team football, and returned to Guernsey, quitting football at the age of just 25. It was a sad ending to a career that had commenced with such promise.
Appearances: FL: 132 apps 18 gls FAC: 7 apps 1 gl FLC: 5 apps 0 gls Other: 2 apps 0 gls Total: 146 apps 19 gls
Honours: FA X1 (who beat Jersey 10-0) 1957. England Under-23 International, 1 cap 1961

LEMON, Arthur
Forward 5' 11" 11st 0lbs
Born: Neath, Glamorgan, 25th January 1931
CAREER: Neath Old Boys. **FOREST 6th February 1951, retired due to injury May 1955.**
Debut v Leicester City (a) 28.2.53, drawn 1-1
At school in Wales, Arthur Lemon's sporting activities were confined to rugby, but during his National Service he took to soccer and did so well that he was recommended to the Forest by one of the club's supporters. In his first full season at the City Ground Lemon was leading scorer for the 'A' Team with 16 in just 15 matches. His progress continued with 32 goals in 35 matches for the Reserves, his total including two hat tricks and five-goal blast in a 9-2 win against Denaby United on 14th February 1953. Sadly, he developed cartilage trouble at a time when he was seriously contesting the leadership of the attack with Wally Ardron and was being tipped for a Welsh cap. Despite a lengthy battle for match fitness, the 24 year-old centre-forward was forced to announce his retirement from the senior game.
Appearances: FL: 24 apps 1 gl Total: 24 apps 1 gl

LEVERTON, Ronald 'Ron'/'Tot'

Inside-forward 5' 8" 11st 2lbs
Born: Whitwell, Derbyshire, 8th May 1926
Died: Bulwell, Nottingham, 19th August 2003
CAREER: Whitwell School. Calverton Colliery. Clowne Town. **FOREST October 1943. Re-registered 12th October 1946.** Notts County October 1953, fee £7,000. Walsall July 1956 to May 1957. Wisbech Town. Arnold St. Mary's. Calverton Colliery August 1962.
Debut v West Bromwich Albion (a) 12.10.46, drawn 1-1
'Tot' Leverton was given his nickname during schooldays, when the tiny left-winger showed up well against boys twice his size. After working for a time as a collier he realised his ambition to become a professional footballer. Beginning with Forest during wartime, he was signed after appearing in just one trial game. Enthusiastic and speedy, he overcame a double fracture of his left leg at Leyton Orient in an accidental collision with Orient's Polish goalkeeper Sam Gerula on 15th October 1949, and went on to record over a century of appearances before crossing the Trent to join neighbours Notts County in October 1953. He was a regular first team player with the Magpies until a double fracture of a facial bone, sustained at Eastville in February1954, halted his successful run of 20 matches. After completing 51 League and Cup appearances and scoring five goals, he rounded off his senior career with a season with Walsall, for whom he scored three goals in 17 League matches.
Appearances: FL: 103 apps 36 gls FAC: 1 app 0 gls Total: 104 apps 36 gls
Honours: (Notts County) FL Division 3 South champions 1951

LIGHTENING, Arthur Douglas

Goalkeeper 6' 1" 13st 0lbs
Born: South Africa, 1st August 1936
Died: Glenwood, Durban, South Africa, October 2001
CAREER: Queen's Park F.C. (South Africa). **FOREST 7th December 1956**. Coventry City November 1958. Middlesbrough August 1962 to May 1963. Durban City (South Africa) 1963 to 1966. Stella FC.
Debut v West Bromwich Albion (a) 8.2.58, lost 2-3
Arthur Lightening was the first-ever player from South Africa to represent Forest in a Football League match. The ideally built goalkeeper's outstanding displays in the Natal League earned him selection to play against the English FA touring side during the summer, and he arrived in Nottingham after a long air trip on 4th December 1956. He quickly impressed with some good displays in the Midland League side, but the headlines on his debut: "Lightening hit by goal storm" marked a shaky first appearance at West Bromwich Albion in which Forest scored twice in two minutes in the second half but lost 3-2. In the following season he took over from Chic Thomson, who had conceded eight goals in the opening two matches, but he conceded a soft goal in the first minute of the match against Tottenham Hotspur on 10th September and two months later he was transferred to Coventry City, along with Ron Farmer, for a combined fee of £6,000. Both players served the Sky Blues with distinction, in Lightening's case, he appeared in 160 League and Cup matches and was a promotion winner from Division Four in his first season. He remained for just one season with his final League club, Middlesbrough, before returning homeward to South Africa.
Appearances: FL: 6 apps 0 gls Total: 6 apps 0 gls

LINAKER, John 'Johnny' Edward
Outside-right 5' 6½" 10st 4lbs
Born: Blowick, Southport, 14th January 1927
Died: Shipley, 14th June 2013
CAREER: Southport & Lancashire schoolboys. Southport (trial) August 1942. Army Training Corps. Everton amateur. Manchester City August 1945. Southport November 1946. **FOREST 2nd September 1947, fee £250**. York City June 1950, fee £1,625. Hull City October 1951, fee £5,000. York City June 1953. Scarborough March 1956. Crewe Alexandra July 1957. Ashington June 1958.
Debut v Fulham (a) 28.8.48, lost 0-4
An all-round sportsman, Johnny Linaker represented the RAF in swimming competitions, and was an excellent golfer who represented Yorkshire, Devon and Lothian, in addition to holding several different posts as a club professional. His talents on the football field were first revealed at Southport, but his availability was sporadic due to his being in the RAF at the time. On moving to join Forest he made a startling debut against Fulham, the Sporting Mirror reporting that: "He played a blinder and actually kept the Cottagers' fine defence, Bacuzzi, Freeman and Taylor, running round in circles. If only there had been someone there to take advantage of his centres and openings." Sadly, after a spell of 13 matches in the first team, and the side looking increasing like relegation candidates, he was dropped into the reserves and was never again a serious contender for a first team place. Subsequently, he recovered his earlier form with York City, and in two separate spells with the Minstermen recorded 98 League appearances and 20 goals.
Appearances: FL: 15 apps 2 gls Total: 15 apps 2 gls

LINDLEY, Edwin
Inside-right 5' 9" 11st 10lbs
Born: Epworth, 22nd April 1931
Died: Scunthorpe, 9th October 1951
CAREER: Scunthorpe United. **FOREST 18th October 1949, fee £1,500**. Scunthorpe United.
Debut v Millwall (h) 31.12.49, won 3-1
An impressive display for Scunthorpe United against Notts County Reserves led to his signing by Forest against competition from Liverpool. Considered a youngster of great promise, Edwin Lindley was a part-time professional who worked on his father's farm. By coincidence, his first game for Forest Reserves was against Scunthorpe United in the Midland League game on 27th October 1949. On his League debut some two months later Forest fielded a reconstituted attack that included Linaker for his first match of the season, and Lindley for the first time ever in senior match. It was Forest's first win at home after four City Ground defeats, but Lindley tired in the second half, and the Reds' attack relied heavily on Ardron and his wingmen. At the early age of just twenty, Edwin Lindley tragically died at The War Memorial Hospital, Scunthorpe on 9th October 1951. He was taken there with a suspected fractured skull after the motorcycle that he was riding was in collision with another motorcycle. A matter of days earlier he had scored two goals for Scunthorpe United Reserves in their 3-2 win against Grantham at London Road.
Appearances: FL: 1 app 0 gls Total: 1 app 0 gls

LISHMAN, Douglas 'Doug' John

Inside-forward 5' 11" 11st 4lbs
Born: Birmingham, 14th September 1923
Died: Forsbrook, Stoke-on-Trent, 21st December 1994
CAREER: St Thomas' RC School. Paget Rangers BC (Birmingham J.O.C. League). Walsall August 1946. Arsenal July 1948, fee £10,500. **FOREST 17th March 1956, fee £3,500 to May 1957.**
Debut v Middlesbrough (h) 17.3.56, lost 2-4 (scored one)
Before the war Doug Lishaman played at centre-half for St. Thomas' R.C. School, Erdington, Birmingham. He later joined the Royal Marine Commandos and served in several campaigns and when demobbed returned home to Birmingham. He then joined Pagett Boys' Club as an inside-forward, and a few weeks later was chosen to play for Birmingham Youths and Old Boys against Tamworth & Trent Valley in the Campbell-Ore Shield Final. Many League scouts were present, and he was in receipt of several offers from first class clubs. He chose one near to his home-Walsall-and turned professional in August 1946. In his first season he made 22 League appearances and scored eight goals, and in the following season (1947-48) he missed only five League games, netting 21 times in League and Cup matches. Manchester City showed an interest but he joined Arsenal on 3rd June 1948, and until January 1st, 1949, played in the Combination side, was coached in the Arsenal style and developed by assistant manager Jack Crayson under Tom Whittaker's direction. A combination of craft and shooting power netted him 137 goals in 244 League and Cup games for the Gunners, before his all-too-brief stay at the City Ground, the highlight of which was his hat trick in the penutitimate Division Two match at Bramall Lane against Sheffield United in the promotion season of 1956-57. In the following month Lishman decided to 'hang up his boots' in order to concentrate on a family furniture business venture at Stoke-on-Trent.
Appearances: FL: 38 apps 22 gls FAC: 3 apps 0 gls Total: 41 apps 22 gls
Honours: England 'B' International. FL representative, 1 app. (Arsenal) FL Division 1 champions 1953.

LOVE, John 'Jack' Thomson D.F.C.

Inside-forward 6' 1" 12st 7lbs
Born: Neweraighall, near Edinburgh, 18th March 1924
Died: Glenfarg, Oerth & Kinross, 14th June 2007
CAREER: Leith Athletic 1941. (Wartime guest player with Hibernian and Raith Rovers.). Leith Athletic 1947. Albion Rovers February 1948. **FOREST 26th February 1949, fee £8,000.** Llanelli player-manager June 1952. Walsall player & assistant-manager March 1955, fee £600, manager September 1955 to December 1957. Wrexham manager December 1957 to November 1959.
Debut v Luton Town (a) 26.2.49, lost 3-4

John Love joined Leith Athletic at the age of 17, and during the war years-when R.A.F. duties permitted-he made guest appearances with Hibernian and Raith Rovers. A flight-lieutenant pilot, he flew both bombers and gliders, and won the Distinguished Flying Cross for his part in the crossing of the Rhine, in which action he was wounded by shrapnel. After the war he rejoined Leith Athletic, moved on to Albion Rovers and assisted them to promotion from the Scottish Second Division in 1947-48, as runners-up to East Fife. His transfer to the Forest came too late to save them from relegation to Division Three South, despite his seven goals in 13 matches. His cracking strike from 20 yards gave Forest their only goal at Hillsborough in March1949, and the unassuming John Love admitted at the time that he had never scored better one. An intriguing headline of the day ran: "Forest waited too long for Love," and certainly with his help the team ended with a flourish, but agonisingly finished just one point from safety in 21st position in the table. In the season that followed, he finished second in the scoring list with 11 goals in League matches, but then made only four League appearances in the championship season, 1950-51, making his first appearance at Norwich on 23rd December, when he was introduced at inside-right for Tom Johnson-the first team change in eleven weeks! In his final season, 1951-52, he scored 20 goals in 31 matches for the Reserves, but made only five first team appearances in which he scored two goals. He then moved into management, initially as player-manager with Southern League side Llanelli, and then as player-assistant manager to Frank Buckley at Walsall. His final appointment in senior circles was with Wrexham and it commenced during the course of the 1957-58 season, which marked the end of the Northern and Southern sections of Division Three. He was able to guide the Robins to 12th place in the table, which ensured Third Division football, rather than soccer's basement Fourth Division. In early November 1959 he resigned his post with the Robins lying in 21st position, but a change of manager did not prevent their ultimate relegation to Division Four. **Note**: *Flight-lieutenant Love was a Bomber Command pilot attached to the Glider Pilot Regiment, and was one of only five DFCs awarded to RAF glider pilots on Operation Varsity, during the course of which 2,700 men were killed, injured, or reported missing.*

Appearances: FL: 59 apps 21 gls FAC: 3 apps 0 gls Total: 62 apps 21 gls

LYALL, George

Midfield 5' 7" 11st 5lbs
Born: Wick, Scotland, 4th May 1947
CAREER: Kingskettle Amateurs. Raith Rovers June 1964. Preston North End March 1966, fee £8,000. **FOREST 23rd May 1972, fee £40,000.** Hull City November 1975, fee £17,500. Scarborough March 1978. Goole Town June 1979, player-manager from February 1980. Grantham February 1981. Bridlington Town August 1981. North Ferriby United October 1981 to May 1982. Debut v Portsmouth (h) 12.8.72, drawn 0-0

George Lyall's all action style and eye for goal attracted the scouts to Starks Park, and he left Raith Rovers to join Preston North End in March 1966. Taking some time to adjust to the demands of English League football, he played in little first team football during his first three seasons at Deepdale. However, under new manager, Alan Ball, father of

the England World Cup winning star, Lyall was handed a starting role and North End won back their Division Two status at the first time of asking, having been relegated in 1969-70. Departing Deepdale with a record of 102/17 appearances and 19 goals, he achieved similar figures during his three years at the City Ground, becoming firmly established in his second season when he became a candidate for Scotland's World Cup squad. His final move to Hull City ended in tragedy. In scoring his team's first goal against Bolton Wanderers at Boothferry Park on 9th February 1977 he suffered a broken leg, an injury that brought his senior career to a close. He had recorded 48 League and Cup appearances and scored five goals for the Tigers.
Appearances: FL: 103/6 apps 22 gls FAC: 11/2 apps 3 gls FLC: 5 apps 0 gls Total: 119/8 apps 25 gls
Honours: (Preston North End) FL Division 3 champions 1971

LYMAN, Colin Charles

Outside-left 5' 10½" 11st 0 lbs
Born: Northampton, 9th March 1914
Died: Cambridge, 9th May 1986
CAREER: East End Rangers. Semilong United. Northampton Town 'A' Team. Rushden Town. West Bromwich Albion (trial). Southend United amateur March 1934. Northampton Town amateur March, professional November 1934. Tottenham Hotspur June 1937. (Wartime guest player with Alderhot, Chesterfield, Coventry City, Derby County, Leicester City, Northampton Town, **FOREST**, Notts County, Partick Thistle and Port Vale.) Port Vale May 1946. **FOREST 25th October 1946, fee £1,500**. Ransome & Marles player-manager June 1947. Notts County August 1947, fee £1,500. Nuneaton Borough player-coach June 1948, and by early 1950 player-manager, resigned January 1951. Long Eaton Town player-manager January 1951. British Timken F.C.
Debut v Leicester City (h) 26.10.46, won 2-0
The outbreak of World War Two curtailed Colin Lyman's promising career which, at the outbreak, had seen a steady improvement and a personal record of 39 goals in 133 matches for his three League clubs. During wartime service with the RAF, Lyman appeared as a guest player for ten different clubs in addition to playing in representative matches for the RAF. Approaching the veteran stage when peacetime football returned, he failed to settle with either Port Vale or the Forest and after a spell of non-League fare with Ransome & Marles, his return to League football with Notts County lasted for less than a season. Initially as player-coach to Nuneaton Borough, he led them to their great run in the FA Cup in 1949-50 when they progressed through the qualifying rounds before losing to Exeter City in Round Three. In his first season, Nuneaton topped the league and won the Birmingham Senior Cup. During his four years with the club their gates had doubled, but he handed in his resignation in January 1951 and was appointed manager of Long Eaton.
Appearances: FL: 23 apps 9 gls FAC: 4 apps 1 gl Total: 27 apps 10 gls

LYONS, Barry

Winger 5' 8" 11st 0lbs
Born: Shirebrook, 14th March 1945
CAREER: Shirebrook Miners' Welfare. Rotherham United amateur June 1961, professional September 1962. **FOREST 11th November 1966, fee £45,000**. York City (loan) August, permanently September 1973, fee £16,000. Darlington July 1976, player-coach June 1977 to July 1978. York City youth team coach August 1978, caretaker manager March 1980 to December 1981, reverting to coach to July 1982 to 1983.
Debut v Sunderland (h) 12.11.66, won 3-1
A fast and tricky winger who appeared in 132 League matches and scored 23 goals in four seasons for Rotherham United, a solid start to a fine career that eventually reached 503/7 League matches and 72 goals for his

four League clubs. Lyons had learned his football in the Mansfield Youth League before joining Rotherham United, and he cost Forest £45,000 in November 1966. He took over the right-wing position from Chris Crowe, and was immediately at home in a fine Forest side that finished runners-up for the First Division championship and reached the semi-finals of the FA Cup, losing 2-1 to Tottenham Hotspur at Hillsborough. In the following season he played in the European Fairs Cup competition, and was selected as reserve for the England Under-23 X1 who played against Italy at the City Ground. Twice during his spell at the City Ground Sheffield Wednesday sought his transfer, on the second occasion, just hours before the transfer 'deadline' in 1971 but he declined to move. In the following season Forest were relegated from Division One, and Barry Lyons played little first team football in 1972-73 before being transferred to York City. From the right side of midfield he played a key role in his new team's promotion to the Second Division in his first season. After 80/5 League appearances and 11 goals he was given a free transfer and ended his senior career with 97 League outings and 10 goals for Darlington. He then returned to York as a youth coach, and for a time as caretaker manager following the dismissal of Charlie Wright. He later worked in insurance before becoming an hotelier in York.
Appearances: FL: 201/3 apps 28 gls FAC: 19 apps 2 gls FLC: 12 apps 2 gls Other: 5 apps 1 gl Total: 237/3 apps 33 gls

McARTHUR, Barry

Centre-forward 5' 9" 11st 3lbs
Born: Newthorpe, Nottingham, 4th May 1947
CAREER: FOREST amateur June 1963, professional 14th May 1965. Barrow July 1968. York City December 1969 to April 1970. Matlock Town.
Debut as sub v Leeds United (a) 4.9.65, lost 1-2
A broken leg sustained while playing for Forest Reserves against Manchester United Reserves at Old Trafford abruptly halted Barry McArthur's bright start to 1967-68 after he had commenced with four goals in his first five outings. Two years earlier he led Forest's attack in Division One, scoring four goals in 7/1 League appearances. Thereafter his scoring form eluded him although his impressive start for the Reserves in 1967-68 had given a brief reminder of his earlier promise. On moving to Barrow in July 1969, his only goal for the club took his side through to round two of the Football League Cup and a home draw against his former club, Forest, who won 2-1 before 8,919 spectators, Barrow's best attendance of the season. He played in only one League match for York City before his release in April 1970. Barry McArthur was the first ever substitute fielded by Forest when he replaced the injured Colin Addison in the 2-1 defeat at Leeds United, the match being his first appearance in the League side.
Appearances: FL: 7/1 apps 4 gls FAC: 2 apps 0 gls Total: 9/1 apps 4 gls

McCAFFREY, James 'Jimmy'
Winger
Born: Luton, 12th October 1951
CAREER: St. Albans and Hertfordshire Schoolboys. Leeds United (trial). **FOREST apprentice 9th August 1967, professional 26th March 1969.** Mansfield Town July 1972. Huddersfield Town January 1977. Portsmouth February 1978. Northampton Town December 1978 to May 1980.
Debut as sub v Arsenal (h) 26.12.69, drawn 1-1
After being rejected by Leeds United, flying wingman Jimmy McCaffrey joined Forest straight from school. A very speedy player, he ran for his county side, as well as representing them on the football field. A frequent scorer for the Colts' team, he was soon appearing for the England Youth side alongside future stars Steve Perryman, Len Cantello and Steve Whitworth. Lacking opportunities at the City Ground he moved on to Mansfield Town and in a stay of five years won two promotions and totalled 195/9 League and Cup appearances, scoring 27 goals. A season each with Huddersfield Town and Portsmouth, and a final eighteen months with Northampton Town

rounded off his career with a League aggregate figure of 262/20 appearances and 29 goals. After football he worked as a newsagent in Rothley, followed by one at the Glenfield Hospital in Leicester.
Appearances: FL: 2/6 apps 1 gl FAC: 0/2 apps 1 gl FLC: 0/1 apps 0 gls Total: 2/9 apps 2 gls
Honours: England Youth International. (Mansfield Town) FL Division 4 champions 1975, Division 3 champions 1977.

McCALL, Robert 'Bob' Henry

Utility 5' 9½" 11st 9lbs
Born: Whitwell, 29th December 1915
Died: Worksop, 6th February 1992
Debut v Bradford Park Avenue (a) 1.2.35, won 4-1
CAREER: Whitwell Colliery. Worksop Town amateur October 1933. **FOREST 5th March 1935. Re-registered 15th June 1946 to 1952.** (Wartime guest player with Derby County, Leicester City, Mansfield Town and Lincoln City.) **Subsequently appointed groundsman and coach to the Forest 'A' Team**. Worksop Town player-manager July 1952.
Signed by Forest at the age of 19 after spending two seasons with Worksop Town as an amateur, Bob McCall began as a forward in Forest's Reserves, but by season 1938-39 his 30 Division Two appearances were made in roles as diverse as right-half, right-back and centre-forward. Certainly Forest's most adaptable player, he served the Reds with distinction on either side of the Second World War, being a regular in the side until 1949-50, with a swansong at Brentford on 22nd September 1951 in the midst of an injury crisis. When appointed to the dual role of groundsman and 'A' Team coach, he still found time to score 13 goals for the Reserves and eight for the 'A' Team. On moving to Worksop Town in 1952, a report of their public trial match in August of that year suggested that Bob McCall was the most outstanding player in the match. His son, David, was in Forest's Youth team at the age of 16, and on the groundstaff of Nottinghamshire County Cricket Club.
Appearances: FL: 162 apps 1 gl FAC: 10 apps 0 gls Total: 172 apps 1 gl

McCANN, James 'Jimmy'
Forward 5' 9" 11st 2lbs
Born: Dundee, 20th May 1954
CAREER: FOREST apprentice June 1970, professional 2nd July 1973 to May 1977.
Stockport County (loan) October 1975. Halifax Town (loan) October 1976. Corby Town.
Debut v West Bromwich Albion (h) 26.4.75, won 2-1
Jimmy McCann failed to progress at the City Ground, despite his deceptive skills and 100 percent effort. Although essentially a striker, he was tried in various positions before being given his first opportunity by manager Brian Clough in the final Division Two match of season 1974-75. One start and four appearances as substitute in 1975-76 included his only goal, from the bench, in a 2-2 draw at Charlton Athletic. Loan spells with Stockport County and Halifax Town added just 6/1 League appearances and one goal to his modest record.
Appearances: FL: 2/4 apps 1 gl Total: 2/4 apps 1gl

McDONALD, Joseph 'Joe'

Full-back 5' 9" 10st 6lbs
Born: Blantyre, Scotland, 10th February 1929
Died: Australia, 7th September 2003
CAREER: St Joseph's School (Blantyre). Lanarkshire Schools & junior football. Bellshill Athletic. Falkirk December 1951. Sunderland March 1954, fee £5,500. **FOREST 10th July 1958, fee £4,450.** Wisbech Town July 1961. Ramsgate player-manager 1963 to 1965. Yeovil Town manager June 1965 to May 1967. Debut v Manchester United (a) 3.9.58, drawn 1-1
Although slightly built Joe McDonald was a most effective full-back, being a good positional player and crisp tackler. He was a goalkeeper during schooldays and then a right full-back for Falkirk, the former coming in useful in the event of goalkeeper injuries. He had an early taste of representative football when picked for the Lanarkshire Youth team against Glasgow Catholic Youth in 1947 and 1948. Another minor honour came later, playing for Scotland 'B' against the Army. He was subsequently capped twice by his country and played for Great Britain v the Rest of Europe in season 1956-57. After 155 League and Cup appearances for Sunderland he was signed by Forest. Deputising for the injured Geoff Thomas on his debut at Manchester United he played a 'blinder' and retained the position thereafter, collecting a Cup winners' medal at the end of his first season at the City Ground. He had missed only a handful of first team matches when he surprisingly allowed toleave after three very successful seasons with the Reds.
Appearances: FL: 109 apps 0 gls FAC: 12 apps 0 gls FLC: 2 apps 0 gls Other: 1 app 0 gls Total: 124 apps 0 gls
Honours: Great Britain v The Rest of Europe, 1956-57. Scotland International, 2 caps v Ireland and Wales. **(FOREST)** FA Cup winners 1959.

McGLINCHEY, Charles 'Charlie'
Outside-left 5' 11" 10st 11lbs
Born: Coatbridge, Lanarkshire, 1942
CAREER: Bellshill Athletic. **FOREST 29th October 1960**. Ramsgate August 1962.
Debut v Gillingham (h), FLC 1, 11.9.61, won 4-1
Like his colleague, full-back Brian Grant, Charlie McGlinchey was a Coatbridge native who commenced his career with Bellshill Athletic. Originally a centre-forward, McGlinchey was switched onto the left wing in the Combination side, but with 'Flip' Le Flem a fixture in the League side, he was restricted to just one first team appearance in the League Cup first round win against Gillingham. A game, played under floodlights, that featured another player making a solitary senior appearance-goalkeeper Noel Wood.
Appearances: FLC: 1 app 0 gls Total: 1 app 0 gls

McGOVERN, John Prescott

Midfield
Born: Montrose, 28th October 1949
CAREER: Henry Smith's Grammar School. Central Parks Juniors. Hartlepool United apprentice July 1965, professional May 1967. Derby County September 1968, fee £7,500. Leeds United August 1974, fee £125,000. **FOREST 22nd February 1975, fee £60,000**. Bolton Wanderers player-manager June 1982 to January 1985. Horwich RMI manager 1985-86. Chorley February 1990. Plymouth Argyle assistant-manager (to Peter Shilton) March 1992. Rotherham United joint manager with Archie Gemmell September 1994 to September 1996. Woking manager. Hull City assistant- manager. Ilkeston Town manager.
Debut v Manchester United (h) 22.3.75, lost 0-1

Commencing as a fly-half at his non-football grammar school, John McGovern nevertheless developed into a very skilful midfielder. He began his career as a winger with Hartlepools United (debut at 16 years and 205 days) and followed his manager, Brian Clough, to Derby County, Leeds United-along with John O'Hare- and Forest in February 1975. Along the way, he set up a record by appearing in all Divisions of the Football League by the age of nineteen. Captain of the side and a fitness fanatic, McGovern grafted untiringly in Forest's finest years when successive European Cups were won. Considered unfortunate not to have been capped at a higher level than Under-23, he left the City Ground in 1982 to move into management, initially with Bolton Wanderers and later as assistant to two former Forest colleagues, Peter Shilton and Archie Gemmell at Plymouth Argyle and Rotherham United respectively. Currently a Nottingham Forest club ambassador, a Radio Nottingham pundit and popular after dinner speaker, McGovern was inducted into the Scottish Football Hall of Fame in 2017.

Appearances: FL: 249/4 apps 6 gls FAC: 17/1 apps 1 gl FLC: 33 apps 3 gls Other: 31 apps 1 gl Total: 330/5 apps 11 gls

Honours: Scotland Under-23 International, 2 caps. **(FOREST)** European Cup winners 1979, 1980. European Super Cup winner 1980, finalist 1981. FL Cup winner 1979, finalist 1980. Anglo Scottish Cup winner 1977. (Derby County) FL Division 2 champions 1969; FL Division 1 champions 1972.

McINTOSH, James 'Jim' William

Winger 5' 7" 10st 8lbs

Born: Forfar, Angus, 19th August 1950

CAREER: Arbroath Victoria. Montrose March 1970. **FOREST September 1970, fee £15,000**. Chesterfield (loan) January 1976. Hull City March 1976, fee £5,000. Dundee United July 1977. Montrose November 1977.

Debut v Everton (a) 7.11.70, lost 0-1

Jim McIntosh joined Forest from Montrose in September 1970 and made his League debut two months later. Despite a lengthy stay at the City Ground he never quite realised his true potential and apart from two seasons between 1971-73 when he made 34/4 League appearances and scored two goals, he played in little first team football, not helped by a cartilage operation during 1973-74 that restricted him to just four League appearances. After a brief loan spell with Chesterfield and three League appearances, a permanent move to Hull City brought only limited opportunities- 20 League matches and one goal.

Appearances: FL: 44/7 apps 2 gls FAC: 6 apps 1 gl FLC: 1 app 0 gls Total: 51/7 apps 3 gls

McKENZIE, Duncan

Forward 5' 8" 11st 2lbs

Born: Grimsby, 10th June 1950

CAREER: Lincolnshire Schoolboys. **FOREST July 1965, apprentice July 1967, professional 12th July 1968.** Mansfield Town (loan) March 1970 and again February 1973. Leeds United August 1974, fee £240,000. RSC Anderlecht (Belgium) June 1976, fee £200,000. Everton December 1976, fee £200,000. Chelsea September 1978, fee £165,000. Blackburn Rovers March 1979 to May 1981. Tulsa Roughnecks (NASL) June 1981. Chicago Sting (NASL) May 1982. Bulova (Hong Kong) June 1983.

Debut v Sunderland (a) 20.9.69, lost 1-2

Duncan McKenzie joined Forest straight from school as a member of the ground staff. He played initially for the Intermediates and the Colts, for whom he scored a hat trick in the Final of the Swiss Shield against the County Police at the City Ground. He was later a member of the Youth team that lost to Rotherham United in the Final of the International Tournament held in Amsterdam. The floppy-haired striker shot into prominence following two loan spells with Mansfield Town-for whom he scored 10 goals in 13/3 League matches. Back at the City Ground he enjoyed a vintage season, his 26 League goals making him the leading goal scorer in the top two Divisions of the Football League. Signed by Brian Clough during his brief spell as Leeds

United manager, this proved to be just the first of several rapid moves, at home and abroad, for a footballer with flair, dribbling skills and a touch of genius, who scored 112 goals in 319/11 League matches for his six League clubs. He retired in 1983 and worked as a florist, and was later involved in a sports management company, helping with financial advice. He additionally worked as an after-dinner speaker and radio and newspaper correspondent. His son, Andrew, played golf professionally and is the owner of the Premier Golf Management Company. In May 2015 he became a PGA teaching professional.
Appearances: FL: 105/6 apps 41 gls FAC: 6 apps 2 gls FLC: 6/1 apps 3 gls Total: 117/7 apps 46 gls

Duncan McKenzie, 1970

McKINLAY, Robert 'Bobby'

Centre half-back 5' 11½" 11st 0lbs
Born: Lochgelly, Fife, 10th October 1932
Died: West Bridgford, 26th August 2002
CAREER: Lochgelly FC. Bowhill Rovers. **FOREST professional 20th October 1949, retired May 1970 to join backroom staff at the City Ground. Later serving as trainer/coach.**
Debut v Coventry City (a) 27.10.51, drawn 3-3
When signed from Bowhill Rovers, following the Fifeshire club's defeat in the Scottish Junior Cup, 17 year-old Bobby McKinley was said to be able to play at outside-right, also centre or wing-half back, but two trial games at outside-right suggested that his best position would be in the middle line. The son of a semi-professional Cowdenbeath player and a nephew of Billy McKinley, a Forest stalwart of earlier years, Bobby was quickly recognised as one of the most promising youngsters at the City Ground. Blessed with an imperturbable temperament and plenty of confidence, he had few first team opportunities in his first three seasons due to the steadiness of Horace Gager, but he was carefully groomed and there was no doubt that he would eventually succeed Gager, who continued to play until 37 years of age. From the 1954-55 season onwards McKinley became the cornerstone of Forest's defence as one of the outstanding pivots in the country. Like his predecessor, Horace Gager, Bobby McKinley played to the age of 37, his consistency and fitness levels enabling him to complete a remarkable run of 265 appearances between April 1959 and October 1965, and a record 682/3 appearances overall. While still some years away from retirement, he was awarded a testimonial match against Celtic on 12th April 1965. If any proof of his popularity was needed, it was underlined by an attendance of over 18,000 at the midweek friendly match. Some of the proceeds of the game he used to take over a large garage and filling station near to the centre of the city. On retirement from the game he worked as a prison officer at the Lowdham Grange *Detention Centre.*
Appearances: FL: 611/3 apps 9 gls FAC: 53 apps 1 gl FLC: 11 apps 0 gls Other: 7 apps 0 gls Total: 682/3 apps 10 gls
Honours: **(FOREST**) FA Cup winners 1959

McLAREN, Hugh
Outside-left 5' 7½" 11st 10lbs
Born: Hamilton, Scotland, 24th June 1926
Died: Beadsall, Derbyshire, 8th December 1965
CAREER: Bothwell F.C. Kilmarnock August 1945. Derby County October 1949, fee £7,000. **FOREST 23rd January 1954, fee £3,900**. Walsall 21st July 1955 to May 1956, fee £2,750. Burton Albion July 1956. Gresley Rovers July 1957 to May 1959.
Debut v Leicester City (h) 23.1.54, won 3-1 (scored two goals)

In what proved to be Colin Collindridge's last season at the City Ground-1953-54-Hugh McLaren was signed as his successor on the left wing. In a remarkable debut the Scottish-born wingman scored two of three goals scored against Leicester City. He then scored a goal in each of his next three matches. By the time he had played only ten games to complete the season, he had scored six goals. In the following season, Forest lost all of their opening five matches and McLaren lost his place when Peter Small was signed from Leicester City. After a lengthy spell on the sidelines McLaren returned to first team action and announced his recall by scoring both of Forest's goals in the 2-0 win against Plymouth Argyle on 12th March 1955. Despite his excellent strike rate for a wide player he was transferred to Walsall at the end of the season. In earlier days he scored 56 goals in 131 senior games for Derby County, where he replaced England international Frank Broome, who left the Baseball Ground to join Notts County in the month of McLaren's arrival from Kilmarnock. The 'Nottingham Post Guide 1954-55' revealed that McLaren was a poultry farmer when not playing football.
Appearances: FL: 33 apps 15 gls Total: 33 apps 15 gls

MARSHALL, Gordon
Goalkeeper 6' 1" 12st 7lbs
Born: Farnham, Surrey, 2nd July 1939
CAREER: Tyneside School. Balgreen Rovers. Heart of Midlothian July 1956. Dalkeith Thistle (loan). Newcastle United June 1963, fee £18,500. **FOREST 10th October 1968, fee £17,500.** Hibernian April 1969, fee £2,500. Celtic July 1971. Aberdeen January 1972. Arbroath June 1972 to July 1975.
Debut v Sunderland (a) 12.10.68, lost 1-3
Although born in Farnham, Surrey, Gordon Marshall was raised in Lothian. He was the son of a Scottish soldier based at Aldershot, and spent the first 23 days of his life in Surrey. He joined Hearts at the age of 17 and in seven seasons made 193 Scottish League appearances, earning League and Cup medals and being capped by England Under-23. He did equally well following his transfer to Newcastle United, being ever-present in 1964-65 when the Second Division title was secured. After 174 League and Cup appearances for the Magpies he joined Forest and became the fourth different goalkeeper fielded in four consecutive matches following injuries to Peter Grummitt and Brian Williamson. Second from bottom in Division One and with home games being played at Meadow Lane following the fire that gutted the main stand at the City Ground, Forest were in crisis mode. They eventually pulled away from the bottom of the table with a fifth goalkeeper, Alan Hill, taking over first team duties. Gordon Marshall returned to Scotland, initially to Hibernian, and eventually took his total of English and Scottish League appearances to an impressive 566 matches.
Appearances: FL: 7 apps 0 gls Total: 7 apps 0 gls
Honours: England Under-23 International, 1 cap. (Heart of Midlothian) Scottish League Division 1 champions 1960. Scottish League Cup winners 1959, 1960, 1963. (Newcastle United) FL Division 2 champions 1965.

MARTIN, Frederick 'Freddie' Arthur
Centre-forward
Born: Nottingham, 13th December 1925
Died: Nottingham, July quarter 1969
CAREER: Cinderford Colliery. **FOREST October 1944.** Ransome & Marles FC (loan) August 1946. Peterborough United August 1949 to May 1956.
Debut v Cardiff City (h) 4.10.47, lost 1-2
Freddie Martin made little headway with Forest, but he enjoyed an excellent seven seasons with Peterborough United of the Midland League. Often opposed to Forest Reserves, one one such occasion in January 1950 the 'Notts. Journal' commented: "Freddie Martin, ex-Forest, was always a danger, and a good scheming inside-forward." A regular for six of his seven seasons

with the Posh, he appeared in 237 Midland League matches, scoring 124 goals, and a further 20 FA Cup appearances and 11 goals.
Appearances: FL: 5 apps 0 gls FAC: 2 apps 0 gls Total: 7 apps 0 gls

MARTIN, James 'Jimmy'
Outside-left 5' 7" 10st 11lbs
Born: Glasgow, 3rd March 1937
Died: Glasgow, 10th September 1994
Career: Baillieston Juniors. **FOREST 27th June 1958' registration cancelled 8th December 1959.**
Debut v Leeds United (h) 22.4.59, lost 0-3
Jimmy Martin alternated between inside and outside-left in the reserves, and it was in the latter role that he made his single senior appearance, as deputy for Stewart Imlach. A match report of his debut, a 3-0 home defeat by Leeds United, ran as follows: "The first team fledgling, outside-left Jimmy Martin, fitted in neatly enough without leaving an indelible impression on proceedings."
Appearances: FL: 1 app 0 gls Total: 1 app 0 gls

MARTIN, Neil

Centre/Inside forward 6' 0" 11st 8lbs
Born: Tranent, East Lothian, 20th October 1940.
CAREER: Tranent Juniors. Alloa Athletic 1959. Queen of the South late 1961, fee £2,000. Hibernian July 1963, fee £6,000. Sunderland October 1965, fee £45,000. Coventry City February 1968, fee £90,000. **FOREST February 1971, fee £65,000.** Brighton & Hove Albion July 1975. Crystal Palace March 1976. Vancouver Royals (Canada) loan 1967. San Antonio Thunder (USA) loan 1976. St Patrick's Athletic 1976 to 1978. Al-Arabi Sporting Club, Kuwait, assistant manager 1978. Walsall youth coach, then joint-manager July 1981, sole manager later that season to June 1982.
Debut v Burnley (h) 20.2.71, won 1-0
Whilst attached to his first senior club, Alloa Athletic, Neil Martin served an apprenticeship as a mining engineer, but his promise induced Queen of the South to pay a then significant sum for his services. His 33 goals in 61 League appearances then attracted the attention of Hibernian. The Easter Road club, a useful side in the mid sixties, reached the semi-finals of both the Scottish and League Cups during Martin's stay, and he earned two Scotland caps, a just reward for netting 56 goals in only 65 League matches. At Sunderland he enhanced his reputation, and just a month after his arrival at Roker won his last cap alongside team mate Jim Baxter (q.v.) in a 1-0 qualifier win over Italy in front of 100,000 at Hampden Park. He then moved to Coventry City, for double the fee that Sunderland had paid. There is no doubt that his 18 League goals in 15 games kept the Sky Blues in the top flight during the final months of 1967-68. The ideally proportioned striker arrived at the City Ground in February 1971, but he had joined a club in decline, and he experienced relegation to Division Two in his second season. It was not until 1974-75 that he led the scoring list, and then with just 10 goals in 26/1 League matches. Released by Brian Clough on a free transfer, he signed for Peter Taylor, Clough's former partner, at Brighton & Hove Albion. Despite netting eight goals in 13/4 League appearances he left before the season was out to join Crystal Palace, for whom he scored his final League goal in 8/1 League outings.
Appearances: FL: 116/3 apps 28 gls FAC: 14/1 apps 4 gls FLC: 5 apps 2 gls Total: 135/4 apps 34 gls
Honours; Scotland International, 3 caps. Scotland Under-23 International. Scottish League representative, 2 apps

MARTIN, Thomas 'Tommy'

Inside-forward 5' 11" 10st 10lbs
Born: Glasgow, 21st December 1924
Died: Blantyre, 6th August 1996
CAREER: Shettleston Juniors. Heart of Midlothian 1942. Stirling Albion October 1949. Doncaster Rovers July 1950. **FOREST 1st November 1952, fee £16,125.** Hull City 22nd June 1955, fee £6,000, Rothes player-coach September 1957 to 1959.
Debut v Rotherham (a) 1.11.52, won 3-2
Tommy Martin joined Forest as an inside-forward after two seasons with Doncaster Rovers for whom he appeared in 71 League matches and scored nine goals. Although described as 'A true Scottish stylist', he never hit his best form at the City Ground, but played outstandingly well at wing-half in the Midland League side. Transferred to Hull City, he appeared in 32 League matches, scoring two goals, before returning to Scotland as player-coach of Rothes F.C., the Highland League club. An excellent golfer, Tommy Martin was runner-up to Ronnie Simpson (Newcastle United) in the 1953 Professional Footballers' Golf Championship at the Little Aston course. Both players posted rounds of 78 and Simpson won in the play-off.
Appearances: FL: 48 apps 4 gls FAC: 2 apps 0 gls Total: 50 apps 4 gls

MEE, George Edwin

Outside-right/Inside-forward
Born: Blackpool, 20th May 1923
Died: Nottingham, April quarter1974
CAREER: Aston Villa. **Wartime guest with FOREST, signing professionally 13th May 1946.** Blackpool October 1947.
Debut v Watford, FAC1 (h) 5.1.46, drawn 1-1
Hailing from a footballing family, George Mee's father was a Bulwell-born star performer at outside-left for Blackpool, for whom he appeared in 194 consecutive matches. He was also a fine tenor singer who 'plugged the pops' in Lawrence Wright song booths on the Blackpool sea front during the summer season. His younger brother, Bertie Mee was on the books of Derby County and Mansfield Town, but was best remembered as Arsenal's manager from 1966 to 1976. George Mee, who was generally regarded as one of the speediest professional footballers in Nottingham, assisted Forest during wartime and in the first season when League football recommenced in 1946-47. Sadly, a cartilage injury that required surgery kept him out of action for three months of the season and although he returned following his enforced absence in March 1947, he played only twice more before being released. He was linked with a move to Portsmouth, but it was Blackpool who signed him but he did not appear for them at senior level.
Appearances: FL: 9 apps 1 gl FAC: 3 apps 0 gls Total: 12 apps 1 gl

MIDDLETON, John
Goalkeeper
Born: Skegness, 24th December 1956
Died: Skegness, 3rd July 2016
CAREER: FOREST apprentice 27th September 1972, professional 28th November 1974.
Derby County September 1977, fee £25,000 plus Archie Gemmill. Retired due to shoulder injury May 1980.
Debut v West Bromwich Albion (a) 19.10.74, won 1-0
John Middleton made his Forest debut at West Bromwich Albion after only eight outings in the reserves. He had established himself as England Youth goalkeeper, helping them to win the Little World Cup in Switzerland in May 1975. Subsequently he gained England Under-21 caps when he played in Finalnd and Norway in the UEFA Under-21 Tournament. He contested the first team jersey with Peter Wells during Brian Clough's first full season as Forest manager. After Forest had won promotion to the First Division in 1977, Clough bought Peter Shilton from Stoke City and transferred John Middleton in exchange for Archie Gemmell and a fee of £25,000. Middleton quickly succeeded Colin Boulton at the Baseball Ground, but at the close of the 1979-80 season, when the Rams were relegated from Division One, John Middleton was forced to retire due to a persistent shoulder injury. He had appeared in 80 League and Cup matches for the Rams.
Appearances: FL: 90 apps 0 gls FAC: 11 apps 0 gls FLC: 6 apps 0 gls Other: 5 apps 0 gls Total: 112 apps 0 gls
Honours: England Youth & Under-21 International, 3 caps. **(FOREST)** Anglo-Scottish Cup winners 1977

MOCHAN, Dennis

Full-back 5' 7" 11st 8lbs
Born: Falkirk, 12th December 1935
CAREER: Beelsdyke United. Carron Villa. Slamannan United. Kilsyth Rangers. East Fife. Raith Rovers. **FOREST June 1962, fee £10,000**. Colchester United September 1966, appointed trainer following final appearance in 1969-70, and briefly caretaker-manager for five matches, July 1972 to November 1972.
Debut v Leicester City (h) 19.2.63, lost 0-2
Stylish full-back Dennis Mochan originally played at centre-forward and outside-left for East Fife. Moving on to Raith Rovers he began as attack leader, but injury to a defender in his fourth match caused his switch to left-back, where he remained for the rest of his career. He arrived at the City Ground having played only twice in England in friendly games against Aston Villa and Gateshead. He had to wait for a first team place with Forest, but when he got it he never looked back, doing so well that he came under consideration by Scottish selectors. Transferred to Colchester United in September 1966 he appeared in 113/3 League matches, scoring two goals. He made his final playing appearance in season 1969-70 but remained as trainer at Layer Road, stepping in as caretaker-manager following the resignation of Dick Graham in September 1972. Following the appointment of Jim Smith as manager, Dennis Mochan resigned in the following month and returned to Falkirk where he took up employment outside of the game. His elder brother Neil Mochan won three Scottish caps as a Celtic player, and spent two seasons with Middlesbrough (14 goals in 38 matches) between 1951-53. Another brother, Willie, was a player with Stenhousemuir.
Appearances: FL: 108 apps 1 gl FAC: 11 apps 0 gls 119 apps 1 gl
Honours: Scottish Junior International. (Kilsyth Rangers) Scottish Junior Cup winners 1955.

MOORE, Alan

Outside-right 5' 8" 10st 9lbs
Born: Hepburn, County Durham, 7th March 1927
Died: Cambridge, 7th April 2008
CAREER: Sunderland amateur, signing professional May 1946. Spennymoor United July 1947. Chesterfield December 1948. Hull City July 1951, fee £7,000. **FOREST 12th January 1952, fee £5,500**. Coventry City 23rd December 1954, fee £10,000. Swindon Town July 1957. Rochdale November 1958. Wisbech Town June 1959. Cambridge United player-manager November 1959, manager only from July to October 1963. Later coach at Cambridge University for two seasons 1967 to 1969.
Debut v Notts County (h) 19.1.52, won 3-2

A 'Geordie' who joined Forest from Hull City in January 1952, Alan Moore made his debut in the local 'Derby' against Notts County at the City Ground, and was very unlucky when a 'goal' was disallowed from his first kick of the ball. His displays on the right wing immediately earned him a regular place in the side and he struck up a very successful partnership with Fred Scott, together they made a very dangerous wing. He headed the scoring list in 1953-54 with 19 goals from the wing, and won many friends with his terrier-like persistency. One of ten brothers, he first played for Sunderland and Chesterfield, and assisted a further three League clubs after leaving the City Ground. He continued to play for Cambridge United until season 1962-63, but then did not register himself as a player in order to concentrate on managerial affairs. In terms of League football he appeared in 269 matches and scored 62 goals for his six clubs.

Appearances: FL: 102 apps 38 gls FAC: 2 apps 0 gls Total: 104 apps 38 gls

MORLEY, William 'Bill'

Wing half-back 5' 8½" 10st 121lbs
Born: Nottingham, 30th July 1925
Died: Aspley, Nottingham, 12th July 1978
CAREER: People's College School. Mapperley Celtic. **FOREST 23rd September 1945, re-registered 25th December 1946 to May 1959**. Wisbech Town August 1959.
Debut v West Ham United (a) 30.11.46, drawn 2-2

Bill Morley began his career with the Forest club in season 1945-46 and made his debut the following term at outside-left against West HamUnited, his only appearance that season. A local lad, he played for an amateur team whose ground was on the Victoria Embankment – just a stone's-throw from the City Ground. During his thirteen years with the club he appeared in the first team in all five forward positions and both wing half berths. Slight of build, his exceptional turn of speed enabled him to figure prominently in either attack or defence. During his spell at the City Ground Morley had a season on the ground staff of Nottinghamshire County Cricket Club but unfortunately an attack of appendicitis prevented his playing very much. That cost him his chance in County cricket, but he

continued to enjoy the summer pastime with Gedling Colliery as a wicketkeeper and batsman. He was due a second benefit from the club in season 1956-57 when he appeared in every match when promotion from Division Two was secured. Sadly, he lost his first team place to Jeff Whitefoot in season 1958-59 and missed out on the opportunity to assist his team to the FA Cup Final, and the 2-1 victory over Luton Town. Having appeared in just five League matches during the season he decided to retire. ***Note****: A familiar name appeared in Football League registrations on 5th December 1950, Geoffrey Morley, younger brother of Bill, was signed as a full time professional by Forest. A wing half-back or inside-forward, he did not make the first team at the City Ground and was transferred to Grantham in August 1951.*
Appearances: FL: 282 apps 10 gls FAC: 19 apps 0 gls Total: 301 apps 10 gls
Honours: (**FOREST**) FL Division 3 South champions 1951

MORRIS, Ernest
Centre-forward 5' 11" 12st 7lbs
Born: Stocksbridge, near Rotherham, 11th May 1921
Died: Hoyland, Barnsley, 29th February 2008
CAREER: FOREST 5th August 1947. Gainsborough Trinity January 1948. York City June 1948. Grantham August 1949. Halifax Town November 1950 to April 1951.
Debut v Bury (h) 23.8.47, won 2-1
Despite scoring a hat trick for Forest's Midland League side on his debut, and his only senior goal against Bradford Park Avenue on his second appearance in the League side, Ernest Morris was replaced at centre-forward after four consecutive matches at the start of the 1947-48 campaign. He had scored a total of 20 goals in first and second team matches when transferred to Gainsborough Trinity, but he subsequently failed to impress in spells with York City and Halifax Town, adding just one League appearance to his modest total, in Halifax's 0-1 defeat at New Brighton on 16th December 1951.
Appearances: FL: 4 apps 1 gl Total: 4 apps 1 gl

MORRISON, Robert 'Bobby' Crossan
Inside-forward
Born: Chapelhall, near Glasgow, 16th February 1933
Died: Airdrie, 6th October 1999.
CAREER: Dalry Thistle. Falkirk 1952. Glasgow Rangers 1956. **FOREST 11th July 1958**. Workington July 1959 to May 1961. Airdreonians coach.
Debut v Wolverhampton Wanderers (a) 23.8.58, lost 1-5
Bobby Morrison appeared in 79 Scottish League matches and scored 19 goals for Falkirk when the Brockville club generally struggled to maintain their place in Scotland's top flight. On moving to the Rangers in 1956 he failed to win a regular berth in the title-winning side of 1956-57, despite scoring six goals in five League matches and one in two Scottish Cup-ties. In his second season he was almost totally unemployed at senior level, being restricted to just one Scottish League Cup-tie. On moving to the City Ground he appeared only once on the opening day of the season, with fellow-Scot John Quigley dominating the inside-right role in the first team. As Forest went on to win the FA Cup, Bobby Morrison's disappointing season at the City Ground was ended when he was placed on the open to transfer list in May 1959. On dropping down to Division Four with Workington, he enjoyed a splendid first season, scoring 18 goals in 46 League and Cup matches. After a further 13 matches and three goals in 1960-61 he retired from playing and took up a coaching appointment with Airdrieoniansa a Scottish League Division One side.
Appearances: FL: 1 app 0 gls Total: 1 app 0 gls

NEWTON, Henry Albert

Wing half-back 5' 8" 11st 4lbs
Born: Nottingham, 18th February 1944
CAREER: Russell School. Firbeck School. Nottingham Schoolboys. **FOREST January 1960, professional June 1961**. Everton October 1970, fee £150,000 plus Tommy Jackson. Derby County September 1973, fee £100,000. Walsall May 1977, retired May 1978.
Debut v Leicester City (h) 8.10.63, won 2-0
Another of Forest's highly promising local youngsters, Henry Newton won many County FA honours and signed professional forms at the age of 17. He was quickly established in the Combination side and made his debut in Division One at 19. In the same season he established a regular first team place following the departure of Trever Hockey to Newcastle United. A tireless worker in midfield with a biting tackle, he was also versatile enough to successful switch to a role at left full-back in 1965-66 to accommodate new signing Terry Hennesey in the number four jersey. In the following season he missed only three League matches and appeared in all FA Cup-ties in the memorable 1966-67 campaign when the side finished as runners-up for the League Championship and reached the semi-finals of the FA Cup. After leaving the City Ground, Newton made 76 League appearances for Everton, and 111/6 for Derby County, where he won his Football League championship medal. His final move to Walsall was marred by injury and he retired after just 16 appearances for the Saddlers, taking his career aggregate figures to an impressive 485/6 League matches and 27 goals. He later ran a sub post office in Derby to retirement.
Appearances: FL: 282 apps 17 gls FAC: 18 apps 0 gls FLC: 10 apps 1 gl Other: 5 apps 1 gl Total: 315 apps 19 gls
Honours: England Under-23 International, 4 caps. FL representative, 1 appearance 1970. (Derby County) FL Division 1 champions 1975.

NICHOLSON, George Henry 'Harry'

Goalkeeper 6' 3" 13st 0lbs
Born: Wetherall, Cumberland, 25th January 1932
Died: Bristol, January 2015
CAREER: Carlisle United amateur. Grimsby Town August 1952. **FOREST 5th July 1955**. Accrington Stanley March 1958. Leyton Orient March 1959, fee £500. Bristol City July 1960. Poole Town July 1961. Bath City 1962.
Debut v Leicester City (h) 31.8.55, won 2-0
As deputy to Clarrie Williams, George Nicholson enjoyed a 17-match run, from 13th February 1954, in the Mariners' goal, despite being beaten seven times in his second outing at Gateshead. He did not feature at senior level again before his free transfer to Forest in July 1955. The tallest man on the staff, he nevertheless impressed with his agility for one so powerfully built. He was given an early chance in

prefence to Bill Farmer and completed 38 League appearances in his first season. He followed with 34 appearances in the following term when Forest won promotion from ther Second Division as runners-up to Leicester City. When experienced goalkeeper Chic Thomson was signed from Chelsea in the close season, Nicholson lost his place, but his 78 League and Cup appearances for Forest proved to be the highlight of his career, as he totalled only six League outings with his next three League clubs
Appearances: FL: 72 apps 0 gls FAC: 6 apps 0 gls Total: 78 apps 0 gls

NORTH, Thomas 'Tom' Williamson

Inside-forward
Born: Barrow-on-Soar, Leics. 31st October 1919
Died: Barrow-on-Soar, Leics. August 1996
CAREER: Banbury Spencer. **FOREST *circa* August 1943, professional 3rd January 1945.** Gainsborough Trinity October 1946.
Debut v Watford, FAC 3, (h) 5.1.46, drawn 1-1
Along with Ernest Jones, Tom North was one of two Forest reserve team players transferred to Gainsborough Trinity in October 1946. Tom North made his first Forest appearances against Leicester City in a 0-0 draw on 30th December 1944, and later in the same season scored in home and away matches against Notts County on 17th and 24th February. He then played in most matches in 1945-46, scoring 10 goals in 33 League South matches. In the month of his 33rd birthday he made his FL debut, and last Forest appearance, in a 1-1 draw against West Bromwich Albion at the City Ground on 12th October 1946.
Appearances: FL: 1 app 0 gls FAC: 2 apps 0 gls Total: 3 apps 0 gls

O'DONNELL, Francis 'Frank' Joseph
Centre-forward 6' 0" 12st 5lbs
Born: Buckhaven, Fife, 31st August 1911
Died: Macclesfield, 4th September 1952
CAREER: St Agatha's School. Denbeath Violet Juniors. Wellesey Juniors August 1930. Celtic September 1930. Preston North End May 1935, along with brother Hugh for a combined fee of £5,000. Blackpool November 1937, fee £8,000 plus two players. Aston Villa November 1938, fee £10,500. (Wartime guest player with Forfar, Preston North End, Blackpool, Liverpool, Wolverhampton Wanderers, York City, Aston Villa, Brentford, Fulham, Tottenham Hotspur, Brighton & Hove Albion and Heart of Midlothian and **Forest) FOREST 1st February 1946, fee £1,125.** Raith Rovers April 1947. Buxton Town as player June 1947, later assistant and then manager to his death in 1952.
Debut v Barnsley (a) 31.8.46. lost 2-3 (scored one goal)
Despite a record of 51 goals in 78 Scottish League matches for Celtic, Frank O'Donnell did not catch the eye of the Scottish selectors until he crossed the border, along with his brother Hugh, to join Preston North End. In his second season at Deepdale he scored in every round of the FA Cup, including five against Exeter City and two against West Bromwich in the semi-final. He also netted in the final, but Sunderland took the trophy by a 3-1 scoreline. In the same season he made his international debut and scored in a 3-1 win against England at Hampden Park. There was just time for two more moves before the outbreak of the Second World War. Firstly to Blackpool (30 League appearances and 17 goals) and then to Aston Villa (29 League appearances and 14 goals). Signed by Forest after playing, and scoring, in two matches as a guest, he was signed on a permanent basis from Aston Villa. On the resumption of normal League football in 1946-47, O'Donnell scored on his debut, and had netted five in his first six matches, but he asked for a transfer in November having lost his place in the side. It was later in the season when his transfer to Raith Rovers was agreed. This lasted for a matter of weeks before a final move took him to

Buxton Town as a player, and later manager. One of a family of 15 children, his premature and untimely death came at the age of just 41.
Appearances: FL: 11 apps 5 gls Total: 11 apps 5 gls
Honours: Scotland International, 6 caps 1937-38. (Preston North End) FA Cup finalists 1937.

O'HARE, John
Forward/Half-back 5' 8" 11st 2lbs
Born: Renton, Dumbartonshire, 24th September 1946
CAREER: St Martin's School. St Patrock's School. Dumbarton Schools. Drumchapel Amateurs. Sunderland amateur 1962, professional October 1963. Vancouver Royals (NASL) 1967. Derby County August 1967, fee £22,000. Leeds United August 1974, fee £50,000. **FOREST 22nd February 1975, with John McGovern for a combined fee of £60,000**. Dallas Tornado, NASL, (loan) 1977. Belper Town August 1981. Subsequently engaged in minor football; assisted Carriage & Wagon F.C. of Derby (East Midlands Regional League) in 1982-83, and managed two other sides in that district, Ockbrook and Stanton. Also scouted for Aston Villa, Leicester City and Celtic.
Debut v Oxford United (a) 28.2.75, drawn 1-1
Totally unselfish and a magnificent team man, John O'Hare had the ability to accept and control the ball in the tightest situations-virtues that outweighed some lack of pace and a modest strike rate in front of goal. He joined Sunderland just before his sixteenth birthday, turned professional at seventeen, and made his League debut a year later. After appearing in 51 League matches and scoring 14 goals, he became one of Derby County's newly installed manager Brian Clough's early signings. O'Hare shared in the Rams remarkable rise to glory, winning all his 13 Scottish caps, a League championship medal and a Division Two title during his seven years at the Baseball Ground. Signed again by Clough during his ill-fated short spell with Leeds United, a third reunion, along with John McGovern, came with his managerial mentor, this time to the City Ground. O'Hare proved a rare bargain, despite his hard work often going unappreciated by supporters. Fittingly, his last appearance for Forest was made as a substitute in the European Cup Final triumph against Hamburg in Madrid. It was a perfect way to end a senior career. He was subsequently employed as a licensee, later taking up a business appointment.
Appearances: FL: 94/7 apps 14 gls FAC: 7/1 apps 1 gl FLC: 14/2 apps 3 gls Other: 122/11 apps 20 gls
Honours: Scotland International, 13 caps. Scotland Under-23 International, 3 caps. (Derby County) FL Division 2 champions 1969. FL Division 1 champions 1972. **(FOREST)** FL Cup winner 1978 (As sub in first game, full game in replay). European Cup winner 1980 (As sub)

O'KANE, William James 'Liam'

Defender 5' 10" 11st 0lbs
Born: Londonderry, N. Ireland, 17th June 1948
CAREER: Derry City July 1964. **FOREST 14th December 1968, fee £10,000, retired May 1977 and joined Forest's coaching staff.** Aston Villa scout.
Debut v Leeds United (a) 30.4.69, lost 0-1
Liam O'Kane's Forest debut came in the final fixture of 1968-69, away at the League champions, Leeds United. Sadly, his debut was marred by injury and it was a foretaste of things to come, as the unfortunate Irishman spent lengthy spells on the sidelines throughout his career. A cultured defender, he became a regular for his country and would have doubtless added to his total of twenty caps, had he not suffered a broken leg in December 1971. This injury kept him out of Forest's League side, and international football, until March 1973. He then enjoyed two injury free seasons between 1973 and 1975, in which he missed only one match,

but in 1975-76 a succession of injuries brought his playing career to a close, his final senior appearance coming on 21st February 1976 at Bristol Rovers.
Appearances: FL: 186/3 apps 0 gls FAC: 20 apps 1 gl FLC: 12/1 apps 0 gls Other: 2 apps 0 gls Total: 220/4 apps 1 gl
Honours: N. Ireland International, 20 caps, 1970-75

O'NEILL, Martin Hugh Michael O.B.E.
Midfield 5' 10" 11st 3lbs
Born: Kilrea, County Derry, 1st March 1952
CAREER: St. Malachy's College. Rosario FC (Belfast). Distillery August 1969. **FOREST 22nd October 1971, fee £15,000**. Norwich City January 1982, fee £250,000. Manchester City June 1981, fee £275,000. Norwich City January 1982, fee £125,000. Notts County August 1983, fee £40,000; retired February 1985. Grantham manager August 1987. Shepshed Charterhouse manager July 1989. Wycombe Wanderers manager February 1990. Norwich City manager June 1995. Leicester City manager November 1996. Celtic manager June 2000 to May 2005. Aston Villa manager August 2006 to August 2010. Sunderland manager December 2011 to March 2013. Republic of Ireland manager November 2013 to 2017. Forest manager January 2019.
Debut v Newcastle United (a) 20.11.71, lost 1-2
For many years, Martin O'Neill was Forest's most capped player, until his total of 36 awards was overtaken by Stuart Pearce's total of 37 England caps. Shortly after scoring two goals in Distillery's 3-0 victory against Derry City in the Irish Cup Final, he joined Forest as an all-action midfielder with an artistic style and the priceless ability to see the move beyond the next. At the time of his signing he was studying law at Queen's University, Belfast. He began well at the City Ground but his form dipped in 1974-75 and he was on the transfer list when Brian Clough arrived as manager. Within a matter of months, O'Neill was back to his very best, and apart from being omitted from the 1979 European Cup winning team, he returned to favour for the final against Hamburg a year later. Then followed two spells with Norwich City, separated by an unsuccessful sojourn with Manchester City, that preceded his return to Nottingham to join Notts County, where his playing days ended because of a knee injury. It was a sad end to a fine playing career as the Magpies suffered successive relegations from Division One and Division Two. Considering his subsequent successes in the field of management, it is surprising that it took him over two years to get started, his first foot on the ladder being three days a week with Grantham. This despite a pedigree of European Cup and championship medals, and having captained his country in the World Cup quarter-final in 1982. Once into his managerial stride, the honours came thick and fast. He took Wycombe Wanderers from the Conference to Division Two before taking Leicester City into the Premier League and to victory in two FL Cup Finals. A Scottish domestic treble in his first season at Parkhead and subsequent entry into the European champions League and UEFA Cup competitions further enhanced his already outstanding reputation. The highlight of four years with Aston Villa was an appearance in the FL Cup Final of 2010. Along with former Forest and Manchester United player Roy Keane as his assistant, O'Neill led the Republic of Ireland to qualification for the 2016 UEFA European Championships. He re-joined Forest as manager in 2019.
Appearances: FL: 264/21 apps 48 gls FAC: 28 apps 3 gls FLC: 34/1 apps 8 gls Other: 22/1 apps 3 gls Total: 348/23 apps 62 gls
Honours: N. Ireland International 64 caps 1972-85. (Distillery) Irish Cup winners 1971. **(FOREST)** FL Division 1 champions 1978. FL Cup winners 1978 and 1979, finalists 1980. European Cup winners 1980

Martin O'Neill 1973

ORGILL, Harold 'Harry'
Goalkeeper 5' 11" 13st 0lbs
Born: Hucknall, Notts. 1st October 1920
Died: Broxtoe, Nottingham, 21st September 1979
CAREER: Basford F.C. Southport June 1939. **FOREST 7th April 1947**. Notts County June 1947 to May 1948.
Debut v Tottenham Hotspur (h) 7.4.47, drawn 1-1
Harry Orgill's seven appearances in Division Two for Forest were made consecutively, before the signing of Harry Walker, the ex-Portsmouth goalkeeper, who proved to be the answer to Forest's problems in the last line of defence. Taking the short trip across the Trent after being released on a free transfer, Orgill spent a season as reserve goalkeeper to Harry Brown at Meadow Lane. He was restricted to just two first team appearances, the last at Swansea Town on 27th December 1947 when he was a late call-up and caught the midnight train from Hucknall, arriving at Swansea at 11a.m. As the 'Football Post' commented: "Orgill rendered his team a marvellous service, which included the saving of a penalty." He had had no sleep, and was on the receiving end of a severe examination from the Swansea attack, but his display was the chief factor in his team sharing the points in a 1-1 draw.
Appearances: FL: 7 apps 0 gls Total: 7 apps 0 gls

ORR, Anderson 'Alan'
Wing half-back 5' 11" 11st 8lbs
Born: Glasgow, 19th December 1923
Died: Lancaster, Pennsylvania, USA, 25th August 1998
CAREER: Third Lanark during wartime season 1942-43. **FOREST 19th July 1951, fee £7,000 to May 1955.**
Debut v Rotherham United (a) 18.8.51, won 2-1
A cool, constructive wing half-back with an ideal physique who began as a teenager with Third Lanark in wartime football while serving in the Scots Guards. Anderson Orr made his debut in Scottish League Division One in 1947-48, and had appeared in 85 matches and scored nine goals at the time of his transfer to Forest in July 1951, in preparation for their first season back in Division Two. After appearing in half of the matches in his first season, he lost his place, and his next real opportunity came following injury to Jack French in January 1954, and he played impressively in 15 consecutive appearances through to the end of the season. His up-and-down experiences continued in his final season when he was dropped after the opening five matches of the campaign ended in defeat.
Appearances: FL: 46 apps 0 gls Total: 46 apps 0 gls

OTTEWELL, Sidney 'Sid'

Inside-forward 5' 8½" 11st 4lbs
Born: Horsley, Derbyshire, 23rd October 1919
Died: Nottingham, 31st January 2012
CAREER: Derbyshire Schoolboys. Holbrook Miners' Welfare. Chesterfield November 1936. (Wartime guest player with Fulham, Bradford City, Blackpool, Birmingham, Chester and Tottenham Hotspur.) Birmingham City June 1947. Luton Town December 1947. **FOREST 24th July 1948**. Mansfield Town January 1950, fee £2,500. Scunthorpe United March 1952. Whitstable Town July 1953. Spalding United player-manager 1954. Heanor Town November 1956. Bourne Town manager. Lockheed Leamington manager 1960 to 1969. Debut v West Bromwich Albion (h) 21.8.49, lost 0-1
Sid Ottewell starred in Schools football, and appeared in England Boy's trials alongside the famous Tommy Lawton. He had made just three appearances for Chesterfield before the outbreak of World War Two and then was called up into the RAF as a physical training

instructor. After guest appearances for six different clubs, he returned to Saltergate following his demobilisation in March 1946. Then followed a number of rapid moves, his transfer to Forest being his third change in 13 months. His best spell came in two seasons with Mansfield Town (21 goals in 67 League matches)
Appearances: FL: 32 apps 3 gls FAC: 2 apps 0 gls Total: 34 apps 3 gls

PALMER, Calvin Ian

Utility 5' 10" 11st 5lbs
Born: Skegness, 21st October 1940
Died: Brighton, 12th March 2014
CAREER: Skegness Town. **FOREST amateur, signing professional 2nd April 1958**. Stoke City September 1963, fee £30,000. Sunderland February 1968, fee £70,000. Cape Town City (South Africa) cs 1970, subsequently player and assistant-manager with Hellenic F.C. Crewe Alexandra October 1971 to January 1972. Hereford United 1972. Durban United (South Africa) 1972. Berea Park (South Africa) 1973-75
Debut v Arsenal (h) 4.4.59, drawn 1-1
Certainly among the most versatile players of his day, Calvin Palmer was well able to make a show in any outfield position, but was likely to be at his best in a wing-half slot. He revealed high promise during his time on the Forest ground staff, representing both the Notts FA and the Thursday League. He gained prominence in 1960-61 with 27 League outings replacing injured right-half, Jeff Whitefoot. Palmer himself lost his place through injury in the following term and asked for a transfer as a consequence. The same thing happened again in 1962-63, after he had become the Forest captain, and it was on the cards that West Bromwich Albion would sign him in a £30,000 deal. However, Palmer did not move for some months, eventually joining Stoke City, where he completed 196 League and Cup appearances, scoring 27 goals. He arrived at Roker Park, Sunderland, a seasoned professional, but his stay was comparatively short (37/5 League and Cup appearances, five goals). Following a spell in South Africa, two League appearances for Crewe Alexandra wound up his playing career, just two games short of 300 League and Cup appearances for his four clubs. Unfortunate not have gained representative honours, he was selected to play for the FA X1 on 4th October 1961 v the RAF but injury caused his withdrawal and he was then selected as reserve for England Under-23 v Yugoslavia in February 1963. Calvin Palmer died in a Brighton Hospice after a long illness and donated his body to medical science to King's College, London.
Appearances: FL: 91 apps 14 gls FAC: 5 apps 0 gls FLC: 4 apps 0 gls Other: 1 app 0 gls Total: 101 apps 14 gls
Honours: (Stoke City) FL Cup finalists 1964

PARR, John Barry
Goalkeeper 5' 11½" 11st 0lbs.
Born: Weston-Super-Mare, 23rd November 1942
CAREER: Ransome & Marles F.C. **FOREST November 1962 to May 1965.**
Debut v Ipswich Town (h) 2.11.63, won 3-1
When John Armstrong was transferred to Portsmouth in February 1963, John Parr stepped up to become Forest's regular goalkeeper in the Football Combination. At the same time he became deputy to Peter Grummitt, but was called upon only once for first team duty, but had the satisfaction of assisting his team to a 3-1 win against Ipswich Town at the City Ground.
Appearances: FL: 1 app 0 gls Total: 1 app 0 gls

PATRICK, Roy

Full-back 6' 0" 12st 0lbs
Born: Overseal, Derbyshire, 4th December 1935
Died: Renfrew, 26th March 1998
CAREER: Derby County June 1951, professional February 1952. **FOREST 11th May 1959**. Southampton June 1961. Exeter City March 1963. Burton Albion August 1965 to May 1966.
Debut v Blackburn Rovers (h) 29.8.59, drawn 2-2
Roy Patrick made his League debut for Derby County against Sunderland at Roker Park in September 1952, at the tender age of 16 years and 277 days. During his stay at the Baseball Ground, the Rams were twice relegated and twice promoted, Patrick's best season coming in 1955-56 when he made 17 League appearances in the side that won promotion from the Third Division North as runners-up to Grimsby Town. He joined Forest on completion of his National Service, which had been deffered to enable him to complete a five-year apprenticeship as a joiner. A resourceful defender with a good positional sense, he fought hard to establish a first team place in his first season, when relegation from the top flight was only narrowly avoided. Following the retirement of Bill Whare in the close season, Patrick appeared in 34 of the 42 Division One matches in 1960-61, but he was given a free transfer at the end of the season. He was quickly snapped up by Southampton, but failed to hold down a first team place at the Dell and requested a move in September 1962. Six months later he joined Exeter City and completed 50 League appearances for the Grecians before returning to the Midlands to work for the Rolls-Royce Company and to play, as a part-time professional, for Burton Albion.
Appearances: FL: 57 apps 0 gls FLC: 2 apps 0 gls Total: 59 apps 0 gls

PEACOCK, Dennis
Goalkeeper 6' 2" 11st 9lbs
Born: Lincoln, 19th April 1953
CAREER: FOREST apprentice 18th April 1970, professional 17th July 1972. Walsall (loan) March 1973. Doncaster Rovers July 1975. Bolton Wanderers March 1980, fee £70,000. Doncaster Rovers August 1982. Burnley (loan) September 1985. Retired May 1986.
Debut v Brighton & Hove Albion (a) 28.4.73, drawn 2-2
After impressing in reserve ranks at the City Ground, the ideally built Dennis Peacock gained some valuable experience during a brief loan spell with Walsall. He made his Forest debut in the final fixture of the 1972-73 season and eventually replaced Jim Barron, commencing 1973-74 as first choice. A change of manager in mid term saw Allan Brown replaced by Brian Clough, and Dennis Peacock did not appear in the League side under the new manager. The first of two separate spells with Doncaster Rovers followed, and although Bolton Wanderers paid a hefty fee for his services in March 1980, he returned to Belle Vue, eventually racking up 329 League appearances, in an overall total of 385 matches for his five League clubs. He was a promotion winner in 1983-84, Doncaster returning to Division Three as runners-up to York City for the championship.
Appearances: FL: 22 apps 0 gls FLC: 2 apps 0 gls Total: 24 apps 0 gls

PEPLOW, Stephen Thomas 'Steve'
Winger 5' 9" 11st 12lbs
Born: Liverpool, 8th January 1949
CAREER: Liverpool apprentice June 1964, professional January 1966. Swindon Town (loan) March 1970, permanently May 1970. **FOREST 2nd July 1973**. Mansfield Town (loan) December 1973. Tranmere Rovers January 1974 to May 1981, fee £6,000. (Loaned to Chicago Sting (NASL) in April 1976).
Debut v Swindon Town (a) 2.10.73, drawn 0-0

Steve Peplow followed his Swindon Town manager, Dave Mackay, to the City Ground but a change at the helm, when Mackay moved on to Derby County and was replaced by Allan Brown in October 1973, Peplow was quickly sent out on loan to Mansfield Town. After three games for the Stags a permanent move to Tranmere Rovers and a return to his native Merseyside saw him produce the best football of his career. He played in all 46 League matches, and scored 11 goals, in 1975-76 when promotion from Division Four was achieved. Less memorable was his record of being the first Tranmere Rovers player to be shown a red card, following the introduction of yellow and red cards in 1976-77, when he received his marching orders on 27th December 1976 at Gay Meadow, in a 2-2 draw against Shrewsbury Town. In a stay of seven years at Prenton Park he made 232/16 League appearances, scoring 44 goals
Appearances: FL: 3 apps 0 gls FLC: 2 apps 0 gls Total: 5 apps 0 gls

PLATTS, Lawrence 'Laurie'
Goalkeeper 5' 10" 11st 7lbs
Born: Worksop, 31st October 1921
Died: Bourne, Lincolnshire, 4th September 2006
CAREER: FOREST 1941, professional October 1943. Chesterfield July 1951, fee £1,000. Burton Albion June 1952. Stockport County February 1953. Buxton manager May 1954.
Debut v Southampton (h) 18.1.47, won 6-0
Laurie Platts made his reputation on the strength of a brilliant performance against Manchester United at Maine Road in 1946-47 when Forest created a football sensation by knocking out their Division One opponents in the fourth round of the FA Cup, winning 2-0. Some ten years later, in a magazine article, Forest's manager, Billy Walker, recalled that his greatest managerial thrill came in the Manchester United Cup-tie of 1947. "I've never seen a better goalkeeping display than that of Laurie Platts that day, he was unbeatable. Laurie lives in Chesterfield these days and I bet that he has never forgotten that match-I know that I never shall." Although his first team appearances were restricted due to the brilliance of ex-Portsmouth FA Cup winning goalkeeper Harry Walker, Laurie Platts did not lack confidence in his own ability, a readiness to take risks, and bravery that showed little regard for his own well-being. After leaving the City Ground, his best subsequent spell came with Stockport County, where he contested the first team jersey with Jack 'Tiger' Bowles, and Dennis Herod, the former Stoke City goalkeeper.
Appearances: FL: 6 apps 0 gls FAC: 2 apps 0 gls Total: 8 apps 0 gls

PLEAT, David John

Winger 5' 8" 10st 9lbs
Born: Nottingham, 15th January 1945
CAREER: Mundella School. Nottingham Schoolboys. **FOREST apprentice June 1960, professional January 1962.** Luton Town August 1964, fee £8,000. Shrewsbury Town 1967. Exeter City July 1968. Peterborough United July 1970. Nuneaton Borough player-manager July 1971. Luton Town reserve team coach July 1972, head coach December 1977, manager January 1978 to May 1986. Tottenham Hotspur manager June 1986 to October 1987. Leicester City manager October 1987 to January 1991. Luton Town manager July 1991 to May 1995. Sheffield Wednesday manager June 1995 to November 1997. Tottenham Hotspur Director of Football January 1998 with two subsequent spells as caretaker-manager September-October 1998 and March-April 2001.
Debut v Cardiff City (h) 17.2.62, won 2-1 (scored one)
David Pleat had already won his third England Youth cap before he joined the professional ranks at the City Ground. He was a member of the successful England Youth side that won the Centenary

International Tournament at Wembley Stadium in April 1963. He had also played for the England Jewish Youth X1 who opposed Israel in Tel Aviv. Considered one of the most promising young players on the books, he scored on his Football League debut at the age of 17, but then had a lengthy wait, before playing in five matches in 1963-64, following the transfer of Trevor Hoockey to Newcastle United. Transferred to Luton Town, newly relegated to Division Four, Pleat suffered a broken leg in training in his first season, and subsequently moved around the lower divisions, his best spell coming with Exeter City (66/2 League appearances and 13 goals). His largely successful career in management commenced with Nuneaton Borough and spanned some thirty years. Highlights included his taking Luton Town to the top flight as Division Two champions in 1982, and the Spurs to Wembley in 1987, where they lost 3-2 to Coventry City. They also finished third in Division One and reached the semi-finals of the FL Cup.
Appearances: FL: 6 apps 1 gl Total: 6 apps 1 gl
Honours: England Schoolboy and Youth International.

PRITTY, George Joseph
Wing half-back 5' 10½" 12st 7lbs
Born: Nechells, Birmingham, 4th March 1915
Died: Birmingham, 3rd July 1996
CAREER: HB Metropolitan Works Old Boys. Newport County May 1933. Aston Villa May 1933. **FOREST 21st December 1938**. (Wartime guest player with Solihull Town and Wrexham.) **FOREST re-registered 22nd June 1946.** Cheltenham Town April 1948.
Debut v Sheffield United (a) 24.12.38, won 1-0
Said to have cost Forest a substantial fee, despite having played in only three League matches for Aston Villa, George Pritty helped to lift a struggling side from the threat of relegation from Division Two. Improving with every game, towards the end of the campaign he produced exceptional form when Forest were extremely hard pressed, escaping the dreaded drop only on goal average. Resuming after the war, he appeared in 26 League and four FA Cup-ties in 1946-47, including Forest's shock 2-0 defeat of Manchester United at Old Trafford in round four. In August 1948 he was released and joined Cheltenham Town. He was living in Birmingham at the time, and training at Villa Park.
Appearances: FL: 49 apps 1 gl FAC: 5 apps 0 gls Total: 54 apps 1 gl

QUIGLEY, John 'Johnny'

Inside-forward 5' 9" 11st 5lbs
Born: Govan, Glasgow, 28th June 1935
Died: Nottingham, 30th November 2004
CAREER: St Saviour's Primary School. St Gerald's Sceondary School. Glasgow Celtic (Provisional). St Anthony's (loan). Glasgow Ashfield. **FOREST 14th August 1957, fee £1,100.** Huddersfield Town February 1965. Bristol City October 1966. Mansfield Town July 1968, fee £3,000, later player-assistant manager and trainer coach to November 1971. Doncaster Rovers coach. Later coached in the Middle East for two years to 1974, and later in Kuwait and Saudi Arabia for five years. Nottingham Dunkirk coach and acting manager August 1996.
Debut v Tottenham Hotspur (a) 5.10.57, won 4-3 (scored one)
The son of a shipyard worker who was spotted while playing for Ashfield Juniors, Johnny Quigley had a meteoric rise into Division One football. A typical ball-playing Scot, he received his big chance when Jim Barrett was injured, and scored on his debut at White Hart Lane.He became the first player to score a post-war First Division hat-trick v Manchester City in

November 1958, and scored the goal that took Forest to Wembley, against Aston Villa in the semi-final in April 1959. Earlier, he had to forgoe his first big honour, having been selected to play for the Scottish FA against the Scottish League under the Ibrox floodlights. His team needed him however for the third round FA Cup replay against Tooting & Mitcham at the City Ground. A regular for seven seasons until replaced by John Barnwell, Quigley gave excellent service to a further three League clubs to bring his career aggregate figures to 473/1 appearances and 64 goals. Whilst with his final League club, Mansfield Town, he helped propel the Stags to two memorable cup runs, to round six, for the first time in their history, in 1968-69 and to round five in the following season.

Appearances: FL: 236 apps 51 gls FAC: 26 apps 4 gls FLC: 5 apps 3 gls Other: 3 apps 0 gls Total: 270 apps 58 gls

Honours: (**FOREST**) FA Cup winners 1959

RAWSON, Colin

Wing half-back 5' 8" 11st 0lbs

Born: Langwith, Derbyshire, 12th November 1926

Died: Sutton-in-Ashfield, 26th March 1969

CAREER: Shirebrook F.C. Welbeck Colliery. **FOREST September 1944. Re-registered 25th December 1946.** Peterborough United August 1947. Rotherham United July 1948, fee £750. Sheffield United March 1953, fee £5,500. Millwall October 1955, fee £4,500. Torquay United July 1959. Alfreton Town player-manager 1959. Taunton Town player-coach 1961-62.

Debut v Watford, FAC 3, replay at White Hart Lane, Tottenham, 16.1.46, lost 0-1

Colin Rawson made his Forest debut in wartime football, first appearing on 7th October 1944, in a 1-0 win at Chesterfield. Fielded at inside-left, he partnered wingman Tom Johnson in 15 matches, but was for a time loaned out to Ollerton Colliery. Finding little opportunity when normal League football recommenced in 1946-47, he refused terms for another season and was granted a free transfer. After a season with Peterborough United, in which he was switched from inside-forward to left half-back, he was transferred to Rotherham United, for whom he made 113 League appearances and scored 12 goals. He followed his old manager, Reg Freeman, to Sheffield United and made 70 League appearances (one goal) before joining Millwall for whom he made 159 League appearances and scored five goals. His final League club was Torquay United, for whom he appeared in 41 League matches in his first season, when promotion from Division Four was secured by a third place finish in 1959-60. He subsequently took his career aggregate totals beyond 400 League matches before dropping out of senior football. In his first season as player-manager of Alfreton Town, he guided them to fourth position in the Central Alliance Division One (North). Incidentally, the 1959-60 season saw Forest 'A' team finish tenth in the table, while another of his previous clubs, Ollerton Colliery, finished at the foot of the table with just five points from 34 matches. Colin Rawson subsequently worked and played for the East Midlands Electricity Board.

Appearances: FL: 1 app 0 gls FAC: 2 apps 1 gl Total: 3 apps 1 gl

Honours: (Rotherham United) FL Division 3 North champions 1951

RAWSON, John **Kenneth 'Ken'**

Centre half-back 6' 1½" 11st 7lbs

Born: Nottingham, 31st March 1921

Died: Belper, 30th March 2005

CAREER: FOREST amateur 20th June 1944, professional 6th September 1944 to May 1950.

Debut v Plymouth Argyle (a) 6.12.47, drawn 1-1

Ken Rawson was one of the mainstays of the Midland League side and later a grand skipper of the 'A' Team, winners of the Alliance Cup in 1952. Throughout the early post war seasons, Rawson was kept out of the first team by the consitency of Horace Gager, who dominated the centre-half position for six seasons. Four consecutive appearances in the final month of season 1949-50 accounted for the majority of his first team involvement, and these ended in a 0-2 defeat against local rivals Notts County on 22nd April 1950, as the Magpies clinched their promotion to Division Two in a game witnessed by an all-ticket crowd of 46,000 spectators. ***Note:*** *Ken Rawson was not related to Colin.*
Appearances: FL: 6 apps 0 gls Total: 6 apps 0 gls

REES, Ronald 'Ronnie' Raymond

Winger
Born: Ystradgynlais, near Swansea, 4th April 1944
CAREER: Merthyr Schoolboys. Coventry City apprentice July 1960, professional May 1962. West Bromwich Albion March 1968, fee £ 65,000. **FOREST February 1969, fee £60,000.** Swansea Town February 1972 to May 1975, fee £26,000. Haverford West 1975.
Debut v Liverpool (a) 15.2.69, won 2-0
Ronnie Rees made an early debut in Division Three with Coventry City, replacing former Forest favourite Roy Dwight for his debut against Shrewsbury Town on 15th September 1962. Under manager Jimmy Hill he enjoyed a wonderful start to his career, the Sky Blues reaching round six of the FA Cup in his first season, and winning the championship of Division Three in his second. He was still a regular in the side when the Division Two championship was secured in 1966-67, but departed in March of the following season, in which relegation was only narrowly avoided. He remained with West Bromwich Albion for less than a year before becoming Forest manager Matt Gillies' first signing to replace the injured Ian Storey-Moore. Rees certainly got off to a good start on an icy pitch at Anfield, where Forest produced a coupon-busting display to win 2-0. Relegation was narrowly avoided, but when the axe fell in 1971-72, Ronnie Rees had lost his first team place, and departed to Swansea City, where he added a further 88/1 League appearances and one goal to his record, taking his career total to 428/11 League matches and 68 goals.
Appearances: FL: 76/9 apps 12 gls FAC: 4/3 apps 1 gl FLC: 6/1 apps 0 gls Other: 2 apps 0 gls Total: 88/13 apps 13 gls
Honours: Wales International, 39 caps 1965-72. Wales Under-23 International, 7 caps, 1962-65. (Coventry City) FL Division 3 champions 1964. FL Division 2 champions 1967.

RICHARDSON, Paul

Midfield 5' 10" 11st 0lbs
Born: Selston, Notts. 25th October 1949
CAREER: FOREST apprentice 23rd July 1966, professional 31st August 1967. Chester October 1976. Stoke City June 1977, fee £50,000. Sheffield United August 1981, fee £25,000. Blackpool (loan) January 1983. Swindon Town July 1983. Swansea City, non-contract September to December 1984. Gloucester City manager May 1985. Fairford Town manager November 1985. Witney Town.
Debut as sub v Sunderland (a) 4.11.67, lost 0-1
An England Youth international in season 1967-68, Paul Richardson made his Forest debut in the same season, initially as a substitute at Sunderland, but later, in the final game of the season, in a 6-1 defeat at Liverpool. This match, incidentally, marked the last appearance for the unfortunate reserve team goalkeeper Mick Harby, whose three

appearances during the season had seen him conceed 15 goals. Over a period of ten years at the City Ground, Paul Richardson averaged roughly 22 League matches per season, mainly in midfield or at left full-back. He had played only twice in his final season before being transferred to Chester, for whom he made 28 appearances and scored two goals. An upward move to Stoke City followed in the close season, and he was instrumental in taking the Potters back into Division One in his second season, his winning header at Meadow Lane against Notts County clinching promotion. In four seasons he appeared in 124/3 League matches and scored 10 goals. From Stoke he moved to Sheffield United who were champions of Division Four in his first season, having lost only four of 46 League matches. It was the first season when 3 points for a win was introduced, at the Blades went up with 96 points. After a brief loan spell with Blackpool, he joined Swindon Town as player coach but made only seven League appearances before the arrival of new manager Lou Macari. A dozen appearances for Swansea City, on non-contract terms, wound up his lengthy career of 409/27 League appearances and 32 goals.
Appearances: FL: 199/23 apps 18 gls FAC: 16 apps 1 gl FLC: 9/1 apps 2 gls Total: 224/24 apps 21 gls.
Honours: England Youth International. (Sheffield United) FL Division 4 champions 1982.

ROBERTS, Gryffydd 'Griff' Orthin
Goalkeeper 6' 0" 12st 0lbs
Born: Blaenau Ffestiniog, N. Wales, 2nd October 1920
Died: Bargoed, October 1991
CAREER: Blaenau Ffestiniog. **FOREST 13th May 1946 to May 1947**. Blaenau Ffestiniog.
Debut v Southampton (a) 16.9.46, lost 2-5
One of five different goalkeepers fielded in season 1946-47, Griff Roberts' opportunity arose due first choice 'keeper Savage being unavailable due to his wife's illness. The 25 year-old Welshman had performed well in the reserves, and despite a shaky opening in the heavy defeat at Southampton, he went on to hold the position for a run of seven matches. Forest's five goalkeepers during the season included outside-left Tom Johnson who was pressed into service at Millwall on 25th March, after Laurie Platts failed to arrive at the Den, having missed his train from Brighton, where he was stationed.
Appearances: FL: 9 apps 0 gls FAC: 2 apps 0 gls Total: 11 apps 0 gls

ROBERTSON, John Neilson
Outside-left 5' 8" 10st 9lbs
Born: Uddingston, near Motherwell, 20th January 1953
CAREER: Drumchapel Amateurs. **FOREST apprentice 13th March 1969, professional 30th May 1970.** Derby County June 1983. **FOREST August 1985 to May 1986**. Corby Town August 1986. Stamford March 1987. Grantham assistant-manager August 1987. Wycombe Wanderers chief scout January 1994. Norwich City chief scout June 1995. Leicester City assistant-manager/coach December 1995. Celtic assistant-manager/coach August 2000 to 2005. Aston Villa assistant manager 2006 to August 2010.
Debut v Huddersfield Town (a) 24.10.70, drawn 0-0
In earliest days the Scottish schools and youth international seemed set to make a big name for himself but needed speed and aggression to compliment his rich promise. Originally a midfielder he was switched onto the left wing under manager Brian Clough to became Forest's most creative player, outwitting opponents with close dribbling skills and always parting with the ball to best advantage. He was sidelined for a lengthy spell in 1973-74 following a complicated cartilage operation, but made a full recovery to become a vital part of Forest's success story of 1978-80, winning the first of his Scottish caps in 1978 and netting the winning goal in the European Cup Final in the same year. A tribunal set fee of £135,000 took him to Derby County but another

John Robertson, 1970

cartilage operation in his first season marked the end of his international career. A return to the City Ground on a free transfer lasted for just one season before he dropped into non-League football and then into management where he linked successfully with former playing colleague, Martin O'Neill.
Appearances: FL: 384/14 apps 61 gls FAC: 35/1 apps 10 gls FLC: 46 apps 16 gls Other: 34 apps 8 gls Total: 499/15 apps 95 gls
Honours: Scotland International, 28 caps, 1978-84. Scotland Under-21 International, 2 caps. Scotland 'B' International, 1 cap. Scottish Schoolboy and Youth international. (FOREST) European Cup winners 1979, 1980. FL Division One champions 1978. FL Cup winners 1978 and 1979, finalists 1980.

ROWLAND, John Douglas

Outside-right 5' 10" 11st 9lbs
Born: Riddings, Derbyshire, 7th April 1941
CAREER: Riddings FC. Ironville Amateurs. **FOREST amateur 1958, professional 18th April 1961**. Port Vale August 1962, fee £6,000. Mansfield Town September 1966, fee £6,500. Tranmere Rovers July 1968 to May 1969. South Shields 1971 to 1973. Derry City.
Debut v Tottenham Hotspur (h) 15.10.60, lost 0-4
John Rowland showed lots of pace and formidable shooting power, but his footwork was said to be in need of improvement. That said, he made his debut in Division One as a teenager, and netted his first goal in a 3-2 win against Manchester United at the City Ground on 25th February 1961. He began 1961-62 by playing at outside-right in the opening four matches, but before the season was concluded no fewer than seven different players had worn the number seven jersey, and John Rowland had departed to Port Vale to enjoy the best spell of his career (147/2 League appearances and 40 goals). Useful spells with Mansfield Town (49 appearances, 16 goals) and Tranmere Rovers (25/1 appearances, 3 goals) took his overall figures to 247/3 matches and 62 goals.
Appearances: FL: 26 apps 3 gls FLC: 3 apps 0 gls Total: 29 apps 3 gls
Honours: England Youth International
Publisher's note. I remain indebted to John to this day. I failed to win a 1959 FA Cup Final ticket in the club's lucky draw. However, my friend in the Boy Scouts, Derek Jones, was John's cousin. Two of John's complimentary tickets enabled Derek and me to stand on the Wembley terraces, bedecked with rosettes, scarves, and a large red and white wooden rattle.

SAVAGE, Reginald 'Reg'
Goalkeeper 5' 11½" 12st 0lbs
Born: Eccles, Lancashire, 5th July 1912
Died: Swinton, 28th September 1997
CAREER: Taylor Brothers (Lancashire). Stalybridge Celtic. Mossley (trial). Leeds United February 1931. Queen of the South July 1939. (Wartime guest player with Bolton Wanderers, Derby County, **Forest** and Blackpool). **FOREST 24th December 1945, fee £1,000**. Accrington Stanley August 1947 to April 1948, fee £340.
Debut v Watford (h), FAC 3, 5.1.46, drawn 1-1
Reg Savage made his Leeds United debut against Blackburn Rovers at Ewood Park on 1st September 1934, making 32 League appearances during the season. The signing of England international Albert McInroy then cast Savage into a reserve role until 1937-38 when he made 32 League appearances, before Jim Twomey, the Northern Ireland international was introduced. A

move to Queen of the South was disrupted by the outbreak of the Second World War, but a rewarding spell as a guest player with Blackpool followed. A very strong side during wartime, thanks to the many guest players stationed in the town, the Seasiders won the 'double' of the Northern Regional League and the Northern Wartime Cup in 1942-43 and were then invited to play Arsenal, the Southern Cup winners, in a game labelled the 'Championship of England' at Stamford Bridge in May 1943. Two goals down after seven minutes, Blackpool rallied to win 4-2 with goalkeeper Savage the star of a hard pressed defence throughout. Joining Forest in December 1945, he made 20 League South appearances, and a similar number in 1946-47 when Forest fielded six different goalkeepers, including outside-left Tom Johnston at Luton Town in an emergency. Transferred to Accrington Stanley in August 1947, Reg Savage failed to get a League outing with Bill Harris, the former West Bromwich Albion and Oldham Athletic goalkeeper, missing only one match during the campaign.
Appearances: FL: 20 apps 0 gls FAC: 4 apps 0 gls Total: 24 apps 0 gls

SCOTT, Frederick 'Freddie' Hind

Outside-right 5' 5½" 10st11lbs
Born: Fatfield, County Durham, 6th October 1916
Died: Nottingham, 14th September 1995
CAREER: Fatfield Juniors. Fatfield FC. Chester-le-Street Schoolboys. County Durham Schoolboys. Chester-le-Street January 1934. Middlesbrough (trial) July 1934. Bolton Wanderers January 1935. Bradford Park Avenue May 1936. York City February 1937. (Wartime guest player with Gateshead and Charlton Athletic.) **FOREST 9th September 1946, fee £3,000, appointed player-coach July 1954, and chief scout June 1957 to May 1958**. Subsequently scouted for Sunderland, Sheffield Wednesday, Blackpool and Southampton.
Debut v Newport County (h) 7.9.46, won 6-1
Freddie Scott was recommended to Forest by 'Sailor' Brown, the pair having played together in wartime football. When Brown departed to join Aston Villa, Scott was chosen to succeed him as captain. Although on the small side, Scott was more than capable of holding his own against the biggest and strongest defenders. A specialist in ball control, he was able to beat his man and centre accurately, a fact much appreciated by centre-forward Wally Ardron. During the course of the 1948-49 season, when Forest were relegated from Division Two, Scott asked for a transfer, and York City's manager, Tom Mitchell, made enquiries with the object of taking him back to Bootham Crescent. When Forest demanded twice the fee that they had paid for him, the idea was quickly shelved. A return to his best form saw Forest bounce back in season 1950-51 with Fred Scott supplying much of the ammunition in a forward line that plundered 110 League goals, Wally Ardron leading the list with a club-record 36 goals. In season 1953-54 he captained the championship winning Midland League side, and devoted even more time to advising the young players on the books. Almost ten years to the day from making his Forest debut, he was drafted in as a last-minute replacement for Jim Barrett for the away match at Rotherham United and fittingly scored Forest's first goal in the 2-3 defeat. With his 40th birthday less than three weeks away, he was thought to be Forest's oldest footballer to play in a senior competitive match.
Appearances: FL: 301 apps 40 gls FAC: 21 apps 7 gls Total: 322 apps 47 gls
Honours: England Schoolboy International 1931. (**FOREST**) FL Division 3 South champions 1951

SERELLA, David 'Dave' Edward
Centre half-back 5' 11" 11st 9lbs
Born: Kings Lynn, 24th September 1952
CAREER: FOREST apprentice 13th November 1968, professional August 1970. Walsall **(loan)** November 1974, permanently December 1974. Blackpool August 1982. Altrincham July 1984. Chorley.
Debut v Coventry City (h) 25.3.72, won 4-0
Luxuriantly moustachioed defender Dave Serella progressed through Forest's junior sides to make his debut in the closing months of the 1971-72 season. One of the quickest players on the books, his strengths lay in his tackling and powers of recovery. His best season was 1972-73, when he made 34 of his League appearances, at other times he found stiff competition from the likes of Sammy Chapman and John Cottam. Initially loaned to Walsall, the move was made permanent just prior to Brian Clough's arrival at the City Ground in January 1975. Eight excellent years with the Saddlers included promotion from Division Four in 1979-80 and an overall record of 302/2 League and Cup appearances and 13 goals. Two seasons with Blackpool in Division Four wound up his senior career with impressive figures of 364/6 League appearances and 15 goals.
Appearances: FL: 65/3 apps 0 gls FAC: 6 apps 0 gls FLC: 2 apps 0 gls Total: 73/3 apps 0 gls

SHARRATT, Harry

Goalkeeper 5' 11" 12st 0lbs
Born: Wigan, 16th December 1929
Died: Lancaster, 19th August 2002
Debut v Portsmouth (h) 1.2.58, won 2-0
CAREER: An amateur throughout with Hindley & Abram Grammar School. Wigan Athletic. Yorkshire Amateurs. Blackpool May 1952 to October 1953. Bishop Auckland. Oldham Athletic March 1956. Bishop Auckland. Manchester United Reserves following Munich air crash. **FOREST 1st February 1958**. Bishop Auckland April 1958.
One of the outstanding amateur goalkeepers of the 1950s, Harry Sharratt appeared for Bishop Auckland in three consecutive FA Amateur Cup winning sides and won four England Amateur caps. He did not have a great deal to do on his Forest debut, but he inspired confidence with his clean handling. An unfamiliar Forest line-up on his debut also included centre-forward Ken Simcoe, in place of the injured Tommy Wilson, and Chris Joyce who made his second senior appearance in place of Billy Gray. Harry Sharratt studied physics at Leeds University and was later a Mathamatics teacher in Leeds. From 1962 onwards he was head of department at Queen Elizabeth School in Kirby Lonsdale.
Appearances: FL: 1 app 0 gls Total: 1 app 0 gls
Honours: Great Britain representative in 1956 summer Olympics, 2 appearances. England Amateur International, 4 caps. (Bishop Auckland) FA Amateur Cup winners 1955, 1956, 1957, finalists 1954.

SHERRATT, Brian
Goalkeeper 6' 0" 12st 10lbs
Born: Stoke-on-Trent, 29th March 1944
CAREER: Stoke City apprentice June 1959, professional April 1961. Oxford United August 1965. **FOREST (loan) 8th October 1968**. Barnsley June 1969. Gainsborough Trinity. Colchester United September 1970 to April 1971. Oxford City July 1971.
Debut v Newcastle United (h) 8.10.68, lost 2-4
Brian Sherratt was signed on loan from Oxford United in the midst of a goalkeeping crisis. Forest had both Peter Grummitt and Brian Williamson on the injured list, and following Sherratt's debut they then paid £17,500 for Newcastle United's England Under-23 goalkeeper Gordon Marshall,

who damaged a finger in his first match! Sherratt made 44 League appearances for Oxford United, where his competitors included Jim Barron, later to star for Forest in 180 appearances in the 1970s. Brian Sherratt later worked at British Leyland, Oxford. He was said to be an obsessive handy man, happily hammering away in his shed from dawn to dusk!
Appearances: FL: 1 app 0 gls Total: 1 app 0 gls
Honours: (Oxford United) FL Division 3 champions 1968

SHUFFLEBOTTOM, Frank

Full-back 5' 10" 12st 0lbs
Born: Chesterfield, 9th October 1917
Died: Chesterfiled, 27th May 2004
CAREER: Dronfield Baptists Boys' Club. Norton Woodseats. Sheffield United amateur September 1934. Margate amateur May 1936. Ipswich Town amateur October 1936, professional June 1938. **FOREST June 1939**. (Wartime guest player with Dundee United, Aldershot, Raith Rovers, Kilmarnock & Clapton Orient). Bradford City October 1946, fee £1,050, to May 1949 when appointed trainer.
Debut v Coventry City (h) 28.9.46, won 1-0
Frank Shufflebottom had made just two League appearances for Ipswich Town when he was signed by Forest on the eve of World War Two. While serving as an army physical training instructor he became a most successful guest player with Dundee United, and in April 1946 the Tannadice club asked Forest for their terms for his transfer. In the event, he played just twice for Forest following his demobilisation, and was then transferred to Bradford City, for whom he made 56 League appearances before being appointed trainer in 1949.
Appearances: FL: 2 apps 0 gls Total: 2 apps 0 gls

SIMCOE, Kenneth 'Ken' Edward

Centre-forward 5' 10" 11st 4lbs
Born: Nottingham, 14th February 1937
Died: Sherwood, Nottingham, 16th September 2012
CAREER: Central YMCA. **FOREST amateur July 1953, professional 13th December 1956.** Coventry City May 1959. Notts County July 1960 to April 1961. Heanor Town cs 1961. Loughborough United cs 1963. Ilkeston Town December 1962. Heanor Town July 1964, retired due to injury February 1967.
Debut v Portsmouth (h) 5.2.58, won 2-0
In October 1956, against Bradford City Reserves, Ken Simcoe became the first Forest amateur to score five goals in a Midland League match, he was 19 years of age at the time and stationed with the RAOC at Chilwell. A centre-forward who commanded respect from opposing defenders, Simcoe won high praise for his goal scoring feats as an amateur. Exceptionally good in the air, he was expected to improve with more experience. However, notes in a Forest programme of December 1956 suggested that the one flaw in his make-up was that he didn't take the game, or himself, too seriously. It was hoped that his demobilisation from the forces, and his subsequent signing as a full-time professional at the City Ground, would help realise his true potential. Despite scoring in his second appearance in a 2-3 defeat at West Bromwich Albion, he failed to mount a serious challenge for the first team centre-forward position with Tommy Wilson a fixture as attack leader from 1956-57 onwards. Simcoe left the City Ground after undergoing a cartilage operation, shortly after the 1959 FA Cup Final against Luton Town. He did little better with his next club, Coventry City (Eight matches and one goal in the Third Division South). On moving to

Notts County in July 1960, he was never likely to challenge his best friend Tony Hateley as attack leader at Meadow Lane, despite scoring 36 goals for the reserve team. Simcoe subsequently prospered in non-League circles, particularly during separate spells with Heanor Town, where his tally of goals was approaching the 200 mark when a knee ligament injury curtailed his career. Despite having missed the boat in terms of a first class career in football, there cannot have been too many locally born men with *the proud record of having worn both the red and black-and-white number nine shirt in League football.*
Appearances: FL: 2 apps 1 gl Total: 2 apps 1 gl

SIMPSON, Noel Harold

Wing half-back 5' 7" 10st 4lbs
Born: Mansfield, 23rd December 1922
Died: Woodthorpe, Nottingham, 21st November 1987
CAREER: Notts County amateur**. FOREST amateur 5th April 1945, professional 11th May 1945.** (Wartime guest player with Notts County.) **FOREST re-registered 13th May 1946.** Coventry City August 1948. Exeter City February 1957.
Debut v Watford, FAC 3 (h) 5.1.46, drawn 1-1
Although on the small side, Noel Simpson was keen in the tackle. His ball distribution was not always accurate but he made rapid development after switching from an inside-forward role to that of a wing half-back. Although better in defence than attack, he memorably scored both of Forest's goals in the 2-0 win at Newcastle United on 8th November 1948 to record the first away victory of a season spent in the lower reaches of Division Two. Transferred to Coventry City in the close season, he quickly established himself in the Sky Blues' middle line, in nine seasons amassing 270 League and Cup appearances, scoring eight goals. He moved to Exeter City in February 1957 but the Grecians were a club in decline, finishing 21st in Division 3 South in Simpson's first season, and rock bottom in the following term. As Noel Simpson departed after 33 League appearances, Exeter City faced the prospect of life in the new FL Division 4.
Appearances: FL: 47 apps 3 gls FAC: 3 apps 0 gls Total: 50 apps 3 gls

SMALL, Peter Victor

Winger 5' 8" 11st 0lbs
Born: Horsham, Sussex, 23rd October 1923
Died: Cambridge, 3rd November 2006
CAREER: Horsham Schoolboys. Horsham Town. Luton Town August 1947. Leicester City February 1950, fee £6,000**. FOREST 1st October 1954, fee £4,675**. Brighton & Hove Albion July 1957 to May 1959, fee £900.
Debut v Ipswich Town (h) 2.10.54, won 2-0 (scored one)
Fast and enthusiastic, and with a good shot in either foot, Peter Small appeared in 188 League matches and scored 44 goals for his four League clubs. After a modest start with the Hatters (28 appearances, five goals) he assisted Leicester City to promotion from Division Two, as runners-up to Everton, scoring 14 goals in 34 League matches, taking his overall record with the City to 16 goals in 65 League matches. He then won a second promotion from Division Two with Forest in 1956-57, but lost his place in mid season to Peter Higham. A final promotion occurred with Brighton & Hove Albion, for whom he scored three goals in eight matches in their Division Three championship team in 1957-58.
Appearances: FL: 87 apps 20 gls FAC: 7 apps 1 gl Total: 94 apps 21 gls

STAINWRIGHT, David 'Dave' Peter
Centre-forward 5' 9" 10st 9lbs
Born: Nottingham, 13th June 1948
CAREER: FOREST apprentice June 1963, professional 5th August 1965. Doncaster Rovers July 1968. York City July 1969. Heanor Town cs 1970.
Debut as sub v Newcastle United 29.1.66, lost 1-2
On leaving school in the summer of 1963, Dave Stainwright joined the Forest staff as an apprentice, and by doing so continued a family tradition as both his father and uncle had assisted the Reds as amateurs during the Second World War. Eventually established in the Football Combination side in season 1965-66, he stepped up to score against Tottenham Hotspur in his full League debut at White Hart Lane on 2nd April 1966. In the following season, when Forest finished as runners-up for the First Division championship, and reached the semi-final of the FA Cup, he was called upon on only three occasions, twice as a substitute. Moving on to Doncaster Rovers at the age of twenty, he appeared only twice, once as a substitute, as the Rovers won promotion as champions of Division Four. A final move in League circles to York City, managed by former Forest and Notts County star, Tom Johnston (q.v.), again failed to come up to expectations, featuring just 6/1 League appearances and one goal.
Appearances: FL: 4/3 apps 1 gl Total: 4/3 apps 1 gl

STOREY-MOORE, Ian

Winger 5' 9" 10st 10lbs
Born: Ipswich, 17th January 1945
CAREER: Scunthorpe Grammar School. **FOREST amateur August 1961, professional May 1962.** Manchester United March 1972, fee £200,000. Burton Albion player-manager September 1974. Chicago Sting (NASL) 1975. Shepshed Charterhouse player-manager 1976 to 1977. Also coached at Forest's academy later becoming chief scout before spending four years in the same role with Aston Villa.
Debut v Ipswich Town (h) 10.5.63, won 2-1
In August 1961 Ian Storey-Moore took part in pre-season trials held at the RAF Watnall ground. He created such a fine impression that he was immediately taken onto the Forest ground staff. On his debut with the Football Combination side, as an amateur against Crystal Palace, he scored the only goal of the game. Le Flem and Hinton initially restricted his progress but from season 1965-66 he made more frequent appearances, often appearing on the right as well as the left wing. A well-built wingman whose close dribbling skills and explosive finishing made him the club's top scorer for four consecutive seasons despite a number of injuries, including a broken leg in the match against Leicester City on 18th January 1969. In March 1972 an abortive transfer to Derby County – he had even been paraded on the Baseball Ground pitch – preceded his £200,000 signing by Manchester United. The flawed deal cost the Rams a fine of £5,000 and an official repremand. On his debut for United he scored against Huddersfield Town to give the Reds their first League win for over three months and he finished the season with five goals in 11 League outings. In the following term a troublesome ankle injury restricted his appearances, and in December 1973 it was officially confirmed that he had been obliged to retire on medical advice. Although able to mount a comeback in non-League football and in the USA, his loss to League football at 28 years of age was greatly regretted. He was later a Nottingham turf accountant with premises adjacent to the City Ground, and coached

part-time at Forest's academy and became the club's chief scout. Though it was reported that he preferred plain "Moore" to "Storey-Moore", we felt we should retain his full name in this book.
Appearances: FL: 235/1 apps 105 gls FAC: 19 apps 6 gls FLC: 13 apps 5 gls Other: 4 apps 2 gls Total: 271/1 apps 118 gls
Honours: England International, 1 cap 1970. England Under-23 International, 2 caps. FL representative, 2 apps.

TAYLOR, William 'Billy'

Utility 5' 9" 11st 3lbs
Born: Edinburgh, 31st July 1939
Died: Manchester, 30th November 1981
CAREER: Bonnyrigg Rose. Leyton Orient August 1959. **FOREST October 1963, fee £4,000.** Lincoln City May 1969 to May 1971. Fulham coach June 1971. (England coach October 1974 to November 1981.) Manchester City coach May 1976. Oldham Athletic coach July 1979 to his death.
Debut v Bolton Wanderers (a) 1.2.64, won 3-2 (Frank Wignall hat-trick)
Billy Taylor was a full-back with Leyton Orient, and followed manager Johnnie Carey to Forest in October 1963. He was sought as an inside-forward by many clubs in Scotland, but preferred to join Orient from Bonnyrigg Rose. Able to play equally well as a striker, schemer or defender, he made his debut at full-back, taking over from Joe Wilson who was recovering from a cartilage operation. Alan Hinton made his Forest debut in the same match, and the Reds won 3-2 with Frank Wignall scoring a hat trick. It was Forest's first win at Burnden Park in Division One since 1898. In his final season Taylor's versatility was underlined when he turned out as a left-winger in place on Ian Storey-Moore, who broke a leg at Leicester in January 1969. On leaving the City Ground Taylor joined Lincoln City and in two seasons scored six goals in 74/5 League appearances. On retiring he joined Fulham, initially as reserve coach, developing to become first team coach and being appointed England coach, a position he held until his untimely death at the age of 42.
Appearances: FL: 10/10 apps 1 gl FAC: 1 app 0 gls FLC: 1 app 0 gls Other: 1 app 0 gls Total: 13/10 apps 1 gl

THOMAS, Gerald Shannon 'Geoff'

Full-back 5' 9¾" 11st 6lbs
Born: Barrow-on-Trent, Derbyshire, 21st February 1926
Died: Nottingham, 18th July 2006
CAREER: FOREST June 1941, professional September 1943. Bourne Town player-manager June 1960 to 1962.
Debut v Watford, FAC 3 (h) 5.1.46, drawn 1-1
A wartime Colt who graduated to first team football, Geoff Thomas was the first of Forest's post war players to receive a benefit of £750 in December 1950. A strong-tackling full-back who had commenced as a wing half-back in wartime soccer, he went on to represent Forest in 14 seasons of peacetime football. A regular in two promotion campaigns, 1951 and 1957, he eventually lost his first team place to Joe McDonald in 1958-59, thereby missing the FA Cup Final win against Luton Town. Thomas scored just one goal in over 400 matches and this came after he had been injured in the match against Leicester City in August 1955. Long before the substitute role was introduced, Thomas was moved onto the wing and had the satisfaction of

scoring his only goal in the 2-0 win. A fine sportsman, he was an excellent golfer, being runner-up in the Professional Footballers' Golf Competition in 1950. In 1957 Forest's manager, Billy Walker, had this to say about his long-serving full-back: "A player who never fails to give his utmost-the type any club would be glad to have." After retiring from the game Geoff Thomas became a season ticket holder at the City Ground and ran a greengrocery business at Woodthorpe.
Appearances: FL: 404 apps 1 gl FAC: 28 apps 0 gls Total: 432 apps 1 gl
Honours: **(FOREST)** FL Division 3 South champions 1951

THOMPSON, Sidney 'Sid'
Inside-forward 5' 10½" 11st 7lbs
Born: Bedlington, County Durham, 14th July 1928
CAREER: Bedlington Terriers. **FOREST amateur 13th May 1946, professional 16th September 1947.** Scunthorpe United August 1955 to May 1956, fee £1,000.
Debut v Barnsley (h) 3.9.52, won 3-0
A Durham discovery who returned home while fulfilling his National Service in the mines, Sid Thompson began as a wing-half, once described as: "A terrier-like tackler, whose great strength enables him to finish a game as fresh as when he started it." During the 1951-52 season he took over in the Reserves as a full-back with much success, and was also renowned for his success with penalty kicks. He had a very long wait for a first team debut and it was not until he finally settled at inside-forward that he enjoyed a run in Division Two, appearing in 14 matches, scoring seven goals in 1953-54. He added a further six matches, and one goal, to his total in the following season before his release. Probably too versatile for his own good, Thompson was able to fill most outfield positions without claiming a regular first team spot in any of them.
Appearances: FL: 22 apps 8 gls Total: 22 apps 8 gls

THOMSON, Charles 'Chic' Richard

Goalkeeper 5' 11" 12st 3lbs
Born: Perth, 2nd March 1930
Died: Bramcote, Nottingham, 6th January 2009
CAREER: Clyde 1949. Chelsea October 1952. **FOREST 21st August 1957, fee £1,500 to May 1961.** Rugby Town 1961.
Debut v Preston North End (h) 24.8.57, won 2-1
The son of a former Scottish League goalkeeper, Chic Thomson was a safe, experienced man beneath the crossbar, signed from Chelsea in readiness for the Division One campaign of 1957-58. After a successful spell with Clyde, he did equally well with Chelsea, sharing first team duties with Bill Robertson for five seasons, with 16 appearances in 1954-55 when Chelsea were crowned Football League champions. A regular with Forest until a series of heavy defeats in the early months of season 1960-61 led to the introduction of Peter Grummitt, who then remained Forest's first team goalkeeper for the best part of nine years. Thomson was a keen golfer who spent his close seasons back at home in Perth where he found a game of cricket a pleasant form of exercise after nine months of serious football. As a mid-order batsman and excellent slip fielder he represented Perthshire in the summer game.
Appearances: FL: 121 apps 0 gls FAC: 13 apps 0 gls FLC: 1 app 0 gls Other: 1 app 0 gls Total: 136 apps 0 gls
Honours: (Clyde) Scottish Cup finalist 1949. Scottish 'B' Division champions 1952. (Chelsea) FL Division 1 champions 1955. **(FOREST)** FA Cup winners 1959

TURNER, Keith John

Inside-forward
Born: Coventry, 9th April 1934
CAREER: R.A.F. Watnall. **FOREST August 1952, professional 10th June 1954 to May 1956.**
Debut v Luton Town (a) 21.8.54, lost 0-3
A reserve inside-forward for two seasons, Keith Turner was spotted by Forest when playing in services football for RAF Watnall. Following his demob from the forces he was given just one senior opportunity in the opening fixture of season 1954-55, a 3-0 defeat at Luton Town. Forest actually lost their first five matches of the season, scoring only one goal while conceding eleven. They eventually recovered to finish in 15th place in Division Two but did better in the FA Cup reaching round five and only losing after a second replay to the eventual winners of the trophy, Newcastle United.
Appearances: FL: 1 app 0 gls Total: 1 app 0 gls

VOWDEN, Geoffrey 'Geoff' Alan

Inside/Centre-forward 5' 10" 12st 2lbs
Born: Barnsley, 27th April 1941
CAREER: First Tower FC (Jersey). **FOREST apprentice 7th May 1959, professional January 1960.** Birmingham City October 1964, fee £25,000. Aston Villa March 1971, fee £12,500. Kettering Town player/assistant-manager July 1974. New York Cosmos (NASL) June-August 1974. Kettering Town manager December 1974 to December 1975. Saudi Arabia coaching appointment 1976 to 1978. Sheffield United Reserve team coach 1980 to 1981.
Debut v Bolton Wanderers (h) 26.9.59, won 2-0
Geoff Vowden owed his chance to a former senior referee and Nottingham resident, George Tedds, who was in Jersey with a party of local referees, when he spotted Vowden playing in a local match and recommended him to Forest. After trials at the City Ground he was signed as an apprentice in May 1959 and was selected for an England Amateur X1 in October of the same year. Leading scorer for Forest's Youth team, winners of the International Tournament held at Wuppertal, Germany, he made his senior debut against Bolton Wanderers while still on amateur forms. He went on to enjoy a successful career as a dangerous marksman for his three senior clubs, netting 141 League goals in 396/12 appearances.
Appearances: FL: 90 apps 40 gls FAC: 10 apps 2 gls FLC: 4 apps 2 gls Other: 1 app 0 gls Total: 105 apps 44 gls
Honours: (Aston Villa) FL Division 3 champions 1972.

WALKER, George Henry 'Harry'

Goalkeeper 5' 10" 11st 2lbs
Born: Aysgarth, Yorkshire, 20th May 1916
Died: Beeston, Nottingham, 9th January 1976
CAREER: Aysgarth School. Leyburn FC. Darlington amateur December 1934, professional November 1935. Portsmouth March 1938. **FOREST 19th May 1946, fee £1,650, retired May 1955.**
Debut v Fulham (a) 26.5.47, drawn 1-1
Harry Walker started his working life as a motor mechanic, and as a youth was well known in the athletic circles of the north-east, winning many prizes as a runner. Before joining Portsmouth in 1938 he 'served his time' with Darlington. A safe handler of the ball and with split-second anticipation he was long remembered by Portsmouth fans for his outstanding display in the 1939 FA Cup victory against the Wolves. With the experience of many seasons of League football before joining Forest at the end of the 1946-47 season, he was acknowledged as one of the best goalkeepers in the Second Division, at either side of a two-seasons spell in the Third Division South. When Forest regained their place in Division Two, he was one of four 'ever presents' in the successful campaign of 1950-51 in which Forest scored the most goals (110), and conceded the least (40), and took the title with a six point margin over runners-up Norwich City. Harry Walker remained Forest's first choice goalkeeper until his replacement by Bill Farmer in his final season prior to retirement.
Appearances: FL: 293 apps 0 gls FAC: 11 apps 0 gls Total: 304 apps 0 gls
Honours: (Portsmouth) FA Cup winners 1939. **(FOREST**) FL Division 3 South champions 1951.

WALKER, Victor 'Vic'

Wing half-back
Born: Kirkby-in-Ashfield, 14th April 1922
Died: Mansfield, June 1992
CAREER: FOREST August 1943, professional 1945. Stockport County June 1946, fee £600, to May 1950.
Debut v Watford, FAC 3 (a) 9.1.46, drawn 1-1
Vic Walker began with Forest as an inside-forward, but was equally at home in the middle line. He commenced with Stockport County in a forward role, occupying all three inside positions, scoring 11 goals in 39 League and Cup matches in 1946-47 and went on to total 107 appearances and 11 goals, having reverted to a wing-half role from 1947-48.
Appearances: FAC: 2 apps 0 gls Total: 2 apps 0 gls

WARD, Denis

Goalkeeper 6' 1" 12st 0lbs
Born: Burton Joyce, 25th October 1924
Died: Carlton, Nottingham, 17th April 2006
CAREER: FOREST 25th August 1947. Stockport County August 1949. Hastings United 1953. Bradford Park Avenue August 1955 to May 1958
Debut v Luton Town (h) 13.12.47, lost 1-2
Denis Ward had an unlucky start in senior football. He had just returned from India to be demobilised when he was promoted from the Colts' team to appear against Plymouth Argyle at the City Ground in February 1947. Unfortunately, the match was postponed due to the arctic weather conditions and it was not until ten months later that he made his solitary outing in a 2-1 defeat against Luton Town. Released on a free transfer in May 1949, he subsequently spent useful spells with both Stockport County (52 League matches) and Bradford Park Avenue (50 matches).
Appearances: FL: 1 app 0 gls Total: 1 app 0 gls

WATSON, Peter Frederick

Centre half-back 6' 1" 12st 2lbs
Born: Stapleford, 15th April 1934
Died: Brighton, 17th August 2013
CAREER: South Notts. Schoolboys. Stapleford F.C. **FOREST cs 1951, professional 25th May 1955**. Southend United July 1959 to October 1966.
Debut v Lincoln City (a) 2.4.56, won 3-1
Said to have trained with Forest players from the age of twelve, Peter Watson joined Forest from local junior football and had many outings as an amateur before turning professional on completion of his National Service with the RAF. A partner in his father's painting and decorating business in the Stapleford district of Nottingham, he was kept busy in the close season, with a preference for outside painting and the benefit of fresh air. On the pitch, rapid improvement culminated in an Easter senior debut at Lincoln City in 1956. Forest refused several offers for a player who would probably have commanded a regular place elsewhere, but was restricted at the City Ground by the brilliance of Bobby McKinlay. Sadly, Watson's final appearance, when he deputised for the injured McKinley, resulted in a 3-0 defeat at Leeds United, with Shackleton, the ex-Burnley centre-forward, scoring a hat trick, Watson being blamed for his failure to 'stick more closely to his man'. As Forest celebratated their FA Cup vicorty over Luton Town in the following month, Watson requested a transfer and was quickly signed by Southend United for whom he clocked up 263 appearances in all competitions before vision problems brought on by a fractured jaw enforced his retirement. Peter's younger brother, Dave, won 65 England caps spread over a period of eight years with five different League clubs.
Appearances: FL: 13 apps 0 gls Total: 13 apps 0 gls

WEALTHALL, Barry Arthur
Full-back 5' 9½" 11st 2lbs
Born: Nottingham, 1st May 1942
CAREER: Nottingham and County of Nottingham schoolboys. **FOREST June 1957, professional 6th June 1959.** Grimsby Town May 1962. York City June 1963 to May 1966.
Debut v Halifax Town, FLC 1 (h) 5.10.60, won 2-0

Barry Wealthall joined the Forest ground staff from school as a centre-half, and was then groomed for the full-back position. All of his four senior appearances were made as deputy to Roy Patrick in the 1960-61 campaign. Without further senior involvement, he joined Grimsby Town, and made nine League appearances. His best spell came with York City, for whom he made 75 League appearances in three seasons. In earlier days, Wealthall was an outstanding junior whose representative honours included an appearance for the National Association of Boys' Clubs at International level, and England Youth International cap, awarded in May 1959.
Appearances: FL: 2 apps 0 gls FAC: 1 app 0 gls FLC: 1 app 0 gls Total: 4 apps 0 gls
Honours: England Youth international.

WHARE, William 'Billy' Frederick

Right full-back 5' 9" 11st 11lbs
Born: Guernsey, C.I. 14th May 1924
Died: Mansfield, 28th May 1995
CAREER: St Martin's FC (Guernsey). **FOREST May 1947 to May 1960.** Boston United.
Debut v Tottenham Hotspur (h) 23.4.49, drawn 2-2
Bill Whare was ten years old when he started playing football at centre-half with St Martin's FC in Guernsey, He eventually moved to left full-back and in 1946 represented Guernsey in the Muratti Cup Final, the greatest event in the Channel Islands calendar. He was then selected for a Guernsey X1 who opposed Southampton in a friendly match and was aked if he would be interested in joining the Saints. It was Forest who claimed him, however, thanks to the advice of Ted Malpas, a former Aston Villa player and colleague of Forest manager Billy Walker. Whare was working as a motor mechanic when he accepted a month's trial and then signed a professional form. In his second season he made his debut at wing-half against the Spurs, but when *Bob McCall was put out of action with a septic knee, Whare was given a first team opportunity in his preferred position at full-back. Despite two serious knee injuries Bill Whare stayed long enough to receive two benefits. A solid defensive player, renowned for his sliding tackles, he rarely ventured over the half way line, scoring just two goals in 322 matches. He retired from senior football at the age of 36 and later became the licensee of The Wagon & Horses at Redhill.*
Appearances: FL: 298 apps 2 gls FAC: 23 apps 0 gls Other: 1 app 0 gls Total: 322 apps 2 gls.
Honours: **(FOREST**) Division 3 South champions 1951. FA Cup winners 1959

WHEATLEY, Roland 'Ron'

Wing half-back 5' 9" 11st 6lbs
Born: Radford, Nottingham, 20th June 1924
Died: Strelley, Nottingham, 27th September 2003
CAREER: Beeston Boys' Club. **FOREST 4th June 1946**. Southampton January 1949. Grimsby Town June 1951. Halifax Town January 1952. Workington March 1952. Corby Town July 1952. Stamford June 1953. Southampton scout 1955 to 1973.
Debut v Brentford (a) 10.9.47, lost 1-3
A former miner and wartime paratrooper who was seriously injured by a mortar bomb during fighting in World War Two. Ron Wheatley failed to establish himself at the City Ground and, rather sadly, asked not be selected for Forest home games due to persistent barracking. Shortly afterwards, Forest agreed terms with Leeds United for his transfer but Wheatley refused the terms offered but later joined Southampton, initially as a player and later as chief scout in the Midlands area, a position he held for eighteen years. His modest playing career totalled just 21 League appearances and one goal.
Appearances: FL: 6 apps 0 gls Total: 6 apps 0 gls

WHITE, Thomas 'Tom'
Defender 6' 2" 12st 0lbs
Born: Brandon, 1953
CAREER: FOREST 7th April 1970, retired due to injury 1973.
Debut as sub v Chelsea, FLC 3 replay (a) 11.10.71, lost 1-2
Injury curtailed Tom White's career before the ideally built defender had progressed beyond outings with the reserves, and his single senior appearance as a second half substitute in a 2-1 defeat in the League Cup replay at Stamford Bridge. Sadly, he lost the sight of one eye in a car crash, and was subsequently employed as a social worker by Durham County Council.
Appearances: FLC: 0/1 apps 0 gls Total: 0/1 apps 0 gls

WHITEFOOT, Jeffrey 'Jeff'

Wing half-back 5' 8" 11st 10lbs
Born: Cheadle, Cheshire, 31st December 1933
CAREER: Stockport Schoolboys. Manchester United June 1949, professional December 1951. Grimsby Town November 1957. **FOREST 26th July 1958, fee £7,000, to May 1968.**
Debut v Wolverhampton Wanderers (a) 23.8.58, lost 1-5
Taught the fundamentals of soccer by his father in the cobbled cul-de-sac outside his home in Platt Street, Cheadle, Cheshire, Jeff Whitefoot graduated to his school team, then Stockport Boys and finally England's Schoolboy International side. He gained four caps in 1949 before Manchester United signed him, initially as office boy on a starting wage of £4 per week. He played a great part in the success of United's Central League team, and made his senior debut against the League champions, Portsmouth, at the tender age of 16 years and 105 days. He won a regular first team place in 1953-54, won a League championship medal in 1956 but lost his place during the course of the season to the emerging Eddie Coleman. In October 1957 he was on the point of signing with Forest but, at the last minute, was persuaded by manager Matt Busby to team up with former Manchester United colleague, Allenby Chilton, player-manager of Grimsby Town. 'Domestic reasons' were given for Whitefoot's decision to leave Grimsby, and Forest finally got their man in July 1958. In his first season at the City Ground, Forest lifted the FA Cup in the 1959 Final against Luton Town. At the time of writing, with the 60th anniversary of the success just a year away, 84 year-old Jeff Whitefoot is the only survivor of the team that lifted the trophy. A memorable occasion for the fair-haired wing-half came in season 1963-64 with Forest trailing Everton by 2-0 and with five minutes remaining, Whitefoot, scored two last gasp goals in a sensational finish that enabled Forest to share the points. For eight seasons a regular in the Forest middle line before losing his place to Henry Newton, Whitefoot remained a valuable member of the reserve team, providing experience and guidance for younger players. During his Forest days, he lived with his wife and two children in West Bridgford, and had business interests in the city. Today, he lives in retirement at Melton Mowbray, and is unlikely to remember your author, although we did both serve in the RAF at Ringway, Manchester, at the time of Jeff's appearance for England Under-23 against Italy Under-23 at Bologna in January 1954.
Appearances: FL: 255 apps 5 gls FAC: 23 apps 1 gl FLC: 4 apps 1 gl Other: 3 apps 0 gls Total: 285 apps 7 gls
Honours: England Schoolboy International. England Under-23 International (Manchester United) FL Division 1 champions 1956. (**FOREST**) FA Cup winners 1959.

WIGNALL, Francis 'Frank'

Centre-forward 5' 10" 12st 0lbs
Born: Blackrod, near Chorley, Lancs. 21st August 1939
CAREER: Blackrod Youth X1. De Haviland Works. Horwich RMI. Everton May 1958. **FOREST June 1963, fee £20,000.** Wolverhampton Wanderers March 1968, fee £50,000. Derby County February 1969, fee £20,000. Mansfield Town November 1971 to May 1973, fee £8,000. Kings Lynn player-manager July 1973. Burton Albion manager August 1974. Quatar October 1975, appointed national coach 1980. Shepshed Charterhouse manager July 1981 to March 1983.
Debut v Aston Villa (h) 24.8.63, lost 0-1
A Bolton Wanderers supporter in schooldays, and a big fan of their England international centre-forward Nat Lofthouse, Frank Wignall was an apprentice aircraft engineer with De Havilland when he joined Everton, initially as a part-time professional. He made a scoring debut against Burnley at Goodison Park and later netted his first hat trick in a FL Cup-tie against Tranmere Rovers. In 1960-61 he scored eight goals in 15 appearances, a total that had increased to 15 goals in 33 appearances at the time of his transfer to Forest. He was the last signing made by manager Andy Beattie, and his £20,000 transfer fee exactly equalled the Reds' record when Colin Booth was signed from Wolves in October 1959. Equally good in the air *or on the ground, Wignall scored a hat trick for the Football League X1 in their 4-0 win against the Irish League in Belfast on 28th October 1964, leading to his first international appearance against Wales at Wembley in the following month, when he scored both of England's goals in the 2-1 win. He retained his place for the 1-1 against Holland in Amsterdam on 9th December 1964. In May 1965 he suffered a minor fracture to the leg in the County Cup Final, and as a consequence missed about half of the matches in the following season. Appearing at inside-forward in his last two seasons, the goals dried up, but he had a very good season in 1966-67 when Joe Baker and Ian Storey-Moore were the main marksmen as the team finished runners-up for the League championship and reached the semi-final of the FA Cup. Spells with the Wolves, Derby County, where he assisted in two promotion campaigns under manager Brian Clough, and Mansfield Town wound up his senior career in which he scored 107 League goals in 300/23 appearances. Forest's matchday programmes in the 1960s carried an advert for 'Frank Wignall Ltd., Bulcote Service Station, Burton Joyce, Nottingham.'*
Appearances: FL: 156/1 apps 47 gls FAC: 14 apps 5 gls FLC: 4 apps 1 gl Other: 3 apps 0 gls Total: 177/1 apps 52 gls
Honours: England International v Wales in November (scored two) and Holland in December 1964. FL representative, 2 apps.

WILKINS Ernest **George**
Inside-forward 5' 8" 11st 7lbs
Born: Hackney, 27th October 1919
Died: Bournemouth, 19th January 1999
CAREER: Townfield School. Hayes Wasps. Wakefield Oil Co. (Middlesex). Tottenham Hotspur (trial). Hayes FC. Brentford amateur November 1937, professional February 1938. (Wartime guest player with Heart of Midlothian, Hayes FC, West Ham United and Portsmouth). Bradford Park Avenue February 1947. **FOREST 29th December 1947, fee £7,700**. Leeds United (trial) September 1949. Boston United October 1949. Hayes F.C. coach in three spells spanning December 1949 to January 1961.
Debut v Doncaster Rovers (h) 27.12.47, won 4-2 (scored one)
Offered a place on the club's groundstaff by Spurs at the age of 15, George Wilkins preferred to stay nearer to home and joined Brentford, initially on amateur forms. He was in the first team at the age of 19, but the outbreak of war halted his progress. He served in the Royal Kent Regiment

Infantry for six years, but managed to turn out for the Bees during the conflict, and was a War Cup winner at Wembley against Portsmouth in May 1942. In 1944 he was a member of the British Army side, along with Bryn Jones and Stan Cullis, who played against the Yugoslav Forces. He was transferred to Bradford Park Avenue in February of the first peacetime season and, during his relatively short stay in Yorkshire, was frequently called: "The brains, general director and schemer of the forward line." He began season 1947-48 as captain at Park Avenue and led his team to a record six consecutive wins. He cost Forest a hefty fee in December of the same season, but failed to lift a struggling side, and early in 1948-49 he was operated upon for cartilage trouble and played in only 13 League matches as Forest, despite a late rally, suffered relegation from Division Two. Hull City's player-manager, Raich Carter, was reported to be watching Wilkin's form in Forest's Reserves, but when he did move it was to join Leeds United. Wilkins had asked for a transfer, and press statements at the time suggested that Forest had had offered Wilkins only £7 per week, and were charging him 35 shillings rent on his clubhouse. This was denied by the club who stated that the player was on the maximum terms of £12 and £10 per week, and the rent was actually 30 shillings per week! After just three matches for Leeds United a reoccurrence of his knee injury enforced his retirement. George Wilkins fathered four sons who all played professional football. Ray (who died recently aged 61) played for England, Dean for QPR, Brighton and Orient, and Graham and Steve were both ex-Chelsea and Brentford.
Appearances: FL: 24 apps 6 gls FAC: 3 apps 1 gl Total: 27 apps 7 gls

WILLIAMSON, Brian William

Goalkeeper 6' 1" 11st 9lbs
Born: Blyth, 6th October 1939
Died: Sydney, Australia, 13th May 2013
CAREER: Seaton Delaval. Gateshead October 1958. Crewe Alexandra July 1960. Leeds United December 1962. **FOREST February 1966, fee £6,000.** Leicester City (loan) August 1967. Fulham November 1968, fee £10,000, retired May 1970.
Debut v Newcastle United (a) 13.1.68, drawn 0-0 (Debut prior to FL registration)
The introduction of Brian Williamson in goal proved a turning point in the fortunes of Gateshead in their first season as members of the new Division Four. His debut at Chester on 7th March 1959 brought a welcome 1-0 win, and a record of one defeat in ten matches eased Gateshead clear of a re-election application and to 20th place in the table. Twelve months on they finished third from the bottom of the table and their application for re-election was rejected and League football at Redheugh Park was ended. With the experience of 55 League matches to his credit, Williamson was quickly back into League football with Crewe Alexandra, for whom he made 54 appearances. Thereafter, he operated mainly at reserve team level with his next four clubs, although he was unfortunate at the City Ground when he broke a bone in his hand in his first senior appearance when successfully deputising for the injured Peter Grummitt at Newcastle United in a 0-0 draw. He recovered to make 12 first team appearances in his debut season, and had made seven consecutive starts in 1968-69 when Fulham signed him in an emergency to cover for their injured Northern Ireland international goalkeeper, Jack McClelland. After 14 League and Cup matches he was again operating at reserve level when he took the decision to retire from the game and take up a position as a security guard.
Appearances: FL: 19 apps 0 gls FLC: 1 app 0 gls Total: 20 apps 0 gls

WILSON, David 'Dave' Edward Joseph

Forward 5' 9" 11st 1lb
Born: Wednesfield, 4th October 1944
CAREER: Wolverhampton Schoolboys**. FOREST amateur November 1959, professional October 1961.** Carlisle United October 1965, fee £8,000. Grimsby Town March 1967, fee £10,000. Walsall September 1968, fee £10,000. Burnley September 1969, fee £15,000. Chesterfield June 1971. East London (South Africa) April 1975. Workington player-manager December 1976 to May 1977. Altona City (Australia) coach.
Debut v Fulham (h) 6.10.62, won 3-1
First discovered by Forest's chief scout, Eric Houghton, the former England outside-left, Dave Wilson made his first team debut at the age of 18, but spent most of his Forest career in reserve ranks. In 1962-63 he was leading scorer in Football Combination matches with 15 in 28 matches, including a hat trick against Peterborough United Reserves in a 4-0 win on 20th April 1963. On moving from the City Ground, he gave excellent service to a further five League clubs, with aggregate Football League figures of 296/11 appearances and 78 goals.
Appearances: FL: 8/1 apps 1 gl FAC: 1 app 0 gls Total: 9/1 apps 1 gl

WILSON, Joseph 'Joe'

Full-back 5' 8" 11st 5lbs
Born: Workington, 6th July 1937
Died: Sydenham, Australia, 25th September 2015
CAREER: Cumbria Schoolboys. Workington July 1952, professional January 1956. **FOREST March 1962, fee £8,000.** Wolverhampton Wanderers March 1965. Newport County May 1967. Workington September 1968 to May 1972.
Debut v West Bromwich Albion (a) 17.3.62, drawn 2-2
A starring performance for Workington against Forest in the third round FA Cup-tie at Borough Park on 6th January 1962 led directly to the strong tackling and enthusiastic full-back joining Forest two months later. Manager Andy Beattie paying £8,000 for Joe Wilson who was immediately elevated from Division Four to Division One, and in his second appearance facing Manchester United's star-studded attack at the City Ground in a 1-0 win attended by 27,682 spectators. Ten days earlier, he had assisted Workington to a 1-1 draw at Southport, a match attended by 3,923! After three years at the City Ground he joined the Wolves and assisted them to promotion to Division One, as runners-up to Coventry City, in 1966-7. A season as captain of Newport County followed before his homeward return to Workington where he passed the career landmark of 500 FL appearances prior to retiring from playing at the end of the 1971-72 season. In his two spells at Borough Park Joe Wilson's impressive figures were: 321 FL appearances and nine goals, and 17 FA Cup and 9 FL Cup matches. After emigrating to Australia in 1972 to work for the Hoechst Chemical Company, he continued as a player and manager of several clubs with outstanding success.
Appearances: FL: 84 apps 1 gl FAC: 7 apps 0 gls Total: 91 apps 1 gl.

WILSON, Thomas 'Tommy'
Centre-forward 5' 9" 11st 0lbs
Born: Bedlington Station, County Durham, 15th September 1930
Died: Tower Hill, Brentwood, 21st April 1992
CAREER: Ellis School. Bestwood Boys' Club. Rigley's Wagon Works. Army service in the Royal Horse Artlery. Cinderhill Colliery. **FOREST 20th April 1951**. Walsall November 1960 to June 1962. Chelmsford City. Brentwood Town manager 1965.
Debut v Luton Town (h) 6.10.51, won 2-0
Tommy Wilson was born in County Durham, but moved with his family to Nottingham at four years of age. Originally signed as a centre-forward from Cinderhill Colliery, an early switch saw him moved onto the right wing, and he became a regular in the Midland League team for three seasons. His big chance came in 1954-55 when Wally Ardron's fine career was reaching its close. Blackman, a prolific goal scorer with Reading, had been signed as his potential replacement, but he failed to find his best form leading to Wilson's opportunity and he responded with 10 goals in 34 League and Cup matches. The signing of Peter Higham from Preston North End in the close season saw Tommy Wilson under employed in the League side, but in the followed term, when promotion from Division Two was achieved, he scored 14 goals in 32 League matches, including a four-goal blast against Barnsley on 9th February, and thereafter his form peaked, particularly in 1958-59, when he netted 27 goals in 50 League and Cup matches, including Forest's second goal in the FA Cup Final victory against Luton Town. At his peak, Wilson was one of the hardest workers in the team; he had a liking for moving out onto the wing, but was extremely dangerous in front of goal. He made his final Forest appearance in the month of his 30th birthday and moved on to Walsall, for whom he scored 18 goals in 53 League matches, assisting them to promotion from Division Three in his first season, lifting the Saddlers into Division Two for the first time in 60 years. The opening match on their return was an all-ticket game at Fellows Park against Sunderland, who fielded Brian Clough for the first time, following his transfer from Middlesbrough. Tommy Wilson scored one goal and made two 'assists' as the Saddlers came from behind to win a rousing encounter by 4-3.
Appearances: FL: 191 apps 75 gls FAC: 25 apps 13 gls Other: 1 app 1 gl Total: 217 apps 89 gls
Honours: **(FOREST)** FA Cup winners 1959

Bob McKinlay, Tommy Wilson and Bill Whare inspect their FA Cup Winners medals at Wembley, 1959

WINFIELD, Bernard **John**

Full-back 6' 0" 11st 11lbs
Born: Draycott, Derbyshire, 28th February 1943
CAREER: Derby Schoolboys**. FOREST amateur June 1959, professional 12th May 1960.**
Peterborough United July 1974 to April 1975.
Debut v Blackpool (h) 3.2.62, lost 3-4 (scored one)
John Winfield joined the Forest staff from school in 1959 and made a scoring debut debut in 1962. Originally a wing-half, he switched to a role in the back four and gave wonderful service to the club, his overlapping runs and high crosses from the wing being a feature of his play. A former captain of the Colts X1, he seized his senior opportunity following Jeff Whitefoot's injury in January 1962. His debut against Blackpool was eventful in the extreme. Three goals in arrears after 26 minutes play in the first half, there then followed a rousing fightback with Winfield netting Forest's third goal to level the scores. Left exposed when chasing the winner, it was the visitors who scored the deciding goal, veteran South African wingman Bill Perry netting his 129th and last goal for the Seasiders. For five seasons between 1966 and 1971, Winfield hardly missed a first team match, forming an excellent partnership with Peter Hindley. After appearing in thirteen seasons with the Forest, he joined Peterborough United but plagued with knee troubles he did not make his first team debut until March 1975 and appeared in only 11 League matches. He then ran a newsagent's business in Woollaton, and is currently living in Alicante, Spain.
Appearances: FL: 353/2 apps 4 gls FAC: 33 apps 1 gl FLC: 16 apps 0 gls Other: 6 apps 0 gls Total: 408/2 apps 5 gls

WOOD, Noel B
Goalkeeper 5' 11" 12st 10lbs
Born: Retford, Nottingham, 25th September 1937
CAREER: Army football**. FOREST 17th March 1961.**
Debut v Gillingham, FLC 1 (h) 11.9.61, won 4-1
Recommended to the club by a supporter who saw him playing in representative army football in Germany, Noel Wood was invited for trials when he was demobilised and joined the professional ranks in March 1961. Some six months later he made his single senior appearance when he replaced Peter Grummitt in goal for the Gillingham League Cup-tie, which, for the first time, was played under floodlighting. Wood's selection came along with a number of team changes, as Forest were due to play Valencia two days later in the first leg of their round one tie in the Inter-Cities Fairs Cup. Forest's initial involvement in Europe competitions proved to be extremely disappointing as they lost 0-2 in Valencia, and 1-5 in the second leg at the City Ground.
Appearances: FLC: 1 app 0 gls Total: 1 app 0 gls

Tony Woodcock, 1973

WOODCOCK, Anthony 'Tony' Stewart
Forward 5' 10" 11st 0lbs
Born: Eastwood, Notts. 6th December 1955
CAREER: FOREST apprentice June 1972, professional 2nd January 1974. Lincoln City (loan) February 1976. Doncaster Rovers (loan) September 1976. FC Cologne (Germany) November 1979, fee £650,000. Arsenal June 1982, fee £500,000. FC Cologne (Germany) July 1986, fee £140,000. Fortuna Cologne June 1988, appointed coach 1990 to 1991. VfB Leipzig coach 1994 to 1995. Debut v Aston Villa (a) 24.4.74, lost 1-3
It took some time for Tony Woodcock to establish himself at the City Ground, and two loan spells came close to being permanent signings before his break through came in the promotion season 1976-77. Depite the fact that he had not started in the first team until November, Forest supporters voted him 'Player of the Year'. A skilful and speedy forward with an eye for goal, he linked up well with Peter Withe and it was success all the way with club and international honours coming thick and fast, the first six of his England caps being awarded in 1978-79, the season in which Forest lifted the European Cup, the FL Cup, and finished runners-up for the League championship. The parting of the ways came in November of the following season when Cologne paid a record £650,000 fee for the transfer of a foreign player. After scoring 28 goals in 81 matches for the Bundesliga side he returned home to join Arsenal after the World Cup Finals of 1982. At Highbury he added a further 18 England caps and was Arsenal's leading scorer in each of his four seasons, a highlight being his scoring five at Aston Villa on 29th October 1983. A return to Cologne and a final spell with Fortuna of Cologne brought his playing career to a close with a record of 176 goals in 526 matches in English and German football, and 21 goals in international matches
Appearances: FL: 125/4 apps 36 gls FAC: 14 apps 10 gls FLC: 21 apps 12 gls Other: 16 apps 4 gls Total: 176/4 apps 62 gls
Honours: England International, 42 caps. England Under-21 and 'B' International. (**FOREST**) FL Cup winners 1978, 1979. FL Division 1 champions 1978. European Cup winners 1979, 1980. Anglo-Scottish Cup winner 1977.

YOUNGER, William 'Billy'

Inside-forward 5' 10" 10st 11lbs
Born: Hollywell, 22nd March 1940
Died: In Northumberland, January 2006
CAREER: Seaton Delaval. **FOREST 15th May 1957.** Lincoln City (loan) February 1961. Walsall June 1961. Doncaster Rovers December 1961. Hartlepools United August 1962. Ramsgate July 1963.
Debut v Birmingham City (h) 7.3.59, lost 1-7
An operation on a damaged ankle in December 1957 was an unfortunate start for 17 year-old inside-forward Billy Younger, but twelve months later he was a member of Forest's travelling party to Newcastle United for the Boxing Day game. His senior debut followed in March 1959 when he appeared as deputy for John Quigley in what was Forest's fourth meeting with Birmingham City in three weeks. A trio of fifth round FA Cup-ties ending with a 5-0 victory for the Reds at Filbert Street, Leicester. With an FA Cup semi-final against Aston Villa due to be played in seven days time, manager Billy Walker rested several players and introduced four reserves for the visit of Birmingham City. The scratch eleven were 1-3 down at half time after leading through a Roy Dwight goal scored after 24 minutes. Billy Gray missed a penalty, his shot hitting the crossbar, and goalkeeper Fraser had an unhappy return to first team duty. After a promising start, Younger faded out and it was not until the final month of the following season that he was reintroduced for six matches. After five appearances and one goal in 1960-61, he was placed on the transfer list, following a loan spell with Lincoln City. His best subsequent spell came with Hartlepools United for whom he scored four goals in 37 League matches.
Appearances: FL: 12 apps 2 gls FLC: 1 app 2 gls Total: 13 apps 4 gls

WAR TIME FOREST 1939-1946

The Football League and FA Cup competitions opened up in August 1939 as usual. Most clubs had played three League games when war was declared on Sunday 3rd September. The football authorities made an immediate decision to suspend all competitions, perhaps recalling that continuing with the Great War season of 1914-15 had proved to be a serious misjudgement. Consequently, players' contracts were cancelled, which meant that no wages would be paid. Footballers than had little choice but to join the armed services or sign on at the local Labour Exchange. Although many of them were eligible for conscription, it took some time for the authorities to organise this process.

With no football, there was of course no money coming in to keep a club running. Rates were due to local authorities for the stadiums, and managers, groundsmen and administrative staff had to be paid. Forest were not the only club facing problems with the bank. The obvious need was to generate gate receipts by getting some kind of football up and running. September 9th was blank, but by the following weekend regulations were relaxed and clubs were allowed to play friendly matches. But how would they find 11 men to form a team? The nation had seen the devastating effect of the German Stuka dive bombers on European cities and feared the worst, so clubs with grounds in sensitive areas were barred at first from playing home matches.

Many players were still undecided about their immediate future. By September 22nd 1939 the Football League and the Football Association decided that clubs should be allowed to pay ex-professional players 30 shillings each to play in the friendly games. This was later increased to £2. Amateur players needed only expenses of course. Players' registrations were not actually cancelled (meaning that they were still tied to their club, even though they were not getting paid) but it was agreed that they could turn out for another club as a "guest". After much discussion, a more formal programme for the season was put together by the Football League, starting in October 1939. Because of blackout rules and travelling difficulties a regional league structure was designed, with a separate cup competition in the second half of the season. In addition, various friendly games were played, often in aid of a particular charity. One such game at the City Ground is worth a mention; in November 1940 an RAF International XI beat Forest 4-1. The RAF line-up was indeed "international"; Swinburne (Newcastle); Turner (Charlton & Wales), Johnson (Newcastle); Crayston (Arsenal & England), Bernard Joy (Arsenal and England), Kirchen (Arsenal & England); Gallacher (Sunderland & Scotland), Fenton (Middlesbrough & England), Doherty (Manchester City and Ireland), Lester Finch (Finchley and England). Played on behalf of RAF charities, 3,497 were in attendance.

The complications of the League structures during the war need not trouble us here. The following pages provide a complete list of players used by Forest in the official competitions and friendly games. Guest players are identified as far as possible. Some well-known names in action for the war-time Reds will be seen to include ten England internationals, amongst them Frank Broome, Wilf Copping, Sammy Crooks and Raich Carter. Andy Beattie and Dally Duncan had Scottish caps. The names of Arthur Clements and Lester Finch might be less well known today; both were amateurs and played together in the Great Britain team at the 1936 Berlin Olympics. Guest players might have moved back to Nottingham for personal reasons, or may have been working for local businesses. Others might have been on leave from the armed services and offered to play for the club. Last minute team changes were common thanks to transport difficulties, sometimes resulting in people being plucked from the crowd. Forest manager Billy Walker was also pressed into action on occasion. Forest's Bob Davies played for Wales for the first ten minutes of the England v Wales international at the City Ground when Dai Astley was late arriving.

Players whose name appears in bold type in the list have a full biography in this volume or its predecessor, which covered the period 1892 to 1939. Players not in bold type and with no lending club were mostly on Forest's books during the war, with many of them playing in the colts team that had an "under 20" age rule. The grid indicates in which of the seven seasons 1939-40 to 1945-46 a particular player made at least one appearance in League, Cup and first-team friendly games.

			40	41	42	43	44	45	46
Adams A	Andrew			x					
Airlie S	Seton (Jock)	Glasgow Celtic					x		
Aldred A	Arthur				x	x			
Allen HA	Tony							x	x
Allen R		QPR					x		
Antonio GR	George	Stoke City	x	x	x				
Armstrong M	Matthew		x						
Arnold D		Leicester City		x					
Ashley H		Guildford			x				
Ashton P	Percy		x			x	x		
Astley J	Dick	Coventry City			x				
Baldwin H	Harry	Brighton & Hove			x	x			
Barks E	Eddie		x	x	x	x		x	x
Barratt H	Harry	Coventry City				x			
Baxter WA	Bill		x			x	x	x	x
Bean AS	Alf (Billy)	Lincoln City				x	x		
Beardall			x						
Beattie A	Andy	Preston North End			x				
Beaumont L	Len		x		x	x	x	x	
Bedford G		Northampton Town			x				
Bee FE	Frank					x	x		
Beswick J	Jeffrey	colt				x	x	x	
Bett F	Fred	Sunderland				x			
Betts A	Arthur							x	
Betts E	Eric						x		x
Bird R		Bournemouth		x					
Blagg EA	Edward A		x			x	x	x	x
Blenkinsopp TW	Tommy	Grimsby Town						x	x
Bosher									x
Bowers JWA	Jack	Leicester City			x				
Bradley					x				
Bramley T		Stoke City	x						
Bray J	Jackie	Manchester City			x				
Brierley B	Bernard		x						
Brook R	Reg	Bristol City	x	x	x				
Broome F	Frank	Aston Villa	x	x	x				
Brown AW	Alan	Huddersfield Town			x				
Brown GS	Gordon							x	x
Brown J		Birmingham		x					
Buck GR	George	colt			x				
Burgess R	Ron	Tottenham Hotspur		x	x				
Butler J	Jack	colt			x	x			
Buttery A	Arthur	Hednesford			x				
Bye W		Birmingham			x				
Cairns WH	Billy	Newcastle United			x	x			
Canning LD	Danny	Cardiff City							x
Carter HS	Raich	Sunderland					x		x
Chadwick C	Cliff	Middlesbrough			x				
Challinor J	Jack	Stoke City	x	x	x				
Chapman GW	George	West Bromwich Alb.				x			
Charles			x						
Clare J	Joe	Lincoln City				x			
Clark TG	Thomas		x						x
Clarke J		West Bromwich Alb.		x					
Clements BA	Arthur	Barking		x					
Coen L	Lawrence	Coventry City						x	
Collins A	Alan	Kilmarnock	x	x	x				
Copping W	Wilf	Leeds United		x					
Corkhill WG	Billy	Cardiff City	x		x				
Corry S	Sidney					x			

George Antonio, Stoke City

			40	41	42	43	44	45	46
Coutts WF	Billy	Leicester City			x				
Crawley T	Tommy	Coventry City		x					
Cressey W		guest		x					
Crisp GH	George H		x	x				x	
Crofts J	Joseph					x	x		x
Cronkshaw J	James							x	x
Crooks SD	Sammy	Derby County			x				
Cummings GW	George	Aston Villa	x	x	x				
Cunningham T		guest						x	
Curtis GF		guest		x					
Cutts A		guest	x						
Davie J	Jock	Brighton & Hove						x	
Davies HJ	Horace						x		
Davies RG	Robert G		x	x	x				x
Dearson DJ	Don	Birmingham		x					
Drury GB	George	Arsenal	x	x			x	x	
Dulson RE	Ralph E					x	x	x	x
Duncan D	Dally	Derby County			x				
Dutton L	Len	Arsenal		x					
Edwards GR	George	Aston Villa		x	x				
Edwards J	Jack							x	
Egan GD	Doug	Aldershot				x			
Egan H	Harry					x	x		x
Elliott BH	Bernard						x	x	
Elliott CS	Charlie	Coventry City		x	x				
Fillingham T	Tom	Ipswich Town		x	x				
Finch LC	Lester	Barnet		x					
Finch R		Hednesford			x				
Firth JW		Bradford PA						x	
Flewitt S	Stanley						x	x	
Flint HG		guest			x				
Flint		colt		x					
Foreman D								x	
Freeman WJ		colt			x				
Fryer JL	Jack		x	x					
Gardiner C	Charles						x		
Gladwin			x						
Godfrey LL		Aston Villa						x	
Goffin WC	Billy	Aston Villa						x	
Graham T	Thomas		x	x	x				
Grant AF	Alick	Leicester City				x			x
Griffin S	Sydney							x	
Guttridge R	Ron	Aston Villa						x	
Hall J	Jack	Tottenham Hotspur							x
Hancocks J	Johnny	Walsall							x
Hannah GL	George	Port Vale				x			
Hardwick R		guest			x				
Harrison C	Clifford						x		
Haycock FJ	Freddie	Aston Villa	x						
Haywood						x			
Hepworth R	Ronnie	Bradford PA					x	x	
Hiatt GA	George					x	x		
Hinchliffe T	Tom	Derby County	x	x					x
Hindley F	Frank	Brighton & Hove				x	x	x	
Hogg F	Freddie	Luton Town					x		
Hollis KB	Kenneth	colt		x		x	x		
Houghton WE	Eric	Aston Villa	x	x	x				
Howe LF	Les	Tottenham Hotspur			x				
Hubbard C	Cliff	West Ham United					x		
Hughes TG	Thomas			x		x			

Eric Houghton, Aston Villa

			40	41	42	43	44	45	46
Hullett W	Bill	Manchester United			x				
Hunt AK	Ashley (Ken)		x	x					
Hunter JB	Jimmy	Preston North End	x	x					
Hutchinson JA	Jack						x	x	
Hydes A		Newport County	x						
Iceton OL	Lloyd	Preston North End						x	
Inskip FC	Charles							x	
Iverson RT	Bob	Aston Villa		x	x				
Jackson J		Bolton Wanderers				x			
Jeffries A	Alf	Sheffield United				x			
Jenkinson F	Fred	Bury				x			
Jennings DB	Dennis	Birmingham		x					
Jepson A	Arthur	Port Vale				x			
Johnson C	Charles				x	x			
Johnson F	Frank	colt			x			x	x
Johnston TD	Tom						x	x	x
Johnstone F		Sunderland				x			
Jones E		guest							x
Jones LJ	Les	Arsenal		x	x				
Jones SH	Stanley						x		
Kaile GW	Gordon							x	
Kilshaw							x		
Kirton J	Jock	Stoke City	x	x	x				
Knight F	Frank		x	x					
Knott B	Bert?	Hull City				x			
Lager EW		Coventry City	x						
Lambert E	Eric	colt			x	x			
Lane H	Harry	Southend		x	x	x			
Langton E	Eddie	colt		x					
Ledger JK	John								x
Leverton R	Ronald							x	x
Lewis J	Jack	Crystal Palace		x	x				
Lewis TG		Watford				x			
Lightfoot							x		
Linacre W	Billy	Chesterfield						x	
Long B	Bruce								x
Long D		colt					x		
Lowrie G	George	Coventry City		x					
Lyman CC	Colin	Tottenham Hotspur			x				
Mansell JE	Joseph					x			
Martin FA	Freddie							x	x
Martin JR		Aston Villa	x						
Mason GW	George	Coventry City		x					
Mason W		Coventry City			x				
Massey AW	Alf	Stoke City			x	x			
Massie A		Aston Villa	x						
Matthew RJ		Bournemouth			x				
Maund B		Hednesford			x				
Maund JH	John H		x	x	x	x	x	x	x
McCall AJ	Andrew J		x						
McCall RH	Robert H		x		x	x	x	x	x
McCarthy D	Dan			x					
McFadyen W	Willie	Halifax Town			x				
McKenzie P		guest	x						
McNab A		guest		x					
McPerson IB	Ian	Notts County							
McPerson T		Glasgow Rangers							x
McStay			x						
Mee GE	George	colt			x	x		x	x

Bob Iverson, Aston Villa

			40	41	42	43	44	45	46
Meek J	Joe	Tottenham Hotspur			x				
Merrick GH	Gil	Birmingham		x	x				
Metcalfe WF	Walter	Coventry City		x	x				
Mettam				x					
Middleton R		Chesterfield					x		
Mills P		Leeds United	x	x					
Mitchell		guest		x					
Moon F	Frederick		x	x					
Morgan C	Charles								x
Morgan W	Bill	Coventry City		x	x				
Morley W	William (Bill)							x	x
Moulson GB	George	Grimsby Town				x			
Mozley H	Bert							x	
Muncie W	Bill	Southend United			x				
Munro JS	John S		x						
Nixon G	Granville	colt	x						
Norris EJ	Eric			x					
North TW	Thomas W							x	x
Oakley JC	Jack	Chesterfield				x	x		
O'Donnell F	Frank	Aston Villa							x
Oxley R		Stockport County						x	
Pallister G	Gordon	Barnsley			x				
Parr J		Derby County					x		
Patten		guest		x					
Paul R	Raymond							x	x
Pawlow M	Maurice	Polish RAF				x			
Payne F	Frank							x	x
Peace RS	Ronald							x	
Peacock T	Tom		x	x	x	x			x
Perry C	Colin		x						
Pimbley DW	Douglas	Leicester City		x					x
Platts L	Laurie			x			x	x	x
Poe S						x			
Poole CJ	Cyril	Mansfield Town					x		
Potts VE	Vic	Doncaster Rovers			x				
Powell T		Grimsby Town						x	
Pritty G	George		x	x					x
Quinton W	Wally	Birmingham			x				
Rawson C	Colin							x	x
Rawson K	Kenneth	colt	x	x	x				
Rhodes A		Cardiff City					x		
Richards S	Stanley		x			x			
Richardson G	Godfrey	colt	x		x	x			
Riley C	Clifford						x		
Riley H	Harry				x	x			
Roberts S	Samuel (Gren)		x						
Robertson J		Bradford PA				x	x		
Robinson J	Jeff	colt		x					
Roebuck N		Sheffield Wednesday		x					
Roulston C		guest	x						
Rutherford J	Joe	Aston Villa		x	x				
Sadler GH	George	West Ham United			x				
Savage R	Reg								x
Seagrave JW		Stockport County		x					
Shaw CE	Cecil	West Bromwich Alb.		x					
Shaw J	John	Birmingham			x				
Shufflebottom F	Frank					x	x		x
Simms T		guest							x
Simpson NH	Noel					x		x	x
Slack L		colt			x	x			

Ronnie Starling, Aston Villa

			40	41	42	43	44	45	46
Smith EF	Ted	Arsenal	x	x					
Smith H	Harry				x				
Smith J	Jack	guest				x		x	
Smith JT	Trevor	Crystal Palace			x				
Smith O					x				
Smith W		Port Vale				x	x		
Southwell A	Aubrey	colt			x	x			
Spelton						x			
Starling RW	Ronnie	Aston Villa	x		x				
Statham A	Alwyne	Mansfield Town				x			
Steele FC	Freddie	Stoke City			x		x		
Stevenson HWH	Horace							x	
Styles W		Birmingham						x	
Surtees J	Jack		x		x	x			x
Taylor ER	Eric					x			
Taylor PD	Peter	colt						x	
Thomas			x						
Thomas GS	Gerald S (Geoff)						x	x	x
Thorpe L	Leonard	colt						x	
Townsend R	Robert	colt			x	x		x	
Trigg C	Cyril	Birmingham		x					
Trim RF	Reginald F	(later at Derby)	x		x	x	x		x
Tudor W	Billy	West Bromwich Alb.		x					
Vause PG	Peter	Rochdale			x				
Vose C		Blackburn Rovers		x					
Wakeman A	Alan	Aston Villa		x	x				
Walker V	Vic						x	x	x
Walker WH	William "Billy"	(Manager)	x	x	x				
Ward J	Jack			x	x				
Ware H	Harry	Norwich City		x					
Waring T	Tom (Pongo)	Accrington Stanley						x	
Watson W		Chesterfield					x		
Wattie J		Dundee					x		
Westland DG	Doug	Stoke City	x	x	x				
Weston T		guest							x
Wheatley R	Roland (Ron)	colt			x	x	x	x	
White F	Fred	Sheffield United							x
Witham R		Blackpool			x				
Wightman JR	Jock	Blackburn Rovers		x		x			
Wilkinson J	Jack							x	
Wilkinson N	Norman	Stoke City			x		x		
Williams A	Arthur								x
Williams BF	Bert	Walsall						x	
Wood HL	Henry	colt		x					
Woodman D		guest							x
Woolley KD	Kenneth	colt			x				
Wright A	Albert	colt						x	
Wyles H	Harold	Leicester City					x		
Young JFH	John					x			

Freddie Steele, Stoke

Years in the column headings are the final year of the season

FOREST MANAGERS 1936 to 1993

		League			*Other*			
	Games	*w*	*d*	*l*	*w*	*d*	*l*	*Win %*
Harry Wightman	120	32	26	57	1	1	3	27.50
Billy Walker	650	254	133	214	20	13	16	42.15
Andy Beattie	135	42	27	48	8	3	7	37.04
Johnny Carey	254	85	60	84	12	4	9	38.19
Matt Gillies	176	43	42	71	6	7	7	27.84
Dave Mackay	44	12	12	15	0	3	2	27.27
Allan Brown	58	17	15	18	3	2	3	34.48
Brian Clough	993	331	208	220	133	54	47	46.73

These are the managers' records at Forest only. "Other" games include FA Cup, League Cup, minor national cups and European club tournaments. Clough's record is his complete career at Forest.

Harold Wightman falls into the scope of the 1892-1939 volume in this series, and we have included him here for completeness. Before 1936, the club committee met every week to select the team. In the pre-war years, players were usually known as "first team" or "reserve team", meaning that the selection process was usually straightforward except in cases of injured players or those not able to play because of other factors. At most clubs, team tactics were rudimentary and coaching almost non-existent. Even training was basic by today's standards, often involving long walks and thermal baths. The need for a team manager, with responsibility for player selection and match tactics, became apparent with the rise of people such as Herbert Chapman, first at Huddersfield Town and later at Arsenal. Even then, club directors were often slow in handing over the reigns to the manager; after all, they were paying the players' wages, and often were instrumental in arranging the purchase of new players. They also paid for a club secretary, responsible for arranging fixtures, transport and other clerical matters. Consequently, today's soccer historian has to try to distinguish between men called managers who were actually secretaries, and some called secretaries who were actually team managers. When Wightman was appointed in 1936, secretarial duties continued in the hands of the then secretary Mr G Noel Watson, so we regard Wightman as the first Forest manager.

HAROLD (HARRY) WIGHTMAN
Position when playing: centre-half/half-back
Born: Sutton-in-Ashfield 19th June 1894
Died: Nottingham 5th April 1945
PLAYING CAREER: Sutton Town 1911. Eastwood Rangers 1912. Chesterfield Town 1913. Derby County 1919 (and assistant manager 1928). Chesterfield 1929. Notts County 1930 (as coach for manager Horace Henshall).
MANAGEMENT CAREER: Luton Town 1.6.1931 to 9.10.1935. Mansfield Town 15.1.1936 to 3.5.1936. FOREST 4.05.1936 to 10.3.1939.
Wightman was a regular guest player in the Forest teams of the First World War, and was a member of the team that won the Victory Shield in a two-legged final with Everton in 1919, collecting the Football League Championship Trophy as their reward. With the return to normal conditions in 1919, Wightman was signed by First Division Derby County, remaining there for nine seasons. He had a full season with Chesterfield in 1929-30 in the Third Division North, and was on Notts County's books in 1930-31 for coaching duties and without playing in the first team. In 1931 he was appointed as Luton Town manager, then in Division 3 (South), where his team's best finish was 4th in 1934-35. After a few months as manager of Mansfield he was given the Forest job at the end of the 1935-36 season. His two complete seasons at Second Division Forest found his club

finishing in 18th and 20th position, with the latter ending in a nail-biting last-day game, the result of which meant the club just avoided relegation. When he left they were again in 20th place. In his resignation statement, Wightman claimed he had not seen eye to eye with the Forest committee for some time, particularly on questions of policy. He said "the parting is quite amicable on both sides". We can assume he selected the team for Forest's game with Fulham on March 11th, with Forest's committee doing so for the next two games.
Playing Appearances: FL: 218 apps 11 gls FAC: 14 apps 0gls Total: 232 apps 11 gls
Managing: Total: 335 matches, 124 won, 81 drawn, 130 lost. Win% 37.01

WILLIAM HENRY (BILLY) WALKER
Position when playing: inside-forward
Born: Wednesbury 29th October 1897
Died: Sheffield 28th November 1964
PLAYING CAREER: Hednesford Town 1913. Darlaston 1913. Wednesbury Old Park 1914. Aston Villa 1919.
MANAGEMENT CAREER: Sheffield Wednesday 9.12.1933 to 8.11.1937. Chelmsford City 1.1938 to 10.1939. FOREST 20.3.1939 to 30.7.1960.
Walker's career at Forest is notable for two things; its longevity and an FA Cup win. By today's standards, holding down the manager's job for 21 years is unimaginable, given that it includes the club's first-ever relegation to the Third Division. Equally, the teams Walker built in the late 1950s were strong enough to head the First Division table in the autumn of 1957 and win the FA Cup in 1959. His playing career at Aston Villa was outstanding and he won international honours for England on 18 occasions. At age 36 he landed his first management job at Sheffield Wednesday. In his second season his club won the F.A. Cup at Wembley Stadium. But then League performances dropped off, Wednesday were relegated in 1937, and Walker resigned. In January 1938 he was appointed manager of non-League Chelmsford City. This might seem an odd choice, but the club were engaged in a battle with near-neighbours Colchester United in a bid to gain election to the Football League. Having just turned professional and moved up from the Essex County League to the Southern League, Chelmsford were keen to see if Walker could use his contacts in the game to build up their playing strength. Some former international players were signed, one of whom, Alex Wood, had represented the United States in the 1930 World Cup. However, Walker resigned just two months into the 1938-39 season. After a short spell out of the game he was appointed Forest manager in March 1939 and therefore was in charge during the hectic last few games, when relegation was again avoided on the last day of the season. Some signings were made in preparation for 1939-40, but plans soon became irrelevant on the outbreak of war. Walker struggled on through the war years and achieved good results from his "colts" policy, which today we would label as "Under 20s". However, the immediate post-war years were difficult and resulted in Forest's first relegation to Division Three in 1949. Unlike today, the committee gave him time to rebuild, and Division Two status was regained in the second season in the third tier. For a man who depended on his youth policy in wartime, his teams of the Fifties were comprised of a few Forest raised players with the rest recruited from other clubs when seemingly past their best. However, cultured football saw his team scramble out of Division Two in 1957, then set the First Division alight in the early part of 1957-58 before dropping back to 10th place. With more signings of established players in the summer of 1958, his team reached new heights which culminated in an FA Cup final victory over Luton Town in May 1959. The following season found him unable to build on that success, and relegation was just avoided. Walker called it a day aged 62 in July 1960 and joined the Forest committee. He was the last of England's pre-war managers still in charge of a club.
Playing Appearances: FL:478 apps 214 gls FAC: 53 apps 30gls Total: 531 apps 244 gls
Managing: Total: 833 matches, 338 won, 198 drawn, 299 lost. Win% 40.58.
Honours as player: FA Cup winner 1920, runners-up 1924. 18 full caps for England, from 10.4.1920 to 7.12.1932
Honours as manager: FA Cup winners 1935. Football League Div. 3(S) champions 1951. FA Cup winners 1935, 1959.

ANDREW (ANDY) BEATTIE
Position when playing: full-back
Born: Kintore, Scotland 11th August 1913
Died: Rushcliffe 20th September 1983
PLAYING CAREER: Inverurie Loco. Preston North End 1.5.1935.
MANAGEMENT CAREER: Barrow 1.3.1947 to 1.4.1949. Stockport County 1.5.1949 to 18.4.1952. Huddersfield Town 18.4.1952 to 3.11.1956. Carlisle United 31.5.1958 to 1.7.1963. FOREST 23.9.1960 to 31.7.1963. Plymouth Argyle 1.10.1963 to 31.5.1964. Wolves 2.11.1964 to 19.9.1965. Notts County 10.62.65 to 18.3.1966, with subsequent caretaker appointments to 28.9.1967.
Press speculation on Walker's successor was rife in August 1960, but the season got underway with no appointment made. Beattie's appointment was announced on 23rd September, meaning he was in charge for the trip to Birmingham City the next day. Beattie's management career was already 13 years and 4 clubs long when he took on the job. Seven successive League defeats was not the best way to start his Forest career but eight unbeaten League games followed to leave Forest in 14th place at the end of 1960-61. After a disappointing 1962-63 season, the following one saw Forest finish 9th in Division One and reach the 6th round of the FA Cup. However Beattie resigned during the summer of 1963 for business reasons (to run a sub post office) but was back in management at Plymouth in October 1963 and later managed Wolves and Notts County.
Playing Appearances: FL:125 apps 4 gls FAC: 21 apps 0gls Other 1 app 0gls Total: 147 apps 4 gls
Managing: Total: 779 matches, 311 won, 182 drawn, 286 lost. Win% 39.92.
Honours as player: FA Cup winners 1938, runners-up 1937. 7 full caps for Scotland
Honours as manager: Promotion from Div. 2 with Huddersfield 1953.

JOHN JOSEPH (JOHNNY) CAREY
Position when playing: full-back
Born: Dublin, Ireland 23 February 1919
Died: Macclesfield 22nd August 1995
PLAYING CAREER: St James Gate (Ireland). Manchester United 1.11.1936.
MANAGEMENT CAREER: Blackburn Rovers 6.1953 to 16-10-1958. Everton 20.10.1958 to 17.4.1961. Leyton orient 1.8.1961 to 7.1963. FOREST 1.8.1963 to 2.12.1968. Blackburn Rovers 21.10.1970 to 8.6.1971.
Carey enjoyed a successful playing career at Manchester United after leaving Ireland. He also played international games for Ireland and Northern Ireland and was captain of the prestigious Rest of Europe XI that played Great Britain at Hampden Park in 1948. His management career started at Blackburn, where in six seasons they finished no lower than 6th in Division 2, and won promotion to Division One, finishing 10th in 1958-59. Tempted to Everton, his best season was 5th in 1961 but was sacked in April that year when the club's directors felt a change was necessary. In his first season at Second Division Leyton Orient he repeated his promotion skills, but the Os were always likely to struggle in the top tier, so it was not a surprise when he resigned in order to join Forest. He had a little over five seasons in charge at the City Ground, with his best team that of 1966-67 which came close to taking the Division One title and reached the semi-final of the FA Cup. In the era BC (before Clough) this was Forest's best-ever season. By 1968-69 some of the magic had gone, and Carey was fired (asked to resign) after a run of 12 games without a win and with the club in 21st place. Assistant manager Bill Anderson was left in charge.
Playing Appearances: FL:304 apps 16 gls FAC: 38 apps 1gls Other 4 apps 1gl Total: 346 apps 18 gls
Managing: Total: 743 matches, 308 won, 168 drawn, 267 lost. Win% 41.45
Honours as player: Division 1 champions 1952. FA Cup winners 1948. 29 caps for Ireland (Eire) and 7 for Northern Ireland. Footballer of the Year 1949.
Honours as manager: Promotion from Div. 2 with Blackburn 1958 and from Div. 3 with Leyton Orient 1962. First Division runners-up with Forest 1967 (and FA Cup semi-finalists that season).

WILLIAM (BILL) ANDERSON (AS CARETAKER)
Position when playing: full-back
Born: High Westwood, Newcastle upon Tyne 12th January 1913
Died: Radcliffe on Trent 19th February 1986
PLAYING CAREER: Medomsley Juniors 1930. FOREST 1931 (no first-team appearances). Chopwell Institute 1932. Sheffield United 1933. Barnsley 1935. Hartlepools United 1938 (no first team appearances)
MANAGEMENT CAREER: Lincoln City 08.1946 to 28 Dec 1965. FOREST assistant manager 1966 to 1975.
An unusual quiz question is "who managed Forest at four different times?" Admittedly the answer depends on how you view the job of caretaker manager. Bill Anderson rose to the challenge four times between 1968 and 1975, finishing with League and Cup results of seven wins, four draws and four defeats. After Carey left he had seven games in charge, then three between Gillies and Mackay, four before Brown, and, amid speculation and confusion about Cloughie's arrival, the cup-tie at the City Ground against Spurs in January 1975. A 1-1 draw in that game gave Clough the replay at White Hart Lane for his debut as Forest chief. After Anderson's playing career ended he was trainer at Lincoln City, then manager in 1946. In a 20-year spell, he took the club to two Third Division championships but the club never quite managed to establish themselves in Division Two.
Playing Appearances: 38 apps 0gls
Managing: Total: 875 matches, 316 won, 195 drawn, 364 lost. Win% 36.11.
Honours as manager: Division Three (North) champions 1948, 1952

MATTHEW MUIRHEAD (MATT) GILLIES
Position when playing: centre-half
Born: Loganlea, Scotland 12th August 1921
Died: Nottingham 24th December 1998
PLAYING CAREER: Winchburgh. Motherwell 1940. RAF Weeton 1941. Bolton Wanderers 1.10.1942. Leicester City 1.1952.
MANAGEMENT CAREER: Leicester City 8.11.1958 to 30.11.1968, FOREST 29.1.1969 to 20.10.1972
Gillies had been fired from Leicester City in November 1968 with his club facing relegation. He was therefore an interesting choice to rescue Forest's 1968-69 season when appointed in January 1969. Results hardly improved, but fortunately other clubs had even poorer records that season, leaving Forest in 18th. Although almost all of Gillies' management career was spent in the top tier, Leicester were relegated after he left in 1968, and relegation with Forest in 1972 led to his resignation in October that year.
Playing Appearances: FL:248 apps 1 gl FAC: 9 apps Total: 265 apps 1 gl
Managing: Total: 682 matches, 249 won, 171 drawn, 262 lost. Win% 36.51
Honours as player: Division 2 champions 1954.
Honours as manager: FA Cup runners-up 1961, 1963. League Cup winners 1964.

DAVID CRAIG (DAVE) MACKAY
Position when playing: wing-half
Born: Musselburgh, Scotland 14th November 1934
Died: Nottingham 2nd March 2015
PLAYING CAREER: Slateford Athletic 1950. Newtongrange Star 1951. Hutchison Vale Boys Club 1951. Heart of Midlothian 1953. Tottenham Hotspur 1.3.1959. Derby County 1.7.1968. Swindon Town 5.5.1971.
MANAGEMENT CAREER: Swindon Town 1.11.1971 to 1.11.1972. FOREST 6.11.1972 to 23.10.1973. Derby County 24.10.1973 to 25.11.1976. Walsall 9.3.1977 to 5.8.1978. Coached in Kuwait. Doncaster Rovers 7.12.1987 to 17.3.1989. Birmingham City 26.4.1989 to 23.1.1991. Managed in Cairo and Qatar before retirement in 1997.
Certainly one of Scotland's greatest-ever midfield players, Mackay enjoyed a trophy-rich playing career at Hearts and Spurs. Mackay was Clough and Taylor's first signing at Derby at the age of

33. He played a significant part in Derby's Second Division championship in 1969, when he was named a joint Footballer of the Year. He became player-manager at Swindon Town in May 1971 and was a popular choice to follow Gillies at the City Ground. Some of this good will disappeared when he upped and left for Derby in October 1973. This followed the departure from the Rams of Clough and Taylor. Mackay's last signing for Forest was Ian Bowyer, though it seems possible that by this time he was already in discussion with Derby County. After the 0-0 draw with Hull on October 23rd, Mackay left and Bill Anderson was back in charge while a new manager was found. With the players and spectators at Derby appearing to want Clough and Taylor reinstated, Mackay had a difficult time at first. No matter: by 1975 Derby were champions of the First Division. If his career in management didn't quite reach the same heights as he did as a player, his Division One championship with Derby was a significant achievement, particularly given the situation he had inherited.
Playing Appearances in English football: FL:415+1 apps 48 gls FAC: 41 apps 4 gls Other: 39 apps, 8 gls Total: 495+1 apps 60 gls
Managing: Total: 484 matches, 179 won, 145 drawn, 160 lost. Win%: 36.98.
Honours as player: Tied with Tony Book for the FWA Footballer of the Year award 1969. 22 full caps for Scotland (4 goals). At Hearts: League champions 1958. FA Cup winners 1956. League Cup winners 1954, 1958. At Spurs: Division 1 champions 1961, FA Cup Winners 1961, 1962, 1967. Missed the European Cup Winners' Cup Final of 1963 through injury. Derby: Division 2 champions 1969. Watney Cup 1970. Honours as manager: At Derby: First Division champions 1975

ALLAN DUNCAN BROWN
Position when playing: inside forward
Born: Kennoway, Scotland 12th October 1926
Died: 20th April 2011
PLAYING CAREER: Kennoway Hearts 1945. East Fife 1946. Blackpool 12.1950. Luton Town 2.1957. Portsmouth 3.1961. Wigan Athletic 1963 to July 1966 (as player manager).
MANAGEMENT CAREER: Luton Town 4.11.1966 to 17.12.1968. Torquay United 8.1.1969 to 11.10.1971. Bury 20.6.1972 to 19.11.1973. FOREST 20.11.1973 to 2.1.1975. Southport 2.1.1976 to 5.5.1976. Blackpool 5.5.1976 to 31.5.1982.
A goalscoring inside forward, Brown spent most of his playing career in the top flight of English football, and was unlucky to miss two FA Cup finals because of injury. He did play for Luton in the 1959 final against Forest, but his club was relegated the following season. He moved to Portsmouth where 2 goals in 9 games did not prevent another relegation, this time to Division 3. His first experience of management came at (then non-League) Wigan Athletic. He returned to Luton for his first taste of Football League management and guided them to the top spot in 1968. Moves to Torquay in Division 3, and Bury in Division 4 followed before he was offered the job at Forest. His tenure at the City Ground got off on the wrong foot with the resignations of coach Colin Murphy and youth coach Alan Hill. A promotion push from Division 2 never materialised in 1973-74, and the club slipped to 13th the following season, four places behind Notts County, who had beaten Forest 2-0 at the City Ground in what turned out to be Brown's last game in charge. Forest's committee met on 2nd January and terminated Brown's contract "by mutual agreement". After a year on the sidelines, he joined Southport in an attempt to help them avoid having to apply for re-election to the League. He then returned to Blackpool, where after a 5th place finish in his first season, he was unable to stop a drop in form which led to their relegation after he had left. Following a job in Kuwait he was back at Blackpool again, but was unable to prevent another relegation, this time to Division 4.
Playing Appearances in English football: FL:378 apps 127 gls FAC: 38 apps 12gls, Other: 6 apps Total: 422 apps 139 gls
Managing: Total: 559 matches, 211 won, 164 drawn, 184 lost. Win% 37.75.
Honours as player: 14 full caps for Scotland, scoring 6 goals. At East Fife: League Cup winners At Luton: FA Cup runners-up 1959. At Blackpool: FA Cup finalists 1951 and winners in 1953, but Brown missed both finals through injury. At Portsmouth: Champions of Division 3 1962.
Honours as manager: At Luton: Division 4 champions 1968.

BRIAN HOWARD CLOUGH
Position when playing: centre forward
Born: Middlesbrough 21st March 1935
Died: Derby 20th September 2004
PLAYING CAREER: Billingham Synthonia 1950. Great Broughton Juniors 1952. Middlesbrough 1.5.1953. Sunderland 1.7.1961.
MANAGEMENT CAREER: Hartlepools United 29.10.1965 to 5.6.1967. Derby County 5.6.1967 to 15.10.1973. Brighton & Hove Albion 1.11.1973 to 20.7.1974. Leeds United 30.7.1974 to 12.9.1974. FOREST 3.1.1975 to 8.5.1993.
We must leave a full account of his career (and the contribution of Peter Taylor) for a later volume. However, this is an opportunity to record Clough's outstanding career as player and manager. Three goals in nine appearances in his first season as a player gave little notice of what was to follow. In five full seasons at Middlesbrough, his goal totals in club games reads 38, 42, 43, 40, and 36. After moving to Sunderland in 1961, he maintained a similar strike rate, but injuries curtailed his appearances. Damage to an anterior cruciate ligament in December 1962 led to a long lay-off until his final three appearances in September 1964. His move into club management began in October 1965 at Hartlepools United. Piloting the Fourth Division club from 18th to 8th was sufficient for Second Division Derby County to offer him their manager's job and the results were immediate; promotion in his first full season. 4th in Division 1 in 1970 was just a foretaste of the delights of 1972 when Derby won the First Division championship. Things fell apart for Clough in October 1973, with he and Peter Taylor washing up at Third Division Brighton and Hove. When Leeds United asked him to replace Don Revie in the summer of 1974 it seemed Clough was back at the level his skills demanded, but as is well documented, it was not to be, and Clough was out of work on 12th September. Following Brown's departure from Forest, it didn't take long for the newspapers to begin to speculate on Clough taking the Forest job, something that duly occurred on January 6th. For the City Ground cup-tie with Tottenham Hotspur on January 4th, Bill Anderson was once again in charge and was rewarded with a draw, meaning Clough could take his seat in the Spurs' dugout for the replay. Before that game, Clough had time to organise a new cooker for the lady in the club's kitchen, and dropped strong hints about signing McGovern and O'Hare from Leeds. The rest, as they say, is history.
Playing Appearances: FL:274 apps 251 gls FAC: 12 apps 5 gls, other 10 apps, 11 gls.
Total: 296 apps 267 gls
Managing: Total: 1,452 matches, 675 won, 367 drawn, 410 lost. Win%: 46.49.
Honours as player: Two full caps for England. Also played at "U23" and "B" level for England.
Honours as manager: At Derby: Champions of Div. 2 1969. Division 1 Champions 1972. At Forest: Promotion from Division 2 1977. Division 1 champions 1978, runners-up 1979. European Super Cup winners 1980. European Cup winners 1979, 1980. Zenith Cup winners 1992. Anglo-Scottish Cup Winners 1977. League Cup winners 1978, 1979, 1989, 1990. FA Cup finalists 1991.

AUTHOR'S ACKNOWLEDGEMENTS

I am, as ever, greatly indebted to friends Jim Creasy and Mike Davage whose continuing researches into the nation's archives has supplied much of the fine detail in this and many other works of a similar nature. I am also most grateful for the continuing support of Peter Holme, Collections Officer of the National Football Museum, and to my friend Mike Jackman. I am also most grateful for the assistance of Rod Evans, Michael Braham, Dave Sullivan (Millwall F.C. Museum), Robert Reid (Partick Thistle historian), Dr. Steve Phillipps, Paul Plowman, Michael Joyce, Gordon Small and last, but by no means least, my friend and publisher Tony Brown.

ABOUT THE AUTHOR

Garth Dykes was born at Mellor, near Blackburn, and was educated at Chadderton Grammar School. Following studies at Oldham Municipal Technical College a career in cotton yarn sales commenced in 1957 at the Wye Mills, Shaw. A career move took Garth to Leicestershire in November1960 and he retired in 1992 at the age of 58. A member of the Football Writers' Association, Garth's lifelong love of football has seen his involvement in twenty-six books to date. His artwork has appeared in many of his publications, also in football programmes, national magazines, and several sets of trade cards issued by David Rowland of Bury. A full list of Garth's publications was included in the previous volume. Recent additions are Stalybridge Celtic in the Football League (Soccerdata 2018) and Gateshead A.F.C. Who's Who (Soccerdata 2019)

CORRECTIONS TO THE 1892-1939 VOLUME

Page 4: The reference to Bury in "Notes on the Text" should of course have said "Forest". This was an error by the publisher, who sincerely hopes he has not included more mistakes in this volume.
Page 10: John Barnsdale. Also played first-class cricket for Nottinghamshire. Later a director or Raleigh in Nottingham, and retired to Frensham in Surrey where he died.
Page 19: John Bullock. Born Llanbeblig, Caernarfon Q4 1869. Died: Nottingham Q2 1894.
Page 24: Fred Chapman. In addition to the details provided, please note that Chapman enjoyed a successful career as an amateur, winning 19 caps for England between 1908 and 1910. These caps included three in the 1908 Olympic Games, where he was in England's team for the 2-0 victory over Denmark in the Final and scored the first goal. Chapman also played for Nottingham Magdala, Port Vale, Reading, South Nottingham, Southall, Brentford, Northern Nomads, Notts County and represented the Nottinghamshire FA.
Page 91: George Richardson. Birth and death details unknown, but possibly b. Mansfield 1876. Replace career record with "Mansfield Grammar School. Mansfield Town 1897. FOREST 02.1898. Mansfield Foresters. Mansfield Town (new club). Mansfield Mechanics. Mansfield Woodhouse." Delete reference to West Bromwich and insert instead "An amateur player from Mansfield Town."
Page 92: Peter Robertson. Full name Peter Neilson Robertson. 5' 10" 12st 7lbs. Born Rosewell 24th September 1875 (not Dundee 1881). Died Macoupin County, Illinois, USA. Career: add Raith Rovers 19th August 1899. Signed for Forest 20th April 1904. Add to notes: Brother of Samuel Robertson of Notts County 1905/06.
Page 107: Frederick Thompson. Born Q1 1870, Died 2nd May 1898
Page 115: John White. Born Annersley 1st August 1877. Died Mansfield 2nd December 1958. Played first-class cricket for Nottinghamshire. Later a professional cricketer in Scotland, then captain of the Mansfield colliery team for 22 years until retiring after an accident in the mine.

FOREST WHO'S WHOs 1866-1891, 1975 to date

Work is underway to scope the contents of an 1866 to 1891 who's who, and we may need two volumes to cover 1975 to date. Some 500 men played in the first team between 1866 and 1891,many of them in just one game. Consequently that volume will focus on the players who made a significant contribution in terms of appearances and goals, and simply acknowledge the rest by listing their names and the year they were active. Any readers with particular knowledge of players from the 1866 to 1891 period should please contact the publisher.

COVER PHOTOGRAPHS

Front cover, 1971. Back, left to right: John Winfield, Bob Chapman, Eric Hulme, Paul Richardson, Jim Barron, Neil Martin, John Cottam. Centre: Ronnie Rees, Ian Storey-Moore, Doug Fraser, Peter Hindley, Tommy Jackson, Barry Lyons, Peter Cormack, Liam O'Kane. Front: John Robertson, Duncan McKenzie, Jimmy McIntosh. Please see page 4 for details of the 1959 group on the back cover.